Books by Selden Rodman

Verse

DEATH OF THE HERO
THE AMAZING YEAR
THE AIRMEN
LAWRENCE: THE LAST CRUSADE
MORTAL TRIUMPH AND OTHER POEMS

Art

THE MIRACLE OF HAITIAN ART
THE ARTIST AS A BLACK AMERICAN (with Carole Cleaver)
THE INSIDERS
THE EYE OF MAN
RENAISSANCE IN HAITI
PORTRAIT OF THE ARTIST AS AN AMERICAN
HORACE PIPPIN: A Negro Artist in America
GENIUS IN THE BACKLANDS: Popular Artists of Brazil

Interviews

TONGUES OF FALLEN ANGELS
CONVERSATIONS WITH ARTISTS

Music

THE HEART OF BEETHOVEN

Travel

SOUTH AMERICA OF THE POETS
THE CARIBBEAN
THE COLOMBIA TRAVELER
THE PERU TRAVELER
THE MEXICO TRAVELER
THE GUATEMALA TRAVELER
THE ROAD TO PANAMA
MEXICAN JOURNAL
THE BRAZIL TRAVELER

Anthologies

ONE HUNDRED BRITISH POETS
ONE HUNDRED AMERICAN POEMS
ONE HUNDRED MODERN POEMS
A NEW ANTHOLOGY OF MODERN POETRY
THE POETRY OF FLIGHT
WAR AND THE POET (with Richard Eberhart)

HAITI:

THE BLACK REPUBLIC

The Complete Story and Guide by SELDEN RODMAN

THE DEVIN-ADAIR COMPANY · OLD GREENWICH · 1980

For information address the publishers,
THE DEVIN-ADAIR COMPANY,
Old Greenwich, Conn. 06870

Printed in the United States of America

ISBN 0-8159-5701-7
Library of Congress Catalog Card Number: 54-10816

First printing November 1954
Second printing March 1955
New revised edition June 1961
Second revised edition December 1973
Third revised edition July 1976
Fourth revised edition September 1978
Fifth revised edition November 1980

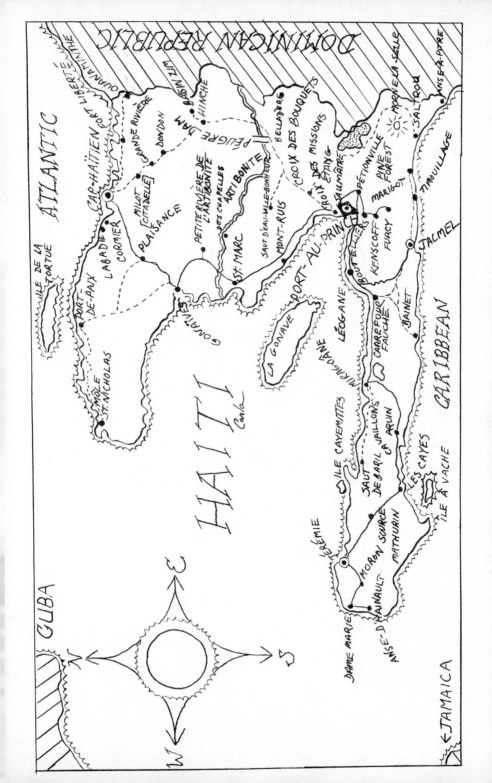

TABLE OF CONTENTS

Contents

INTRODUCTION

How on those upswept hills
The sway-backed spidery houses seemed to hang
Together by some wind-defying logic
While clouds of pink dust through the blue haze fell,
And unrepentant songbirds out of season
In royal palms miraculously sang
For delight only, was enough of magic
To make one want to ask, beyond all reason,
What is Man? And can art make him well?

What is Haiti's special appeal to the foreigner? Why are Americans—who can find better beaches, more luxurious hotels and climates as agreeable without leaving home—beginning to come to Haiti by the thousands? Is it a particular kind of visitor who finds in Haiti something unique and compelling? And if so, who is he? And what is he looking for?

The Haitian himself, if he has the means to travel, does not travel in Haiti. If he is from the provinces, he moves to the capital when he can. If he is from Port-au-Prince, he stays there. If he is well-off, he goes to Paris or New York as often as possible; and if he is not well-off, and can still get away, he may never return. The adventurous visitor's interest in Haiti's wild interior perplexes the *élite* Haitian; the tourist's insatiable anxiety to "see voodoo" amuses or repels him. The spectacle of the twenty-four-hour guest snapping pictures of barefooted peasants carrying Esso cans on their heads in front of African-type thatched huts makes him wince with shame. He is so sure that his country is being held up to ridicule abroad that in his propaganda for tourism he pictures Haiti as a a band of overdressed Creoles performing "folklore dances" between an airconditioned hotel and a kidney-shaped swimming pool. Is it surprising that this Haitian is confirmed in his suspicion that

Americans are a race of plutocratic sunbathers, cold-blooded and self-centered?

Some of them are, of course, and these are the kind that hop from island to island. They can afford to. Why they come to Haiti, apart from the misleading advertisements which promise golf and surf-bathing, is a mystery. Or maybe it isn't a mystery if we can overcome our own prejudice against their pathetic inability to leave for a moment what is expensively familiar. Perched over the glittering bars of Pétion-Ville, faced with the Continental croupier's reassuring ability to separate them from their money at the Casino Internationale, or peering from taxis at the overburdened market-women climbing the poinsettia-lined road to Le Perchoir—these jaded folk are human too. Behind the conventional facade they are driven, we must assume, by at least a remnant of the same yearning that brings the rest of us here.

What is it we all seek—and find, to the extent of our capacities—in Haiti?

Primitivism is a loaded word. Bandied about by people with little knowledge and less respect, it can become a synonym for savagery, ignorance and want of skill. These attributes exist in so-called "backward" countries—and, taking different shapes, in the most civilized. But in the sense we choose to employ the term here, primitivism stands for essential simplicity.

Far from being a savage, the Haitian peasant, though sharing one of the lowest standards of living in this Hemisphere, accepts life with a grace, a courage, an exuberance, a responsive friendliness and a capacity for hard work and cooperation that are heroic. For the most part illiterate, and lacking (through no fault of his own) even such primary agricultural implements as the plough and the wheelbarrow, he is not ignorant of the means of living in peace with his fellowmen and the spirits of his cosmos. This is a basic knowledge that has been lost to the more "favored" races of mankind throughout a good part of recorded history. The peasant has not yet acquired the skill to operate machines or to organize collectively for intricate enterprises. He cannot lay a mathematically precise foundation or draw a straight line. Yet none of these techniques, with a little teaching, are out of his reach. And when given no more than the tools, it has been amply demonstrated that the self-taught Haitian can mould a figure or paint a picture with a directness of inspiration and a sureness of "taste" that are beyond any but the most gifted of the sophisticated. In the arts that belong naturally to his tradition—ceremonial dancing and drumming, and the creation of imaginative disguises—his skills are incomparable.

The characteristically "Haitian" story with which the travel-ler comes home is two-edged. To the insensitive visitor, who looks in all countries for an image of himself, and rates other cultures on the degree to which they approximate standards of technological efficiency, these stories are told with a superior smirk. To others the same stories are no less amusing—but for what they reveal of the limitations of "modernism." It depends on one's values. How im-portant, in the last analysis, is economic well-being? Is inner peace related to caloric consumption? Do advanced systems of communi-cation contribute to understanding between people? Are plumbing, super-markets, bank accounts and double-entry book-keeping pre-requisites of the good life? What is happiness?

To answer these questions either way quickly is dangerous. The therapeutic value of a visit to Haiti is that one is forced to *ask* them. Consider three typical stories.

The manager of a drydock is wringing his hands because the rusted paint has not yet been removed from the steel hull of a freighter. Thirty half-naked Haitians are banging away lustily with improvised hammers. The visitor approaches to see why so much industry is having so little effect. He discovers that the workers are beating out basic drum-rhythms, and that each of them is sing-ing a song to his own accompaniment . . .

During the War the Haitian Coast-Guard, cooperating with the American Navy, patroled the isolated beaches to prevent pro-visioning of Nazi submarines. Hearing that a German crew had come ashore near Bayeaux and received the bounty of the peasants, an officer asked the local *chef-de-section* whether it was true that an enemy of Haiti had been served. The magistrate replied that the peasants might not be sure who were the friends and who were the enemies, but that in this case at least the officer had nothing to wor-ry about. "To be sure, they took the food aboard," he said, smil-ing, "but after the door was closed, there was a tragic mishap: the iron canoe sank to the bottom of the sea with everybody inside and never was seen again!" Could one have explained to those peo-ple what the War was about without being a little ashamed of one's "civilization"?

An enterprising American furniture dealer saw that the chairs the peasants make for their own use were sturdy and beautiful. He bought one for a dollar. Then he went to the little shop in the country where the chairs were carved and woven and asked the pro-prietor how good a price he could give him on a hundred. The proprietor spent almost an hour arguing with his neighbors and adding up rows of figures. "We can make a hundred chairs," he said finally, "for two-hundred dollars." The dealer was astonished and irritated. "But for such a large order," he said, "surely the price per chair should be *less* than a dollar, not more!" "Ah, but Monsieur," the carpenter replied tolerantly, "you have neglected to figure on all the extra work for us that such an order would involve!"

There are three special reasons why Americans of more than average sensibility find in Haiti something the other Caribbean islands fail to offer. The first has to do with skin-color. There are Negroes in all the islands, of course, but Haiti is the only one from which the white colonial master was ejected, and which has in consequence experienced a hundred-and-fifty years of proud if troubled independence. The most obvious contradiction of American democracy has been its treatment of the Negro. Most Americans, openly or subconsciously, are ashamed of that record. If their sense of justice has not been blunted, they are grateful to be tolerated by a race that welcomes them with far more hospitality and humanity than America as a nation can claim to offer. And in the few instances where they are actually snubbed or discriminated against by a proud colored aristocracy, Americans can experience (with proper humility, one hopes) their share of the national guilt.

A less subtle aspect of Haiti's extraordinary hold over the imaginative visitor is the opportunities it still offers for exploration. With the opening-up of Africa, the conquest of the poles, and now the scaling of Everest, there are few corners of the earth still denied to adventurous eyes. Oddly enough Haiti, though crisscrossed by airliners and within napping-time of Miami, is one of them. It is not, of course, that any inch of Haiti's soil is really inaccessible; it is rather that the country's deliberate policy of isolation during the Nineteenth Century, and its concomitant lack of a road-net, makes the wilder and more beautiful parts of a country no larger than Maryland as untouched (and still unglimpsed) as the Matta Grosso jungle. Only a millionaire can afford what it takes to explore the Matta Grosso. But anyone with a few hundred dollars and a taste for virgin waterfalls can get lost in Haiti. By jeep, on horseback or on foot, any mysterious underground labyrinth or Indian burial-ground in Haiti may be investigated; yet one locality less than thirty air-minutes from the capital is so isolated that the appearance of an American there made a whole village scatter in terror to the hills. Even for those who don't enjoy roughing it, being so close to the fabled fastnesses of the *bocor* and the *zombi* (and reading about them) is thrill enough. As for the man-made miracles of Haiti—the fairy-land architecture of Port-au-Prince, the Italian hill-town aspect of balconied Jacmel, the astonishing pastel symphony that is Cap Haïtien, the awesome ruins at Milot and the great murals of St.-Trinité—they are accessible to everyone.

Americans are a race of reformers and improvisors. Improving the bicycle led to the invention of the airplane. The New Deal is history but its social innovations remain. America is an increasingly complex organism, however, and invention as well as reform have tended to become institutionalized. In Haiti it is pathetically obvious that vast improvements, in the material sphere, could be effected with relatively little technical know-how and money. To cite but one instance: as overpopulated Haiti cuts down its few remaining trees for cooking-fuel, the last thin layer of topsoil is being washed away by torrential floods. The man farsighted enough to plant a single tree is giving Haiti what it needs most. The efficiency-minded American, frustrated in his will to reform at home, comes to Haiti and has a field day. Sometimes, though not often enough, he returns, as a member of one of the many governmental or privately-financed agencies that have helped Haiti solve some of its most desperate problems. But in any case our latent reformer has the fun of reconstructing Haiti's fabulous colonial prosperity in his imagination. If he talks only to himself he is not a menace!

These aspects of Haiti's magnetism, and others less tangible, combine in a mysterious way to renew our confidence in ourselves. The newcomer may look about him and ask petulantly why the peasant does not revolt. The oldtimer, if he has not buried himself behind the sterile barrier of the capital's American Colony, acquires an admiration for the peasant's independence and fortitude that makes him proud of belonging to the human race. To free himself from tyrants, black ones as well as white, the Haitian fought a series of insurrections as violent as any in recorded history. If, when he finally acquired his freedom and his parcel of land, he preferred to sit tight, rather than gamble with the laws, the gods and the promises of city folk, he had his reasons. Politics left him, and still leaves him, unmoved. Like the man from Missouri, he wants to be shown.

It is easy for the visitor to Haiti to romanticize—easy and dangerous. The snapshot of the "picturesque" market-woman swinging down the steep trail from La Vallée to Bainet with a basket of manioc and calabashes on her head may reveal, when enlarged, the open infection of yaws on the forearm; it will not reveal the inroads of tuberculosis or hookworm. Nor will it reveal the after-effects of carrying for long distances loads too heavy for the human spine to endure. The grown man "loafing" in a sunny arcade is thought to be a "typical" victim of the lassitude induced by the tropics—if one knows nothing of the effects of malaria.

Conversely, however, the visitor to Haiti will be wise to refrain from congratulating himself on his superior lot. Haiti has at least as much to teach him as he has to teach Haiti. If he turns up his nose he will not be likely to see what is under his feet. But if he gives his curiosity free rein, and looks about him with even a little sympathy, he will partake of an experience rich indeed. From the *élite* and the poor alike, if he accepts them, he can acquire an insight into the meaning of true hospitality. From the seemingly interminable festivals of Mardi Gras and *Ra-Ra* he may rediscover the lost art of amusing others by unrestrainedly amusing oneself, and how to laugh heartily. From the *coumbite*, the peasant's method of killing (with rhythm and satire) a piece of work too big for one man, he can learn more of communal enterprise than Marx ever dreamed. From *vaudou*, if he approaches it neither as a sensation-seeker nor a cultist, he may find what it means to *live* one's religion.

There is a point of land six thousand feet above the sea, beyond Pétion-Ville, beyond Kenscoff, beyond Furcy itself, but only forty-five minutes drive on asphalted roads from the heart of Port-au-Prince, where a view of miles upon miles of the most breathtakingly rugged mountain-ranges on earth is suddenly revealed. The road that is intended some day to cross the Massif de la Selle to Caribbean Jacmel comes to an end there. The visitor is urged to drive first to that point, get out, walk a few steps further—and pause. The stillness is as deafening as that which envelops one stepping into a Gothic cathedral. At first there is no sign of human habitation. But slowly, as the eye and ear become accustomed to the tremendous scale of nature, the landscape comes to life. Far to the right across a distant ravine, where banana plants punctuate the red earth with sabres of green, a tiny figure in blue denim threads his ant-like way. A thousand feet straight down, where it seems impossible that even a Haitian goat could find foothold, a woman with a crimson bandana on her head is bent double over her potato patch. Miles to the left plumes of smoke behind a cluster of white *cailles* in a mango grove indicate the preparation of new fields for millet or the smothering of charcoal-pits. The stillness is accented but not broken, first by the wild notes of an African work-song, plaintively falsetto; then by an even more distant melody played on a bamboo flute or conch-shell; and finally, if one is patient and lucky, by the chorded whistle of the almost extinct but incredibly haunting singer of the rainforest dells, the *oiseau musicien*. One is aware, if one brought a camera to this spot, that the scene is inaccessible to photography. It is, in fact, beyond the power of any machine, or any organism but the human eye—and one is glad that this is so.

It is here—and the place may be multiplied with local variations from the fortress-prow of the Citadelle in the North to the chalk-and-limestone cliffs overhanging Jérémie's Anse d'Azur in the extreme South—that one acquires perspective. What an astronomer takes to himself by contemplating dead worlds may be acquired by the traveller to Haiti, more meaningfully perhaps, by absorbing the timeless rhythms, the visual pattern and the ever-responsive heartbeat of the living.

1953

Twenty years (and ten visits) later, how much has changed? Surprisingly little. The capital's population—augmented by an influx from the provincial towns whose access-roads deteriorated during the decade of 1959–1969 when foreign aid was cut off—almost doubled. And by the same token the smaller towns, especially in the South, suffered from poverty and neglect. But Port-au-Prince, with a surge in small industry, electric power, functional telephones, hotels, beaches and art galleries, has become the fastest-growing tourist-Mecca in the Caribbean. And Cap Haïtien—with cruise ships, which now account for 50% of all visitors to Haiti, making almost daily stops in season—promises to develop almost as rapidly.

What is most surprising to the casual visitor is that the Haitian people remain wholly unaffected by the wave of ugly racism that originated in the United States and that has infected every other part of the West Indies. With no record of servility to colonial domination to live down, and justly proud of their own culture, Haitians regard pan-Africanism as childish and Black Power ideologies as barbaric. Visitors to Haiti without such preconceptions or other prejudices are invariably welcomed as friends, whatever their race, creed or nationality.

An incident of 1972 illustrates the unique attraction which Haiti exercises over those who come to it with an open heart. In that year an American, making his first visit to Milot, stepped backward on the Citadelle without looking, to get a better photograph. Falling into one of the shafts that ventilate the gun galleries, he broke his back and came close to losing his sight. Without anaesthetics, peasants and their donkeys carried him to Cap Haïtien, and the trip to a hospital in New York took two days. A year later, the American was organizing a charity auction of Haitian art in New York City, and later that year he was bringing his family to Jacmel where he bought a house for permanent residence.

1973

ACKNOWLEDGMENTS

I am grateful for this opportunity to express my thanks to at least a few of the many Haitians and friends of Haiti who helped me gather material, gave me advice, or accompanied me on visits to most parts of the Republic during my visits there.

Jean Saurel, Director of the National Office of Tourism, André Théard, former Director, and Aubelin Jolicoeur, former Deputy Director, for their unfailing kindness and patience in helping me with the revisions of this book in 1973 and 1978.

Also, for their generous help to me during the same period, I would like to thank Théo Duval of the Office of Tourism, Marc and Miriam Ashton of ABC Tours, Alix Pasquet and Robert Garrison of New Haiti North, Georges Deslandes of the *Avis* Rent-a-Car Agency, Robert, Tamara and Jacques Baussan of the Hotel Ibo Lélé, Pierre Monosiet and Francine Murat of Le Centre d'Art, Issa El Saieh of the Galerie Issa, Andrew Saba of The Red Carpet, George Nader of Nader Gallery; Bill Negron and Manu Sassoonian. In Cap Haïtien, Walter Bussenius of the Hotel Mont Joli, and Kurt Beck, of the Hotel Beck, were most helpful. And in Jacmel, Axel and Monique Madsen, Hervé Boucard, Mme. Alexandre Vital, and Eric and Marlene Danise of the Pension Craft.

During trips to Haiti in the 1960s I owe particular thanks to Mme. Carmelle Oland of the Hotel Quisqueya in Pétion-Ville, Dr. and Mme. Rindall Assad of the Hotel Villa Créole, and to former American Ambassadors Benson E. L. Timmons and Claude Ross whose guest I was on two occasions.

Without the help of former President Paul E. Magloire and the members of his government, in particular Pierre Chauvet, Denys Bellande and Jean Brierre, who facilitated my travel throughout the country, my original research for this book in 1954 would have been most difficult. Other friends of that period who helped in putting the original book together were Robert Théard, John Hersey, Lavinia Williams, Bishop Alfred Voegeli, Luce Tournier, René Kenswill, William Negron, Fortuné Bogat, Lorraine Wallace, John Goodwin, Howard and Betty Schermerhorn, Roger Baldwin, my former wife Maia Wojciechowska Larkin, and Wilson Bigaud.

On still earlier visits to Haiti in the 1940s I am indebted to Edouard Mathon, William and Margaret Krauss, DeWitt Peters, Patrick Leigh-Fermor, Elsa Voelcker, Ralph Thompson, Arthur and Ryerson Vervaet, and the late Hilda Clausen.

Without the help over the past ten years of my wife, Carole Cleaver, and of my children Oriana, Carla and Van Nostrand, the revision of this book would have been a chore rather than a joy.

PICTURE CREDITS

With the following exceptions, all photographs reproduced in this book were taken by the author and all paintings and sculptures belong to him:

The photographs of the *vevers*, the woman possessed, the women seated behind candles, the *Ra-Ra* musicians and the waterfall of Saut d'Eau were taken by Odette Mennesson-Rigaud.

The photographs of Miragoâne Cathedral and of the peasant woman with a pipe were taken by Arthur O'Neill.

The photographs of Sans Souci, the Citadelle, the *vaudou* drummer, the peasants with mortar and pestle, the cockfight, the murals in St.-Trinité Cathedral, and the *élite* beauty, Adrienne Déjoie, who took the lead in Morisseau-Leroy's creole *Antigone*, were taken by Byron Coroneos.

The photographs of the National Palace, the seine caster, and the peasants cultivating in the mountains were taken by Edouard Peloux.

The photographs of the Catholic Cathedral, sugar-cane loading, coffee sorting, and of the *camion* were taken by Hugh Cave.

The photographs of 'Ti Ro-Ro, the *élite* wedding reception, the Déjean Choir, the four poets, the luxury hotels, and of Gustav dalla Valle spearing a shark, were contributed by Bernard Diederich from the files of the *Haiti Sun*.

The photograph of the *coumbite* was taken by André Roosevelt.

Bazile's 'Triumph' is from the collection of Edward Bragaline in New York.

Ciappini's 'Toussaint Louverture' is from the collection of Gomez Sicré in Washington, D.C.

The two coins reproduced are from the collection of Kurt Fisher.

For permission to photograph Jasmin Joseph's sculpture for the visitors' gallery of the Cathedral St.-Trinité, I am indebted to the Centre d'Art, representing Jasmin Joseph.

To Carol and Bob Boyar I am indebted for their Dimanche sculpture, and to Lynn Grossberg for her photos of the Mellons and of President Duvalier.

The pictures by André Pierre, André Normil and Gerard Valcin are from the collection of Issa El Saieh. The photograph of President Jean-Claude Duvalier is reprinted from *Ebony* with that magazine's kind permission.

HAITI:

THE BLACK REPUBLIC

CHAPTER I

A BACKWARD GLANCE:

From Columbus' First Voyage to the Battle of Vertières

SITUATION

EVER SINCE Columbus sighted the harbor of Môle St. Nicholas the evening of December 5, 1492, and possibly before, the physical fact of Haiti's ruggedness has influenced its history. The Buccaneers a century and more later found the mountains a good place to retire to after their sweeps of the Main. Spain was influenced to cede Haiti to France in 1697 because the terrain seemed so unpromising for either mining or cultivation. The African slaves who worked for the French were able to organize a successful revolt in 1791 because their masters had never been able to effectively control more than the towns and the few rich coastal plains. Napoleon's efforts to take back the colony failed, in part, for the same reasons. And all through the Nineteenth Century independent Haiti was able to maintain the isolation that gives it its unique character today because the land's physiognomy rendered it uninviting to either foreign conquistadores or native "civilizers." The Sixteenth Century English Admiral's description of Haiti—he had answered his sovereign's request by crumpling a sheet of paper in his fist and tossing it on the royal table—is still a good one.

'Haiti' was the aboriginal word for 'mountainous land' and though it has at various times been used to describe the whole large island lying between Cuba and Puerto Rico, it was first appropriated in 1804 as the name for the country we are writing about. Up to that time the Spaniards had referred to their colony, comprising the eastern two-thirds of the island, as Santo Domingo, while the French named their more mountainous western domain Saint-Domingue. The island as a whole is best described in Columbus' original name for it, Española, or Hispaniola.

Haiti (Saint-Domingue), the western third of the island, comprises today little more than 10,000 square miles. This includes a stubby (50-mile long) northern peninsula separated from Cuba at its extremity (Môle St. Nicholas) by the 70-mile wide Windward Passage, and a long peninsula on the south pointing 150 miles toward Jamaica, 130 miles west-southwest. Between these upper and lower jaws extends a wide-open mouth (the Gulf of Gonave), a detached tongue (the large island of La Gonave), and a throat, only twenty-five miles from the Dominican (once Spanish) border, the Bay of Port-au-Prince, protecting at its extremity the capital city of that name. No larger than Maryland or Vermont, Haiti conveys its impression of vastness by verticality. The ubiquitous mountains, rising to 8900 feet, drop generally into the sea without the grace of a plain or even the brief luxury of a beach. Its uncountable valleys and chasms defy communication. And farmers, they like to say, have been killed falling out of cornfields.

THE INDIANS

Three waves of Indian migration broke over the island of Hispaniola before Columbus so named it. The earliest, and most primitive, the Ciboneys, are supposed to have come from the North American continent around 450 A.D. Their stone knives and axeheads have been found at such places as Cabaret, Fort Liberté and Tortuga.

Supplanting the Ciboneys in the Seventh or Eighth Century, came the Arawaks or Tainos, an agricultural tribe from the Orinoco and Amazon basins. The Arawaks lived in big villages. They made beautiful baskets and carved furniture and sculptured pottery. Due to the intensive cultivation of the soil of Haiti itself by the French, the sites where Arawak artifacts may most easily be found today are the off-shore islands of Cabrit, Vâche, Gonave and Tortuga. Columbus described the Arawaks, who were in full possession when he arrived, as "loveable, tractable, peaceable and praiseworthy." But as early as 1512, when the first Africans were imported to work the almost-exhausted gold mines of Santo Domingo, all but a handful of the loveable Arawaks had been exterminated.

The third wave of Indian migration to the West Indies consisted of Caribs from South America, but they had barely overrun Puerto Rico and reached the eastern tip of Hispaniola by 1492. The Arawak women they enslaved retaliated, it is said, by refusing to learn the Carib language, and ridiculing their conquerors' war-

2

like pretensions in their own tongue. But it was a fortunate thing for Columbus' soldiers that they could hoodwink the amiable Guacanagari and his beautiful queen Anacoana; the fierce, nomadic invaders would have given them trouble.

> The Arawaks, believing war
> Ill-bred, or agriculture saner,
> Retreated to this island shore
> Pursued by Caribs from Guiana.

> The pacifists set out to teach
> The warriors peace was civilized,
> When Spaniards landed on the beach
> And wiped out both to honor Christ.

THE SPANIARDS

Columbus' first descriptions of Hispaniola were ecstatic. The harbors, he declared, were the best in the world. The plains were the most fertile. The rivers could hardly be counted. The trees "reached to the stars" and the nightingales were always singing. As for the natives, "they show greater love for all others than for themselves; they give valuable things for trifles, being satisfied even with a very small return, or with nothing." He added that the Arawaks far from being idolatrous "believe that all strength and power, and in fact all good things are in heaven, and that I had come down from thence with these ships and sailors; and in this belief I was received there after they had put aside fear." [1] Even climate and conditions of health were found to be faultless:

> . . . for I certify to Your Highness that it seems to me that there could never be under the sun lands superior in fertility, in mildness of cold and heat, in abundance of good and pure water; and the rivers are not like those of Guinea, which are all pestilential. For, praise be to Our Lord, up to the present among all my people nobody has even had a headache or taken to his bed through sickness; except one old man with pain of gravel, from which he has suffered all his life, and he was well at the end of two days.

Only in one passage of this communiqué to his Sovereigns did the Admiral reveal that intention to take advantage of the natives' good nature which was to have such terrible consequences:

[1] *The Letter of Columbus on the Discovery of America.* New York, Lenox Library, 1892. All other quotations in this section are from Samuel Eliot Morison's *Admiral of the Ocean Sea*, Boston, 1946.

> These Indians [he said] bear no arms, and are all unprotected and
> so very cowardly that a thousand would not face three; so they are
> fit to be ordered about and made to work, to sow and do aught
> else that may be needed, and you may build towns and teach them
> to go clothed and to adopt our customs.

Columbus' progress east along the north coast of Haiti between December 6 and 25, 1492, was interrupted on the latter
date by the wrecking of his flagship, the *Santa Maria*. The site of
this mishap, and of the subsequent planting of the ill-starred colony
of La Navidad, is believed to be the present fishing-village of Bord-
de-Mer Limonade, a few miles east of Cap Haïtien. Here, relieved
of the discipline of the Admiral, the Europeans paid the penalty of
their lust and avarice. And here, a few years ago, the anchor of the
Santa Maria was found. The fact that Columbus did find gold in
the riverbed of the Yaque del Norte (a principal river of the present Dominican Republic, to the east) accounts for the fact that the
Spaniards established their first colony in the New World there,
and the still more important circumstance that Haiti itself remained
virtually untouched for the next hundred and fifty years.

Leaving Haiti behind him, Columbus had founded his principal
base at Isabela on the Northern Dominican coast and, while he
was away from there exploring Jamaica and Cuba, had left a lieutenant in command with instructions to leave the Indians alone
(unless they stole, in which case their ears and noses were to be
cut off) and to report on the island and its products. Neither instruction was obeyed. The Spaniards needed food—Las Casas wrote
that "one Spaniard ate more in a day than a whole family of natives
would consume in a month"—and to get it they resorted to whip-
pings and enslavement. It is amazing that in this most fertile of
countries the Spaniards never did become independent of imported
food supplies. Why? "Although the soil is very black and good,"
reported Michele de Cuneo, "they have not yet found the way nor
the time to sow; *the reason is that nobody wants to live in these
countries.*" Only Columbus himself and a few idealists thought in
terms of a permanent colony and of Catholicizing the natives; the
rest of the Spaniards were out for gold and only gold.

When Columbus returned to Isabela he found that bands of
Spaniards were ranging the island, looting, raping and killing the
natives, but instead of disciplining the Spaniards he hunted down
those who had resisted them and made slaves of 1500. These slaves
were shipped to Spain, in lieu of the promised gold, but since almost all of them died en route or shortly after landing, the pres-

sure for a return on the royal investment increased. In consequence, Morison says, a tributory edict was issued: "Every native
of fourteen years of age or upwards who submitted (as the only
alternative to being killed) was required to furnish every three
months a Flanders hawk's bell full of gold dust; and one of the
caciques, Manicaotex, had to give a calabash full of gold valued at
150 castellanos every two months." Not only was the Indians' store
of gold trinkets, accumulated over generations, gone, but the river-
beds themselves were becoming exhausted of the rare dust. The
edict, in Las Casas' words, was irrational, impossible, intolerable
and abominable. The delinquents took to the mountains where they
were hunted by hounds. Others, by the thousands, took casava poison. Of an estimated original island population of 300,000 in 1492,
60,000 were counted in 1508 and in 1548 less than 500.

As to what is to this day called "the Spanish end of the island,"
it enjoyed a few more decades of feverish activity as the principal
base for Cortez' and Pisarro's expeditions west and southwest in
search of gold. Then began its slow decline. As the fortunes of the
French colony rose spectacularly in the mountainous unpromising
West, the dwindling possessors of the incredibly rich Dominican
plain did less and less. Haiti, as we shall see, was to rule the whole
island for a spell in the Nineteenth Century, but it would not be
until the spur of Trujillo in our time roiled Dominican flanks that
the favored acres of the eastern two-thirds of the island would
realize their promise.

THE BUCCANEERS

Into the vacuum that was Haiti after Columbus' progress eastward, stepped years later, and little by little, the adventurous ma-
rauders of the High Seas. Freebooters in search of haven for their
ships and treasure, a mixed crew of English and French, they settled Tortuga in 1630. Fanning out over the western forests of the
main island shortly thereafter in search of cattle and wild boar,
they became known (from their practice of cooking the meat over
Indian spits or *boucans*) as buccaneers. A lawless, independent lot,
acknowledging no sovereign, these settlers gave their character to
the planters that were to follow.

THE FRENCH

By 1663 the English element in Haiti had been assimilated and
the Spaniards to the east repulsed. In 1697, following the War of

the Grand Alliance in Europe, Spain acknowledged a *fait accompli* by ceding to the French the western third of Hispaniola. The 94 years that followed this Treaty of Ryswyck witnessed a miracle of economic exploitation. Sugar, which had been introduced to the island by the Spaniards in 1506, became the principal export product, supplying the needs of all Europe, but coffee, indigo, cocoa and cotton were not far behind. The fabulous colony's combined annual export and import trade of $140,000,000 dwarfed that of the thirteen American colonies; it even exceeded the production of all the colonies of Spain.

The rich alluvial Plaine du Nord, off which *Santa Maria* had foundered, boasted a thousand plantation houses behind monumental pillared gateways. It sparkled at night with the gay illumination of elaborate balls, lighted carriages, and the glaring ovens and stacks of boiling-houses refining sugarcane 'round the clock. At its western extremity Cap Français (now Cap Haïtien), a city of 25,000 with fine public buildings and theatres of stone and brick, was properly known as "The Paris of the Antilles." In prosperous years as many as 80,000 seamen and 700 ships were employed to move Saint-Domingue's products to the Mother Country, two-thirds of whose foreign commercial interests it supplied.

To the south, connected by splendid roads, Port-au-Prince, a town of 8000, was beginning to assert itself as the outlet for a naturally dry region brought under cultivation by artificial irrigation. As the capital of the southernmost province, Les Cayes, with its own small but very fertile plain, was flourishing, but on the whole the South Peninsula remained undeveloped, partly because of its intractible physique and partly because of its proximity to the English in Jamaica who were already beginning to dispute with the French its control.

Who was responsible for this immense productivity, a wealth so suddenly come by that its brash spenders were regarded with envious dislike by even the gilded courtiers at Louis XV's Versailles?

The 36,000 Whites who administered the affairs of Saint-Domingue up until 1791 were not only convinced that it was their work alone. They regarded the Paris of the Bourbons with its social snobbism, its increasing import duties, and its codes of fair treatment for (colonial) labor, with contemptuous distrust. That they should regard the Paris of Mirabeau, Marat and Robespierre with more than merely distrust was inevitable.

Next in line of privilege, 28,000 *gens de couleur* comprised all free persons who had African blood in their veins. These *affranchi*, who by 1791 owned almost one-third of the land, including the better part of the fertile parish of Jérémie, owed their existence to Louis XIV's *Code Noir* of 1685, an article of which had stated that a slave acquiring freedom either by gift or purchase was to become a full French citizen, with all rights, even including the ownership of slaves of his own. The position of this enterprising new class may be compared in many respects to that of the Jewish middle class in Germany under Hitler. The Mulattoes, living in constant fear of the mass of Negro slaves—at least of falling back into their wholly unprivileged ranks—were in turn held in check by the less enterprising but politically dominant and socially secure ruling caste of "pure" Whites; and the means of doing so consisted of imposition of the most humiliating and cruelly enforced racial legislation ever up to that time conceived by man. Leyburn [1] quoting the contemporary Moreau de St.-Méry who listed ten major and 250 minor blood combinations recognized by the courts of Saint-Domingue, enumerates the steps by which the white planters discriminated against the Mulattoes:

> One by one his rights in the Code were abrogated. He might not fill any responsible office either in the courts or the militia, for that would elevate him above white persons. Certain careers, such as goldsmithing, were closed to him because they brought wealth; others, notably medicine and the apothecary's art, were forbidden on the ground that whites might be poisoned; law and religion were barred to him because of their public and honorific nature. Colored women were forbidden in 1768 to marry white men. In 1779 began a series of laws designed to humiliate the colored person in public: his clothes must be of a different material and cut from the white person's; he must be indoors by nine o'clock in the evening; he might not sit in the same section of churches and theatres with whites.

Unlike the Whites and the Mulattoes, the 500,000 Negro slaves could not claim title to the unparalleled wealth of Saint-Domingue; they were too busy producing it. In addition, of course, they were illiterate, without spokesmen or recognized means of protest—without privileges of any kind. So relentless, indeed, was the pace at which the slaves were driven to work, that it is estimated their entire number had to be replaced every twenty years. The inexhaustible source of supply, of course, was Africa. Chained

[1] *The Haitian People.* By James Leyburn. Yale University Press. 1941.

7

neck-to-neck in the pestilential holds of slave-ships, only the very strongest survived even the hazards of the "Middle Passage."

Dahomeans, Nagos, Congos, Aradas, Fans, Ibos, Mandingues, Capalaous and members of a hundred other proud tribes from the West Coast were driven to work in Saint-Domingue with whips and if they showed a disposition to protest were flogged to death, buried alive, thrown into ovens or horribly mutilated. Fear makes men capriciously brutal, and a French visitor in 1790 (Baron de Wimpffen) tells of witnessing an incident near Jacmel that left him with a sense of incredulous horror. A planter, strolling in the fields with his neighbor, admired one of the neighbor's trees to the extent of ordering one of his slaves to dig it up and replant it in his own yard. When the neighbor protested, the master had his slave strapped to a ladder and given a hundred lashes—for theft.

Two things alone sustained the slaves in this seemingly hopeless ordeal: their hatred of the master race and their participation in the religious ceremonials of their ancestors. Both consolations, of course, had to be indulged in secret. Slaves who could escaped into the mountain fastnesses; known as *marrons*, they descended upon the more isolated plantations from time to time. In 1758 the ablest leader of these outlaws, Macandel, almost succeeded in a plot to poison the reservoirs supplying the Plaine du Nord and fall upon the Whites while they were in convulsions. But the religious rites (*vaudou*), sometimes disguised as innocent "dances" and therefore tolerated by the planters as a kind of "safety valve," provided the real means of subversive organization and of contact between the *marrons* and their unliberated comrades.

THE INSURRECTION

The spark that was to ignite this magazine of suppressed fury was the French Revolution. When word came in 1789 that delegates were to be nominated to the States-General after a lapse of 150 years, the planters made two strategic blunders. They sent no fewer than 37 delegates to Paris to air their "grievances," and they asserted by implication that the only solution to their problems was complete freedom to determine their own course regardless of Paris. The answer of the National Assembly came quickly. A resolution was passed granting political rights to the *gens de couleur*. Two young leaders of the Mulattoes, Ogé and Chavannes, observing that the Whites had no intention of obeying this directive, organized a demonstration at Cap Français to which the colonial police replied in March of 1791 by seizing them and breaking them on the wheel in public.

It was at this juncture, when the Mulattoes were beginning to see that their rights were not to be gained except by force, that the unexpected happened. The 500,000 Negro slaves revolted. Their insurrection was plotted at a *vaudou* ceremony in the Plaine presided over by a *papaloi* (priest) named Boukman. Six days later, on August 20, the slaves set fire to the plantation houses and drove those masters they could not lay their hands on into the fortified towns. The Mulattoes, with no alternative, tried at first to make friends with the leaders of the Blacks and turn the insurrection to their advantage.

In the two years of confused struggle that followed, the French, with revolutions and foreign wars of their own to contend with at home, attempted to keep the disastrous situation in their richest possession in hand by sending Commissioners with instructions to appease the three [1] warring factions. But when one of them, an unscrupulous Jacobin named Sonthonax, exceeded his orders by decreeing the immediate freedom of the slaves and giving them the keys to Cap Français, Rigaud, the able leader of the Mulattoes who had played a major part in expelling the British from the undefended Southwest, broke with the Negroes.

TOUSSAINT LOUVERTURE

At this critical moment there came to the front of the stage the ablest figure in Haitian history, and perhaps the most remarkable man in the annals of the Negro race. Nearly fifty years old at the time of the 1791 revolt, in which he took no part except to assist the family of his master to escape, Toussaint Louverture had early in his life been recognized for his intelligence, taught to read French, and elevated from stable-boy (in which capacity he may have learned the superb horsemanship he later exhibited) to coachman. He was a small man and very homely, but shrewd and fearless and capable of inspiring a fanatical devotion among his followers. When a French general, during the truce that preceded his ultimate kidnapping, asked Toussaint where he would get arms should the fighting be renewed, he answered: "From your advanced guard!"

When war broke out between France and Spain in 1793,

[1] Actually there were five by this time as both the English and the Spaniards were attempting to take advantage of the confusion.

Toussaint had joined the Spanish with six-hundred disciplined Negroes and induced a number of French regular troops who had deserted to train and officer his ragged but growing army. By the spring of 1794 he was in command of 4000 men. That summer, when the English were threatening to take advantage of the French debacle by appearing as champions of the Whites and Mulattoes, Toussaint without warning deserted Spain and arrived in Cap Français as the saviour of Sonthonax and his nominal superior, the French Governor-General Laveaux. In a series of brilliant campaigns Toussaint and Rigaud succeeded in all but eliminating the British. Toussaint then turned his attention to the Mulatto general, whose relationship with Laveaux he first undermined with charges of conspiracy to detach Saint-Domingue from France. Coming to Laveaux's rescue when the French general had been imprisoned by two of Rigaud's lieutenants, Toussaint made the Governor so much his debtor that the latter appointed him Lieutenant-Governor and promised to do nothing thenceforth without his advice.

Sonthonax, meanwhile, who had had no difficulty in outwitting Negro leaders in the past, made the fatal mistake of trying to increase his own power by backing Toussaint and getting Laveaux recalled to France. Laveaux departed, but Toussaint promptly had the surprised Commissioner "elected" deputy to France, and, backed by several thousand troops, politely escorted him to shipboard. Writing conciliatory letters to the increasingly alarmed Directory in Paris, Toussaint, now in complete control of the North, determined to "integrate" the Mulatto South.

Rigaud had managed to restore prosperity in Les Cayes by following Toussaint's lead and introducing forced labor. The English, in their last remaining footholds—Jérémie, Port-au-Prince and Môle St. Nicholas—were inactive. By a master stroke of diplomacy Toussaint succeeded in convincing them that if they should surrender these strong points to *him*, not only would the French be embarrassed but opportunities for future trade would be theirs. They complied. At once Toussaint fell upon the South. It was January of 1800. Dessalines, Toussaint's ferocious lieutenant, drove Pétion, Rigaud's second-in-command, from Jacmel; and Toussaint himself, at the Battle of Aquin defeated Rigaud, forcing him and his 700 Mulatto *corps d'élite* to evacuate the country. According to an eyewitness, Pamphile de Lacroix, later a lieutenant-general in the Napoleonic army, the racial hatred engendered in this campaign was so great that disarmed combatants attacked each other with their teeth. Dessalines, who was now instructed to "pacify"

Peasant Woman

In Haiti, the peasant woman does all the marketing, most of the work, smokes a pipe. Her ancestors came from Africa to a land from which the Indians had been dispossessed. Is the wisdom of both races in this ancient face?

Toussaint Louverture

The primitive artist (Ciappini) painted him on wood, inspired by an old engraving which caught the pride, the craftiness and the determination of the Negro race's first great man.

Christophe or Pétion?

These symbolic likenesses on coins of the period point up the great decision in Haiti's early history—to go the way of industry and wealth under a dictator or of individual freedom and poverty under a benevolent patrician.

Sans Souci and the Citadelle

The palace bespoke leisure and culture—though not for the people. The fortress rose out of pride, vanity and death.

Charlemagne Péralte Martyrdom

As portrayed by Obin who knew the guerrilla leader (and his mother, here shown mourning for her son), Péralte's death at the hands of the Marines was a "crucifixion" for the nation's Second Coming.

The National Palace

... on the Champ de Mars symbolized Haiti's rebirth even before the Marines left.

Tides of Color
Rapprochement between the Mulatto and the Negro, old-time foes, is being achieved today.

Tides of Health
This little girl on the beach at Çaçra poses the question of undernourishment in the West's most overpopulated land.

Permanence

In a country where disease and suffering are as ubiquitous as death and taxes, selflessness is the rarest of virtues and the only symbol of hope. Dr. & Mrs. Lorimer Mellon at the great Albert Schweitzer Memorial Hospital, Déschapelle.

Change
The transition from François Duvalier's austere isolation to the relaxed régime of his son, Jean-Claude, was effected peacefully.

The Élite

Famed for the beauty of its women and the luxurious graces of its social life, Haiti's aristocracy is mostly light-skinned, light-hearted, French in its outlook.

The Peasant

He grows his own food, cultivates with a hoe or a *machete*, and grinds his grain with a mortar and pestle.

Agricultural Big Three

Coffee, grown in shade; sorted in sun. Sisal flourishes in the near-desert, is processed by machines. Sugar is loaded onto "Mademoiselle Diesel," refined in the capital.

Men of the Sea

. . . are not necessarily sea-dogs, nor are their craft always sea-worthy. The Haitian is unrivalled as a caster of seines; and in the coastal waters (as here at Ile à Vache) he manoeuvers his hand-made boats most skillfully.

Man-Power or Water-Power?

In this country of shocking contrasts, none symbolize better the primitive past and the pushbutton future than the peasant *coumbite* and the Péligre dam, here being surveyed by an American engineer while bulldozers level the ground in the Artibonite gorge 200-feet below.

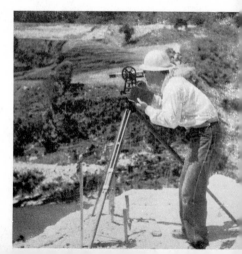

the province, followed up the campaign with a methodical extermination of the survivors. He was reproached but not disciplined
by Toussaint who remarked mildly: "I told him to prune the tree,
not uproot it."

1801 was Toussaint's year of full power, his *annus mirabilis*,
and his last year on the stage of history. It began with the capture
of Santo Domingo, the Spanish capital in the East, and the subjection of the entire island to Black rule. Ten years of revolution had
left Haiti in ruins. The towns were destroyed, the fields were no
longer cultivated, the great irrigation works in the Artibonite and
Cul-de-Sac plains were destroyed beyond repair. In that year, partly by appealing to the pride of the Negroes, partly by using his
armies to enforce discipline on the plantations, and partly by nego-
tiating favorable trade agreements with France's enemies, England
and the United States,[1] Toussaint managed to restore most of the
prosperity of the old Colony. This ex-slave who had once assisted
his white master to escape from Boukman's incendiaries now welcomed back the former planters as administrators; respected contracts; and sought to heal the terrible wounds inflicted by racial
warfare. When General Moyse, his nephew, disobeyed orders and
condoned a massacre of Whites, Toussaint had him executed by
a firing squad. The Constitution of May 9, 1801, was drawn up by
a committee consisting of seven Whites and three Mulattoes. Toussaint neglected nothing to convince a hostile world that the first
Negro state was prosperous, law-abiding and enlightened. But it
was not to be.

In fact it was inevitable that Napoleon, whose star had risen in
the meanwhile, should look with irritation upon this growing menace to his colonial ambitions. This "gilded African," as he called
Toussaint, had re-awakened dreams of the fabulous lost treasure
of Saint-Domingue—and there he stood athwart the road to empire
in North America! All during the year 1801 the shipyards of Brest
and Marseilles rang with preparations for the largest combined operation and transoceanic expeditionary force in history. The dictator's private orders to the commander of this force of 20,000 vet-
erans of Campo Formio and Arcola, his brother-in-law Leclerc,
were succinct: in the first fortnight the coastal towns were to be
taken; that accomplished, a converging movement would smash re-

[1] "The supplies and ships that [President John] Adams sent enabled Toussaint not
only to defeat Rigaud but to achieve independence of France in all but name."
(Leyburn)

sistence in the interior; in the third phase, flying columns would hunt down the remaining resistors:

> "In the first period you will not be exacting: you will treat with Toussaint, you will promise him everything he asks—in order that you may get possession of the principal points . . . Gain over Christophe and all the other black leaders favorable to the whites. In the first period confirm them in their rank and office. In the last period, send them all to France . . . Toussaint . . . must be put on board a frigate and sent to France . . . Declare Moyse and Dessalines traitors and enemies of the French people . . . White women who have prostituted themselves to negroes, whatever their rank, shall be sent to Europe."

That Toussaint should be the principal victim of this plan, which succeeded only its first phase, and that he should be betrayed by his own lieutenants, was the tragic destiny of this great man:

> Toussaint, the most unhappy man of men! . . .
> Though fallen thyself, never to rise again,
> Live, and take comfort. Thou hast left behind
> Powers that will work for thee; air, earth and skies;
> There's not a breathing of the common wind
> That will forget thee; thou hast great allies;
> Thy friends are exultations, agonies,
> And love, and man's unconquerable mind.

Had Wordsworth foreseen the terrible consequences to Haiti in Toussaint's kidnapping and subsequent death by starvation and cold in the Jura Alps, he might have written as feelingly, but otherwise.

INVASION: THE EXPULSION OF THE FRENCH

On February 5, 1802, Leclerc, with a detachment of 5000 men, went ashore off Cap Français. Christophe, the Negro commander whom Toussaint had placed in charge of the capital of the North, followed his instructions far enough to fire the city and retire to the hills. By February 6 Leclerc controlled the Plaine du Nord. The same day Port-au-Prince fell to another detachment, its principal fort which Toussaint had entrusted to a Mulatto surrendering to the French with shouts of "Vive la France!" Another Mulatto officer, Laplume, voluntarily surrendered the South Province. Only Dessalines at St. Marc and Maurepas at Port-de-Paix offered resistance as they retreated inland. The time which Napoleon had allotted for capture of the coastal towns had not been exceeded. The fortnight that followed could be devoted to the pursuit and reduction of Toussaint's main forces in the interior. On February 23 Toussaint's strong point in the Ravine de Couleuvres was stormed and the French drove on into Gonaïves, but Toussaint, thanks to Dessalines' support of his left flank, was permitted to escape with the bulk of his army and retire into the eastern Artibonite Valley. It remained for Leclerc to dispose of this concentration.

The decisive battle took place at the entrance to the valley the final week of March. Crête-a-Pierrot, an almost impregnable position, was garrisoned with a picked regiment of 1200 Negroes commanded by Dessalines. Leclerc took it at a cost of 2000 men, allowing half the garrison to cut its way to freedom. But the Black resistance was broken. Christophe went over to the French, and exposed by this defection, Toussaint and Dessalines capitulated on the promise of generous terms May 1.

Toussaint and Leclerc had each made a major mistake. Toussaint had put too much trust in his trained army of 20,000, and its officers, many of whom were motivated more by envy of his brilliance and hatred of the Blacks than by hostility to Leclerc; if he had armed the 400,000 remaining ex-slaves and instructed them in guerrilla warfare the French general's position would have been hopeless from the outset. Leclerc's mistake, if it can be called one, was in being unable to disguise Napoleon's real intention: the reimposition of chatel slavery on Saint-Domingue. The news that people had already been re-enslaved on Guadaloupe leaked out, and this, confirmed by the seizure of Toussaint, made it impossible for Leclerc to dissolve popular resistance before the advent of his ultimate and fatal adversary: Yellow Fever.

Already weakened by the loss of half his effectives in battle—to the point where he was in no position to risk guerrilla warfare by dealing with Christophe and Dessalines as he had with Toussaint—Leclerc encountered, June 1, his first case of the terrible disease. By the end of the month 4000 officers and men were dead. Leclerc himself was fighting off bouts of malaria when the news spread over the island that the French—contrary to his promises—had officially restored slavery in *all* their colonies. At once the fanatical North was up in arms. The Black generals slipped away and made peace with the Mulattoes, now regrouping in the South under the leadership of Pétion. Through July and August with his reinforcements dropping dead almost as soon as they landed, Leclerc wrote letters of desperation to Paris. The fear that Toussaint might escape from France and return to head up the rebellion became an obsession. On November 2, while writing a last frantic appeal to Napoleon for more troops, Leclerc himself succumbed to Yellow Fever.

Rochambeau, the new Governor-General, took over, and in his desperation went so far as to import from Jamaica 1500 bloodhounds at over $100 apiece to track down the Blacks and disembowel them, but it was too late. The resumption of war with England on May 12 cut Rochambeau's lines of communications. Defeated by Dessalines and Capoix-la-Morte at Vertières outside Le Cap on November 18, 1803, the French general surrendered his sword to the waiting English admiral on his flagship. The French, who had spent millions and sacrificed 50,000 men to recapture Saint-Domingue, were gone never to return. And Napoleon's ambition of making Hispaniola a stepping stone to Louisiana and the ultimate conquest of the New World came to nothing.

INDEPENDENCE

On January 1, 1804, at Gonaïves, Dessalines proclaimed the independence of the colony, re-naming it 'Haiti', and settled down to the task of restoring order and prosperity in a land devastated by thirteen years of unremitting combat. But his first act in the presence of the victorious army was symbolically fateful. Seizing the tricolor of France from its standard he tore out the white section and announced that henceforth the new nation's flag would be red and black alone.

CHAPTER II

THE FIRST HUNDRED AND FIFTY YEARS:

From Dessalines to Magloire

DESSALINES

"WHATEVER THE MEANS he employed to accomplish his ends," remarks Louis Mercier, one of Haiti's foremost educators, "Dessalines remains the most powerful spirit in our history . . . One cannot be a real Haitian unless one is Dessalinian." Modern friends of Haiti have been puzzled by this persistent devotion to the savage chieftain, even on the part of the country's predominantly Mulatto *élite*, a devotion that has overshadowed the towering figure of Toussaint Louverture, the genius of the masterbuilder Christophe, and the Olympian benignity of the Mulatto progenitor, Pétion himself. There is a disposition to overlook not only Dessalines' well-established brutalities, including his relentless persecution of the Mulattoes, but also the unyielding absolutism and libertine personal conduct that characterized his brief, unhappy reign.

The fact of the matter is that it was Dessalines who established Haiti's independence, and while the methods he used to prevent a recurrence of White overlordship—such as promising clemency to the remaining French and then butchering them in cold blood when they emerged from hiding—may not be condoned, the fact is also that no foreign master dared set foot on Haitian soil for one hundred and ten years after the famous statement purported to have been made by his secretary at Gonaïves.[1] It is felt, and perhaps not unreasonably, that without the violent passions and relentlessness that characterized this illiterate ex-slave's temperament, Haiti would not have weathered the storms that attended its birth.

In 1805 Dessalines had himself crowned Emperor in imitation of Napoleon, but without a complement of subordinate titles. "Mois seul, je suis noble!" he is said to have ordained, and this was

[1] "We will write this act of Independence using a white man's skull for an inkwell, his skin for parchment, blood for ink and a bayonet as pen."

a strategic blunder for it underlined an unpopular policy: all but Dessalines' soldiers would be forced to work with their hands. And work they did! The army was given two tasks: to build fortified works on the mountains behind the ports as notice to Napoleon that further invasion would be resisted; and to drive the rest of the population to the task of rebuilding Haiti's economic prosperity— not with whips, as had the hated Franch overseers, but with *lianes*, a whiplike vine that left an identical impression. Seizing both the French-owned plantations and those acquired since by Mulattoes, Dessalines moved swiftly toward a monopoly of the land by the State. Complete order and a large measure of the old prosperity were restored—but at a price of totalitarian subservience. The practice of *vaudou*, representing a threat of subversion, was stopped with the bayonet; and to a counsellor who suggested religious education as a consolation for the workers, the Emperor replied: "You are wrong: the laborers can be controlled only by fear of punishment and even death; I shall lead them only by these means; my 'morale' shall be the bayonet."

Dessalines was a tyrant, but he was a tyrant, as Leyburn says, whose tyranny eventually prepared the way for control by the Mulattoes over the Blacks. There is every reason to believe that Pétion, if he did not actually instigate the conspiracy that ended with the Emperor's assassination at Pont Rouge October 17, 1806, closed one eye.

CHRISTOPHE

Because the Mulattoes alone were able to read and write (many of them, in addition, like Pétion, had been able to complete their education in France) they had managed to occupy most of the administrative and diplomatic positions in the Haitian government under Dessalines. As a result, one of their first moves after the Emperor's ambushing, was to rewrite the Constitution in such a way that his Negro second-in-command, Christophe, would be deprived of Dessalines' absolute powers. Christophe refused to take the Presidency with these limitations, and in the struggle that ensued between him and Pétion, seized the North, including St. Marc, Gonaïves and Le Cap, leaving the Mulatto general in control of Port-au-Prince and the South.

Christophe had been born of free Negro parents on the English island of St. Christopher, from which he took his name, adding later the Christian name Henry in token of his admiration for everything English. He is said to have participated, with 800 other colored volunteers including Rigaud and Chavannes, in the American Revolutionary Battle of Savannah. When the insurrection of 1791 broke out he was working as a waiter in the Crown Hotel at Cap Français. Very soon he distinguished himself as an officer under Toussaint, rising later under Dessalines to the position of deputy commander-in-chief.

Christophe was like Dessalines in believing that he and he alone knew what was best for his people—work, with discipline. But he was unlike Dessalines in having no immovable prejudices against either Whites or Mulattoes. He was also unlike him in having a very high regard for culture and in being driven by a passion to make Haitians the most civilized, educated and creative people on earth. In the beginning, at least, his subjects regarded him as a benevolent "Papa." Crowning himself King Henry I and renaming Le Cap 'Cap Henry,' he had the astuteness to create at the same time a peerage, thus identifying the interests of his subordinates with his own. For the education of his daughters, the Princesses Athenaire and Amethyst, the King hired as governess a Quaker lady from Philadelphia.

Christophe's accomplishments in the early years of his rule were solid. Without changing the over-all system of state lands and policed labor inaugurated by Toussaint and Dessalines, he allowed tenant-proprietors to make a profit after paying one-fourth of their annual crop yield to the royal treasury and one-fourth in wages. Laborers were given Saturday afternoons and Sundays off, but were not permitted to leave their place of work or change occupation. The work day was marked by regular hours. Bugles sounded reveille, mess, prayers and taps. The strictest rules governed even dress. Honesty was promoted by planting purses on unsuspecting persons and meting out punishments if they were not turned in. Commerce was encouraged and foreign traders were given every protection. A sound currency was established. Education, under the latest English system, was made compulsory. Books were printed and beautiful coins issued. The wealth of Saint-Domingue returned briefly; for when Christophe died no less than $6,000,000 worth of his splendid silver coins found their way back into Boyer's half-empty treasury.

Dramatic in everything he did, Christophe concentrated the resources of his increasingly prosperous kingdom on the erection of two stupendous monuments. Consciously or not, they were conceived as symbols of the first Negro state's ability to compete in grandeur and ingenuity with the most enduring memorials of the white race. The shape these monuments took corresponded accurately with the two phases of Christophe's rule. Sans Souci, a magnificent palace of brick and mortar against the rising foothills back of Milot, symbolized the early effort of the benevolent monarch to provide primitive Haiti with a lasting emblem of cultural leisure and good living. The Citadelle, on a peak of the range behind it, characterized the tyrant into whom Christophe grew. Threatening, useless, inaccessible, conceived in needless fear and militarily absurd, it was constructed at untold cost of toil, tears and blood.

The Citadelle became, in 1820, the appropriate immediate cause of Christophe's overthrow, suicide and ignominious burial. Whether the story is true that the King ordered a platoon of his Royal Dahomets to march off the parapet of the fortress to impress a visiting dignitary with their loyalty to him, it is a fact that Christophe in his last years had to police his entire border to prevent desertions to Pétion's and Boyer's easy-going South. The end came when Christophe, suffering a paralytic stroke that prevented him from mounting his horse, was deserted by his army and most of his courtiers. He is said to have shot himself with a silver bullet at Sans Souci, following which the Queen and one faithful courtier dragged his huge body up the precipitous trail to the Citadelle and dumped it in a vat of quicklime.

PETION AND BOYER

The paradox of Alexandre Pétion's place in history is that he was at once Haiti's best-loved ruler and the architect of her economic ruin. The contemporary Haitian historian, Dantès Bellegarde, says that the key to the Mulatto general's character was good will, "but this trait betrayed him into an excessive indulgence with the actions of others, to a tolerance that degenerated very often into weakness . . . Of spotless honesty himself, he did not believe in honesty in others, considering as inherent in human nature the vices he had observed in Colonial society." [1] This tolerant cynicism and certainty that human nature could not be changed combined to mould Pétion's policy of *laissez faire*.

He began by redressing the balance in favor of the Mulattoes of the South, giving them subsidies when the coffee crop was poor,

[1] *Histoire du Peuple Haïtien* (1492-1952) by Dantès Bellegarde. Port-au-Prince. 1953.

bolstering their social position. Next, he abolished Toussaint's law prohibiting the holding of plantations of less than a minimum acreage. Then he began giving away the State lands: fifteen acres to every soldier in the army. Finally most of the remaining public domain was either parcelled out by sale or made available for squatting. The immediate result of this "democratization" of the land was that a peasant class came into existence. Growing sugar on a few acres is not profitable; growing vegetables is a necessity. Coffee became the major export crop, but whereas the French had pruned, fertilized and grafted their bushes, nature (as now) was allowed to take its course. Pétion, who had taken over a Haiti rich and united, left it divided and poor.

Naturally aristocratic in his nature, Pétion managed to moderate the social antagonism between Mulattoes and Blacks to such an extent that the former accused him of betraying his own caste. He established schools, ruled constitutionally, gave sanctuary and money to the Latin-American liberator Bolivar, and was mourned when he died by a nation of little people he had befriended, dark-skinned as well as light. As even his severest critic Leyburn admits, Pétion was "the one man among the early rulers who seemed to have any realization of the human values involved. Material gain is desirable but not at the expense of liberty. Freedom means something, even in poverty."

Pétion's successor, Jean-Pierre Boyer, another Mulatto aristocrat of good intentions, completed the division of Haiti's land into small parcels and of its society into two rigidly separated classes. Whereas under Dessalines there had been the rulers (the army) and the ruled, under Pétion and Boyer more and more of the people enjoyed less and less, with the aristocratic Mulatto caste distinguished from the peasantry not so much by their wealth as by the fact that they had a "classical" education, spoke French and did not work with their hands. The pattern has persisted to this day.

Boyer made an attempt, the last in Haitian history, to regiment agriculture to the prosperity of colonial days, but his instrument, the so-called *Code Rurale* of 1826 failed completely because its provisions (attaching the peasant to his land and requiring a certain fixed rate of production) were not enforced. The peasants simply ignored it. They had had a taste of liberty with economic anarchy and they preferred this to compulsion and the signing of dubious contracts. Even if they had made an effort to cooperate with the military, the Code would probably have failed. For one thing, the Army was occupied elsewhere. In 1822, two Haitian corps had taken advantage of Spain's current colonial troubles by enveloping Santo Domingo. For the next twenty years the whole island was under Haitian rule; but occupation by Negro troops, though it replenished the scattered population and noticeably darkened it, did not sit well with the Dominicans. Keeping their conquerors busy and finally throwing them out, the ex-Spaniards to the East emerged as an independent state in 1844, unified by their ordeal.

The second reason the Code failed was that Boyer, believing he was freeing Haiti from the threat of re-conquest, at last gained French recognition of Haiti's independence. This was accomplished, however, at considerable expense to the treasury; moreover the Army in consequence seems to have relaxed to such an extent that its own officers were no longer obeyed.

SOULOUQUE AND THE LONG NIGHT

The physical aspect of Haiti during Boyer's long rule had changed radically. Coffee grew wild, and the organized cultivation of sugarcane, cocoa and cotton for export had ceased altogether. The French buildings, factories and irrigation works that had survived the Revolution and been rebuilt under Dessalines or Christophe fell into disrepair. Earthquakes leveled the ruins. The neat coastal cities gave way to villages of jerry-built one-story wooden houses, while African-type thatched huts of wattles and mud began to dot the countryside. It was generally acknowledged that the Mulatto attempt to rule Haiti in behalf of an *élite* caste, while making economically disastrous efforts to appease a predominantly Negro population, had failed. Between 1844 and 1915, when the American Marines occupied Haiti and backed a series of Mulatto puppets, only three light-skinned presidents held power and for a period totaling only nine years.

The four presidents thrust into power between 1844 and 1859 were tools of the Negro army which had finally resolved to lessen the power of the Mulattoes in government; all of them were incompetent, and one of them was notorious. Faustin Soulouque many years before had been singled out by Boyer when the latter was prophesying trouble ahead. "Anyone," said the assured Mulatto president, "could become president in such a time—even that stupid Negro over there!" Soulouque, at whom Boyer was pointing, is said to have replied: "Please, Mr. President, don't make a fool of me." When word came to the lazy soldier, lying in his hammock, that he actually had been chosen by the drawing of his name out of a hat (to avoid conflict among the generals), he thought it was a practical joke.

The decision turned out to be no joke for Haiti. In the first year of his regime, Soulouque suppressed an attempted Mulatto coup by massacring every alleged participant. In the second, he had himself crowned Emperor. "After four years of his reign," writes J. C. Dorsainvil, "Christophe had but seventy peers, including three princes and eight dukes. At the beginning of *his* reign, Faustin I named four princes, fifty-nine dukes, ninety counts, two-hundred barons, three-hundred and forty-six chevaliers. Later the deputies and senators became in their turn barons . . ."

Wholly illiterate, Soulouque practiced *vaudou* openly, devoted hours of every day to fantastic court ritual, and diverted himself further with disastrous military expeditions against the Dominican Republic. The fact that following one of these a treaty was signed legalizing the incorporation of the villages of Las Cahobas and Hinche in the Haitian state is cited by Bellegarde as evidence that Soulouque's reign was not a total loss. But when the Emperor was finally unhorsed in 1859, everyone, including the Army, breathed easier.

The administration of Fabre-Nicolas Geffrard that followed was a popular one. This handsome general, as much at home in the salon as on the battlefield, "neither Black nor Mulatto," and something of a poet, reestablished a measure of unity in the country. The republic was restored. Geffrard encouraged the growing of cotton, making gins available to planters, and set up an agricultural credit corporation. He attempted to form a much-needed middle class, even importing Negroes from the United States to serve as artisans and professional men. He gave his blessing to an intracoastal steamship company. And he promoted public works, including construction of the first reservoirs and gaslight companies in Port-au-Prince. Reorganizing the primitive school system, he established scholarships in foreign universities for outstanding pupils and opened schools of law, architecture and painting. Under Geffrard's presidency a sixty-year breach with the Vatican was healed and such educational-charitable organizations as the Brothers of Christian Instruction and the Order of St. Joseph de Cluny were allowed to entrench themselves firmly.

Nevertheless Geffrard, for all his good will and enterprise, did nothing to arrest the increasing division and subdivision of the land. Under Haitian law, which follows the French in not recognizing primogeniture, holdings were becoming smaller and smaller. Geffrard put through a law by which national property could be leased in lots of fifteen acres *at most*, and though he attempted to legalize squatters' rights by registering their claims, he was not successful; the peasant saw no reason to sign a paper securing what he already occupied and had no intention of leaving.

Geffrard was driven into exile by his own palace guard in 1867. He was succeeded by four presidents of slight consequence. A fifth, Louis-Félicité Lysius Salomon, Soulouque's Minister of Finance, turned out to be another reformer of considerable gifts. Even under Soulouque's regime he had been distinguished for his honesty. But he was inflexible and vengeful. Suppressing another conspiracy of the Mulattoes, this one intended to restore their domination in the South, Salomon executed in reprisal so many innocent Mulattoes in the capital that business came to a virtual halt. His monetary reforms—the retiring of the public debt, the lowering of tariffs and the founding of the National Bank—were offset by the issuance of blizzards of paper money resulting in inflation. Salomon's attempt to solve Haiti's perennial problem, agricultural inertia, by outright grants of land to peasants who would cultivate a certain acreage of sugar or tobacco on provisional grants, was ignored by the peasants as soon as they saw that the state rather than themselves was the beneficiary. Following what had now become a pattern, Salomon was overthrown when he atempted to extend his tenure in office beyond its constitutional limit.

One other exceptional president, during this Dark Age of the Nineteenth Century that saw Haiti slipping steadily backward into barbarism, was Florvil Hyppolite (1889-96). Hyppolite, though dark-skinned, was a member of the *élite* and at the beginning of his regime a liberal. Establishing a Ministry of Public Works, he took advantage of a momentary upswing of the economic pendulum by introducing telegraph and telephone systems and building the scores of iron markets and bridges still to be seen from Jacmel to the Cape. Jacmel, however, proved to be Hyppolite's *ville fatale*. He had put down an uprising there with notable severity in 1891, but the superstitious Jacmelians, observing that the President's hat fell off as he proceeded to the "pacification" of nearby Bainet, predicted in a famous *Congo* that the southern seaport would prove his undoing:

En sortant la ville Jacmel . . .
Panama'm tombé . . .

When the President five years later set forth to give Jacmel another lesson in good conduct, he fell dead from his horse just as he was passing the Portail Léogane.

But the history of Haiti's Dark Age cannot be written in terms of well-recorded facts, nor can its dimly-remembered enormities be charged exclusively to the accounts of the dark-skinned generals who were its rulers. No matter how anti-Mulatto the latter might be, Mulattoes continued to hold the key ministries. Politics in those times could be reduced to the single question of who controlled the annual millions of the coffee tax—not only the government's sole source of revenue but the financial plum on which the Mulatto caste, through its accountants, lawyers and treasury officials, managed to subsist.

Since it was the latter who wrote such histories of the period as were written, the romantic, heroic episodes are fairly well documented but the record of graft survives mainly in legend. We know, for example, a good deal about Boyer Bazelais, the swashbuckling leader of the light-skinned opposition to President Salomon—how he recruited a hundred dashing young exiles in Jamaica, landed with them at Miragoâne, and held an army of 13,000 Negroes at bay from March 26, 1883 to January 8, 1884, accounting for 8000 of them, until every last Mulatto had been killed. But we know a lot less about Frédéric Marcelin, an *élite* politician, poet and financial wizard who held a variety of key posts under many Black presidents to whom he made himself indispensable. One legend tells how he managed to pass repeated inspections of the Treasury's books by oppositionists suspicious of his growing personal fortune; he is reputed to have always managed to show assets because he had built a secret tunnel connecting the Treasury with a German banking house which would wheel carts of gold into the Palace whenever an inspection of the empty coffers was contemplated. Another story relates Marcelin's coup against the Dominican ambassador who had abetted the murder of his cousins. It seems that the Haitian government owed the Dominicans $100,-000 in gold and that Marcelin, who was then Premier, persuaded President Hyppolite to transfer it with much ceremony to the neighboring capital on a warship. Honored guests on the voyage included most of Hyppolite's political enemies—and the Dominican Ambassador. A few hours after the ship steamed out of Port-au-Prince harbor, a massive explosion rocked the nearby coast. The vessel with all aboard vanished—save for a single seaman who was washed ashore clinging to one of many crates marked 'GOLD' which had floated because they were entirely empty.

OCCUPATION BY THE MARINES

When American Marines landed at Port-au-Prince from gunboats the afternoon of July 28, 1915, their unwelcome visit had been prepared by three circumstances. Several corrupt Haitian presidents had prolonged their terms in office by heavy borrowing abroad so that the National Bank and the railway that supplied the principal sugarmill in the capital had become virtually mortgaged to American interests. The opening of World War I offered a pretext to both France and Germany to collect their Haitian debts by force—and to the United States, which then had imperialistic ambitions of its own, to block any such possibility of European naval concentration in the Caribbean by invoking the Monroe Doctrine.

The third circumstance denied to Haiti any possibility of resisting occupation either by moral arguments or military force. In 1912 President Leconte had been blown up in the National Palace. The following year President Auguste was poisoned. During 1914 Presidents Oreste, Zamor and Théodore were disposed of by more conventional means: revolutions. But on the morning of July 28, 1915, President V.-G. Sam, having returned to the temporary presidential residence on the Champ-de-Mars from a massacre of his political foes in a nearby prison, and feeling that he would be safer in the French Embassy next door, was detected peering from behind a curtain by vigilant oppositionists. While the body of President Sam was being torn into small pieces by an infuriated mob in the square, 300 Marines landed at Bizoton from Rear-Admiral Caperton's cruiser, which had been waiting for just such an occasion in the harbor, and seized the strong points of the capital.

Reinforced by 300 more troops, the Marines fanned out over Haiti, disarmed the demoralized and over-officered Haitian Army of 20,000, and began opening recruiting centers for a native constabulary of 2400 men. Commanded at the outset by 100 Marine officers, this police force, out of whose ranks Haitians later rose to become commissioned officers, was the nucleus of the present small but well-disciplined Garde d'Haiti.

During their first two years of occupation the Marines encountered little overt resistance. The country was tired enough of revolutions to welcome a respite of law and order. Adequate gravel roads with bridges and concrete culverts were built connecting the principal towns. Hospitals and clinics were established; sewage systems and reservoirs constructed; telephones and electric systems installed. Mulatto business and professional men, with the threat of the Negro army removed, returned to commercial power, and the Marines, looking for political acquiescence as well as economic stability, backed into office a series of light-skinned presidents.

It was inevitable that trouble between the proud Haitians and their often tactless overlords would develop. In the early days of the Occupation the Americans had sent Marines from Southern states to Haiti on the fantastic theory that they would "know how to handle" Negroes. It was observed that American administrative officers were not hurrying to train native replacements as they had promised to do. As to the road-building, the Marines had re-awakened memories of slavery by impressing peasants into labor under the *corvée* system, in consequence of which political highwaymen who had terrorized the countryside during decades past (they were called *cacos*) regrouped and commenced organized guerrilla warfare against the Americans.

The so-called Cacos War that followed (1918-22) has been somewhat magnified and romanticized in recent years. Law-abiding Haitians at the time had little sympathy for activity they had come to regard as banditry since 1860. However many of the 6000 Haitians who were killed died in consequence of stupidity and inflexibility on the part of their pursuers. A crowd at Cayes, for example, was decimated in a burst of machine-gun fire by a trigger-happy noncom; innocent peasants were shot at St. Marc in "reprisal" for the activity of snipers. At the peak of the struggle, 3000 Marines under the command of the famous Smedley Butler were required to exterminate the Cacos in the Central Plateau. The climactic event was the ambushing of their leader, Charlemagne Péralte, near Grande Rivière du Nord and the roping of his dead body to a door as a warning to future guerrillas.[1]

FROM VINCENT TO MAGLOIRE

Order having been restored and government re-established, it was patent, writes Leyburn, "that any Haitian administration which could effect the withdrawal of the Marines would be immensely popular; it was equally patent that if the Americans left

[1] The foregoing account is based for the most part on the testimony of Fortuné Bogat, a patriotic but not anti-American Haitian business man who served in the constabulary under Marine officers as a young man.

the country, the benefits of their efficiency and material improvement would remain as a tangible boon to Haiti."

Bogat tells this story of the period immediately following the withdrawal. It seems that the telephone system continued to function with remarkable efficiency, every employee arriving for work on time, until one day somebody entered the central exchange and, pointing to a Marine officer's hat hanging over the director's desk, asked scornfully "What's that?" When told it was the director's hat, he tweeked it from its nail, laughing loudly and long. "Don't you know that Captain —— left Haiti a month ago?" he roared. And placing the hat on his own head at a rakish angle he sauntered out the door whistling "The Halls of Montezuma." From that day on, it seems, the employees relaxed and the telephone system began to develop those exasperating peculiarities for which it has since become notorious.

All during the Occupation, vociferous American groups, opposed to continuation of the Theodore Roosevelt-Woodrow Wilson policy of armed intervention in Latin-American affairs, had been hammering at the State Department.[1]

The withdrawal took place under the administration of Sténio Vincent, a Mulatto elected in 1930 without American interference, and was in part the consequence of the new Good Neighbor doctrine in Washington. It was formalized by the visit of President Franklin D. Roosevelt to Cap Haïtien in 1934. An American fiscal agent was left behind to control customs until the Haitian debt should be paid.

Vincent, calling himself Haiti's "Second Liberator," benefited, and the *élite* caste seemed firmly in the saddle for the foreseeable future. Reform of the Constitution—the one under which the Occupation functioned had been written by F.D.R. himself at the

---

[1] The Chief of Police for the Marines accuses President Hoover and his Forbes Commission of causing the ouster of their own man, President Borno, and the selection of his successor, President Roy, at the behest of the opposition party simply to mollify "liberal" opinion in the States. Of the Occupation in general he adds: "I am an honest imperialist. I believe we had a perfect right to go into Haiti, just as I believe the police have a right to go into the house of any man who maintains a nuisance. I believe that our Occupation was honest, conscientious and benevolent, and that we conferred immeasurable benefits on the Haitians. But often I blush at the transparent maneuvers to which we resorted to make it appear that the Haitians were accomplishing their own regeneration in accordance with democratic principles as understood in the United States . . . We were continually obliged to manufacture flimsy evidence to prove that they really wanted us to occupy their land." —John H. Craige in *Cannibal Cousins*, 1934.

time he was Assistant Secretary of the Navy—was Vincent's first task. This consisted principally in enormously increasing the power of the executive at the expense of the deputies and senators who had ridden high during the Occupation. It gave the president, moreover, the right to name 10 of the 21 senators and to submit a list of the 11 others to the Chamber of Deputies for their nominal approval. A later amendment written by Vincent went further and gave him the power to *remove* any one of these senators at any time he chose.

On its surface, the Constitution gave to the people the right to choose the Executive and the members of the Assembly, but it must always be born in mind that Haiti, with 90% of the people illiterate and exercising no voice in the affairs of government, is not, and never has been in our sense of the word, a democracy. Bellegarde himself sadly admits that "with the same docility with which they had accepted the share of sovereignty that was bestowed on them in 1935, the people renounced in 1939, by plebiscite, their precious prerogative to choose directly the Chief Executive and to revise the Constitution." Exactly what group he had in mind when he spoke of "the people," Bellegarde does not say.

On the whole Vincent ruled wisely and well. He retired, albeit grudgingly, in favor of his lieutenant, Élie Lescot, and he acquired in so doing the unique distinction of handing over the reins of office peaceably to his successor and of being permitted to remain in Haiti.

Only one humiliating episode mars the otherwise constructive record of Vincent's tenure. In October of 1937 word trickled in from the northeast provinces that Trujillo, the Dominican dictator, had rounded up thousands of migratory Haitian cane-cutters, penned them in stockades, and cut them to pieces with carbines and *machetes*. The Rivière Massacre at Ouanaminthe was red with blood for a week. Trujillo denied nothing, except having actually given orders for the atrocity—which from a man who supervised even the private lives of his people was patently absurd. Vincent has been excused for accepting gratefully Trujillo's sop, an indemnity of $750,000 for the rehabilitation of the families of the victims, but not only was most of the sum never paid at all, but Vincent had the bad taste to express his thanks by permitting the Haitian capital's principal thoroughfare which had just been renamed "Avenue Trujillo" to so remain.

Lescot's four years in office (1941-5) were marked by a disposition to cooperate fully with wartime America's policy of Latin-

American pump-priming while at the same time using the emergency (Haiti declared war on the Axis the day after Pearl Harbor) to nail down Vincent's executive authoritarianism. Neither policy was designed to enhance Lescot's popularity with the Haitians. Cut off from its Euroepan trade by the Nazi U-boats, American financial and technical assistance, unfortunately, took the form of a joint Haitian-American development corporation (SHADA), $4,000,000 of whose resources were devoted to the experimental growth of a rubber-substitute weed known as *criptostegia*. SHADA became a political football. Haitians claimed that it threw peasants out of their homes without proper compensation, destroyed the best land and fruit-trees in the Republic, produced no rubber. Americans denied all charges except the last, but added that rubber or no rubber Haiti's economy would never have survived the War without this shot in the arm.

Lescot, meanwhile, had amended the much-amended Constitution to prolong his term of office, giving himself not only the right to re-election but clamping the lid on any elections whatever for the duration of the "emergency." It was at this precise moment, Bellegarde mordantly points out, that the United States, with millions of men fighting all over the world, was conducting a perfectly orderly contest between Messrs. Roosevelt and Dewey.

With the War's ending, Lescot's spree was over. It took no more than a student strike to set in motion the capital's seething discontent. The Army folded its arms while a mob of market-women stormed the home of the President's hated Interior Minister, reportedly tearing out some of the nails that held it together with their teeth. On January 11, 1946, Lescot and his family took flight for Canada. In his place at the National Palace sat a military executive committee consisting of the chief-of-staff of the Army, Colonel Franck Lavaud, the director of the Military Academy, Major Antoine Levelt, and the commander of the strategically placed Palace Guard, Major Paul Magloire.

Behind the opposition to Lescot lay the time-honored complaint that a Mulatto president had used his high office to feather the nests of the *élite*. The complaint was sound, if one gave Lescot credit for having attended handsomely to his own family first—and if one made the reservation that historically speaking Mulattoes had no monopoly on raiding the public treasury. Nevertheless there was a new element in the complaint, a by-product of the War. Intellectuals the world over were becoming conscious of racial injustices as never before. No one could deny that the masses of the Haitian

28

people received little consideration from the light-skinned politicians and entrepreneurs of Port-au-Prince—or that these masses were black. The military executive committee affirmed its support of a national unity beyond skin-color, but it gave its support to a Negro who was well-educated and familiar with political office but who was definitely not a member of the *élite* caste.

There is some question whether the committee realized, however, that in elevating Dumarsais Estimé to the presidency it was giving its support to a man who had every intention of establishing himself as a leader of the working-man—and of the Blacks. Outwardly, Estimé's administration accomplished much good. At a cost of $600,000 the frontier village of Belladère was transformed into a modern two-story town, complete with plumbing, electricity, paved streets and a hotel. That it would symbolically counter Trujillo's model outpost of Elias Piña across the frontier was considered to outweigh the fact that Belladère was completely off the beaten track—and connected to the accessible parts of Haiti by a track not even beaten. More tangible in its benefit to Haiti was Estimé's expenditure of $6,000,000 on the Bi-Centennial Exposition of Port-au-Prince in 1949. The clearing and landscaping of the capital's malodorous waterfront slums has been of inestimable value to tourism, which soon thereafter became Haiti's second greatest source of revenue. A law requiring peasants to wear shoes in town and merchants to install plate-glass windows and neon-signs was one of this humorless President's less serious accomplishments. A story of the time relates that peasant offenders were taken to Gonave Island where they were stranded with a pick and shovel. When arrests mounted, the government investigated. The prisoners, they found, were exchanging their shovels for rides back to the capital with local fishermen, whereupon they would sell the picks for a good price and promptly get arrested again.

Estimé's attempt to create collective farms by giving peasants who cooperated 16 acres of land, tools and seed, proved no more successful than the rural reforms of Boyer and Salomon. But Estimé's discharge of the American debt, thus effecting recall of the last hated caretaker of the Occupation, and his signing of an agreement with the Export-Import Bank of the United States for the financing of a $6,000,000 irrigation and land-reclamation project in the Artibonite Valley, were substantial achievements. Under Estimé's presidency, Haiti's first income tax became law.[1]

[1] The scale now runs from 5% on incomes of $3000 or under to 30% on incomes over $40,000.

Late in 1949 it became apparent that the socialist Estimé intended to go much further than public works in changing Haiti's face. On April 18, 1950, the Senate refused to amend the Constitution to permit him to succeed himself, and less than a month later the Army handed Estimé his passport and sent him into exile.

Paul E. Magloire, who was elected president by a direct vote of the people in an unopposed election following the Army's dissolution of the two legislative chambers, was as dark-skinned as his predecessor. Trusted by the *élite* and the business community, however, he made it clear that skin-color would have nothing to do with his choice of officials. And as the Army's favorite son he was able to count on the complete loyalty of the real power in Haiti.

The social and economic stability which General Magloire was able to achieve was short-lived. Even before the expiration of his term in 1957 it had become apparent that this stability had been bought at a cost of unprecedented family graft. But by the time Magloire and entourage had fled abroad, in the wake of an abortive attempt to extend their six-year term, it was futile to estimate how many millions had been siphoned from the Peligré Dam and other American-financed projects. Haiti was virtually bankrupt.

There followed a period of anarchy with "provisional" governments succeeding each other in rapid succession. It culminated with a free election involving Louis Déjoie, prominent mulatto businessman, and the Black-Peasant Left, variously represented by Dr. François Duvalier, Clément Jumelle, and Daniel Fignolé. Duvalier won.

Why the American government supported the victorious candidate, doubled its commitment in 1959 to aid-programs in the Artibonite Valley and the North designed to make Haiti self-sufficient in food, and then from 1963 on threw a *cordon sanitaire* around Haiti withdrawing all personnel except the Ambassador and a skeleton staff, are questions still unanswered. The American explanation was that President Duvalier insisted on politicalizing the Haitian staffs of the various projects. According to the Haitian ruler, the programs were shut down because he objected to having most of the loans go for American salaries, equipment, and sale of surplus foods to the States—familiar charges throughout Latin America. Whatever the cause, Haiti became isolated and increasingly impoverished during the '60s; and the now-embattled "Papa Doc" spent the nation's dwindling resources repelling a series of American-based attempts to assassinate or overthrow him, and consolidating his power at the expense of the largely-mulatto *élite* that had held economic power in Haiti since the Occupation.

To frustrate his enemies within and without, Duvalier did not hesitate to shake up the Garde d'Haiti, trained and still supplied by the U.S. Marine Corps, ousting its American advisors, closing its *élite* Military School, and transferring ultimate power from its officer caste to a triumvirate of military chiefs at odds with one another and wholly dependent on him. The arsenal was transferred to the Presidential Palace compound, and the instrument through which compliance of both the military and the business community was secured was the secret police (popularly known as Tonton Macoutes). Whatever effect these strong-arm plainclothesmen had on the local opposition and on Haiti's image abroad—an image melodramatized by Graham Greene and by Duvalier's many enemies in exile—a genuine transfer of power was effected.

A new ruling group, predominantly middle-class and black, was in the saddle; and its philosophy, technocratic rather than exploitative in a commercial sense, began to be applied. Schools where the student population had been 90% mulatto or white are now more than 50% black—with the average constantly approaching a proper reflection of Haiti's actual demography. And a similar shift took place in the non-Catholic priesthood (once imported *en masse* from Brittany) and hierarchies of various Protestant sects.

Now invulnerable to oppositions, foreign and domestic, the President-for-Life as the decade ran out began to moderate his controls and apply his powers constructively. Factories to make Haiti independent of imported flour and cement were built. Electric-generating turbines were installed at the Peligré Dam. The moribund telephone system in the capital was given new equipment. By 1972 more than a tenth of Haiti's non-domestic wage-earners were employed in the so-called Transformation Industries, processing out of U.S.-imported materials such products as baseballs, computer switches, brassieres, screw-drivers and toupées, for sale in the U.S. And low though the wages were, these 10,000 new jobs, with the figure expected to double annually, were giving a tremendous boost to the Haitian economy. Tourism, down to less than 20,000 annually in the '60s, spurted to over 200,000 in 1973, with new hotels and beach-clubs sprouting by the dozen.

By late 1978, with young President Jean-Claude Duvalier seemingly in firm control after five years as his father's anointed successor, Haiti's cultural primacy in the Caribbean was beginning to be accompanied by material improvements. The new North-South superhighways sparked the needed decentralization of the crucial tourist industry.

CHAPTER III

HAITI TODAY:

Ways of Life Among the Rulers and the Ruled

THE PEOPLE

HAITI'S FOUR MILLION, as we have already noted, fall into two primary castes, the *élite* (comprising less than 10% of the population, and for the most part, though by no means exclusively, light-skinned), and the peasants who are predominantly black. The Blacks are descendants of the African slaves imported into Hispaniola between 1510 and 1791. The Mulattoes are descendants of these slaves intermarried with French colonials or white foreigners who came to Haiti during or after the Revolution. But money, as everywhere, can dissolve barriers. A Creole proverb wisely observes: A rich Negro is a Mulatto, but a poor Mulatto is a Negro.

A middle-class, of varying complexion, is slowly emerging in Haiti. Many of its members are Syrians, Lebanese, Corsicans, etc. who came to Haiti in this century and constitute a majority of the shopkeepers in the towns. These tradesmen, even in the small communities where caste-consciousness is almost unknown, tend to think with the *élite*, though the *élite* for their part regard them as social inferiors.

Haitians with Indian features are not uncommon and it may be that some interchange of blood took place in the Sixteenth Century between the African slaves and those Indians imported from the mainland to replace the exterminated Arawaks. Traces of the Spanish, and their language, are noticeable along the 194-mile Dominican frontier.

There are about 3000 permanent white residents in the Republic, most of them concentrated in Port-au-Prince and engaged in business.

THE LANGUAGE

French is the official language of Haiti, but a patois called Creole is spoken informally by everyone, and exclusively by the peasants. According to one theory, Creole was already well-developed as a dialect when the mass of African slaves was imported. The French buccaneers, most of whom came from Normandy and Brittany, spoke it and contributed to it most of its words and constructions. The slaves spoke it with an African softening and suppression of "r's," adding a considerable number of words having to do with their religious beliefs and appropriating others from the Indians. Certain Spanish, English and American words were added later. According to a second theory Creole emerged as a language only when it became necessary for the French and the Africans to find a common means of communication.

To those familiar with French, Creole is not difficult to understand when spoken slowly. It rarely is spoken slowly, however. Americans with a good ear who speak no French at all are more likely to speak Creole fluently since the word-order in some respects is similar to English. Because Creole developed independently in Louisiana, French Canada and the French West Indies, people familiar with those dialects can get along readily in the Haitian.

Creole is rich and salty, and nothing will demonstrate better its terseness than to quote a few of the thousands of class-conscious proverbs for which it is justly famed. *Lo mapou tombe, cabrit mangé feuille li.* When the (giant) Mapou tree falls, the (little) goat eats its leaves. *Ça Neg fait Neg, Bon Dieu rit.* When Black hurts Black, God laughs. *Bon Dieu grand passé Roi.* God is bigger than the King. *Malheuré pas rêve poule; c'est boeuf li rêve.* The poor man doesn't dream of a chicken; he dreams of an ox. *Chien derrié chien; devant chien: Monsieur Chien.* A dog is a dog except when you're facing him; then he's Mr. Dog.

Unquestionably Creole has played a part in keeping the peasant isolated on his acre. Until recently, classes in even primary schools were conducted in French which meant that most children were listening to a half-foreign language. However efforts to make Creole the sole vehicle of primary education have not succeeded. It is felt that teaching children to read in a language that boasts no more than a dozen printed books would serve to cut them off even more completely from the rest of the world. Advocates of a Creole education, however, ask pertinently: Is it more important to turn the peasant into a Frenchman with a consciousness of the problems of the outside world or to equip him to cope with the problems of his own environment by his own means?

THE PEASANT

It has been said of another semi-primitive culture—that of the Italian island of Sardinia—that "neglect, injustice and backwardness have created a climate in which the law is thought of only in terms of the tax-gatherer and the policeman. Poverty has led to a tradition of honorable stealing . . . and violence." The Haitian peasant, in contrast, as everyone who knows him well can testify, is peaceable, law-abiding,[1] good-humored and philosophical. Why? There are several explanations. One is that the Sardinian's background is feudal where the primary values were "honor" and individual vengeance; the Haitian peasant, a descendant of slaves, avoids trouble,[2] puts the best face on things, rarely complains and finds his ultimate salvation in the group.

It has been said that the position of the governing group would be threatened if the peasant improved his lot, and this is true. However, things being as they have been for 150 years, the peasant is non-political. Revolutions have always left him worse off. He is content to remain scattered rather than cluster in villages, the better to avoid the surveyor, the tax-gatherer and the police. He is not lazy—he has to work hard to make a precarious living—but he could not be described as industrious either, and certainly not ambitious. "If work were a good thing," another proverb runs, "the rich would have grabbed it all long ago." For more than a century the idea of work was linked with the idea of slavery, and teaching the peasant that work can also mean freedom has been difficult. Moreover militarization, in the early days of the Republic, made it incumbent on the peasant to avoid work. Nor was there any puritan tradition to glorify industriousness for its own sake. Nevertheless, if it can be said that Americans live to work, it is equally true that Haitians work to live.

The Haitian peasant woman must be considered separately. She is always working. She rarely tills the fields, as did her African ancestor, but taking care of the family and the domestic animals, drawing water often from great distances, beating the laundry in the riverbed with a club, and doing all the marketing (selling as well

[1] Tourists beset by beggars, fresh children, arrogant young men and petty thieves in Port-au-Prince will do well to remember that the first and last belong to the declassed riffraff found in any large city, and that the others are insecure members of a rising and still unaccepted middle-class.

[2] The response *'en principe,'* equally popular with the *élite,* reflects this attitude. So does the popular saying 'To nod your head Yes won't break your neck.'

34

as buying), keeps her busy from earliest childhood on. In the days of *cacos* and *corvées* it was not safe for the men to go to market, and today women derive too much enjoyment from bargaining and market gossip to willingly give it up.

Part of the social life of the male peasant expresses itself in the *coumbite*. The *coumbite* is what New Englanders used to call a work-bee. The cultivator who has a big job to do enlists the aid of his neighbors, helping them later in his turn. The work is done in rhythm, with a drum or a *lambi* (conch shell) providing the accompaniment. Sometimes a singer provides barbed comments on the shirkers.

Zami nous cila c'est gros neg assez!
Tous temps li gagn travaille pour nous.
Lé nous besoin yo, hanh!
Li gagnin zaffai nans ville, oh!

Our friend here is an important Negro!
All the time he has work for us.
The day we need him, hanh!
He has something to do in the city, oh!
    (after Courlander)

After the work a feast, or party (*bamboche*) is held.

Seabrook tells this story of a legendary peasant's shrewdness; he got it, he says, from Ernest Chauvet, now publisher of *Le Nouvelliste*:

Théot Brune, at twenty, ragged, barefoot, and without a copper, wanted a bottle of *clairin*, which is colorless, like moonshine corn whiskey. He found an empty bottle, half filled it with water, and approached a woman who sat retailing her wares, dried herring, little bundles of tobacco leaves, food and drink, beneath a roadside booth. "Replenish my bottle," he ordered, and she filled it, unsuspecting, from her jug. "Thirty cobs" (six cents), she told him.

"Thief! *Criminelle!*" he cried in a passion. "Never!"

"What would you pay?"

"I will not trade with robbers. Take back your *clairin*, pour it out."

And with his bottle still half-filled, but now with rum and water mixed, he played the trick successively at other roadside booths until the pure water he had started with was transformed into pure rum.

At thirty, Théot moved to Port-au-Prince, where he acquired a house and family; but he still had no money and wanted a pair of shoes. He sent a child to a neighborhood merchant, saying, "Théot has rheumatism. Send one shoe, size thus, for Théot to try on, and if it fits, I will return with the money and get the other shoe." There seemed no sense in Théot's trying to cheat him out of one shoe; so the merchant acquiesced. But Théot sent the child with the same tale to another merchant, and Théot rejoiced in a pair of shoes which had cost him nothing.

At forty, Théot, who had risen considerably in the world, had begun to dabble in politics. His shrewdness and trickery had made him valuable to men higher up. He decided privately that the time had come for him to go higher up himself. There were some senatorial vacancies to be filled by senatorial ballot. For Théot to aspire to a senatorship was quite absurd, but this is what he did: He went confidentially to one senator and said, "I have a little favor to ask you which can do nobody any harm. On the first balloting for such and such a vacancy, I want you to vote for me, so that when the minutes are published in the newspaper reports, Théot's name will appear written in that honorable company; it will make my wife so proud and happy, and it will increase my prestige with all my neighbors. They will say, 'So, this Théot is getting to be a man of importance!' and it will not do anybody any harm. You can vote afterward for your serious candidate, of course. It is just a little confidential favor you can do me, my vanity perhaps, and no one need ever know who did it. Neither of us need mention it to a soul. But I do want just that one vote." He confided his harmless wish, "in confidence" to other senators, who must have been subsequently somewhat astonished when they discovered that they had elected Théot senator almost without a dissenting vote.[1]

Haiti is probably the only country in this Hemisphere where neither the plough nor the wheelbarrow are generally used. Crop rotation is unknown. Congo peas, millet (*piti mi'*) or yams are grown over and over again on the same hillside until a very low yield forces the peasant to burn off and move nearby; when nature and cattle-grazing restore some fertility, he returns to the original plot.

In addition to the basic food crops already mentioned, the peasant may grow maize, rice, red beans, sweet potatoes, manioc and plantains. Common fruit trees include mango, avocado, papaya and lime. The typical peasant may have a few chickens and pigs, a *bourique* (donkey), a dog, and perhaps some goats. Goat's milk, unaccountably, is not drunk. The more prosperous peasant may have, in addition, a cow or two and a small horse for transport. The qual-

[1] Quoted from *The Magic Island* by W. B. Seabrook.

ity of all these animals except the goats is poor since their food depends entirely on forage. A small dairy industry is to be found near the larger towns.

The typical native hut (*caille*) is built by the man at a cost of from $10 to $50. There are three types, all having a hand-hewn wooden frame. The poorest is walled with mud-daubed wattles and thatched with palm branches or guinea grass. The second is plastered inside and out with lime over lathes and thatched with good straw. The third is painted over the plastering, sometimes with a superimposed design in color; it has a ceiling and wooden floors, sometimes a tin roof and a porch; and there are two or more rooms. The houses, and the large families that live in them, are as clean as circumstances and proximity to water allow. Sanitary facilities and running water are unknown in the rural areas. Sleeping mats are made of banana branches. All cooking is done over three stones and a brazier outside the house; black coffee for breakfast, and one prepared meal a day, is the usual fare.

There are two classes of peasants, the more prosperous being generally descendants of soldiers who were given small estates in the mountains at the time of the Revolution. In spite of unremitting efforts by the Catholic Church, *placage*—a polygamous arrangement whereby a man establishes common-law wives on different plots of land as overseers and labor suppliers—is more often the rule than marriage. Marriages cost money. Nevertheless, with or without legal sanction, the family dominates Haitian life. Children are treated well, start working as soon as they can carry sticks or cans of water, mate early. Sex is regarded as normal, not sinful. Old people—the few that survive disease and hard work—are respected.

When death comes to a peasant, the deceased is often dressed in his best clothes and seated at a table with food in front of him. Sometimes a cigarette is placed in his mouth—or a clay pipe, if it be a woman. Then the wake begins. All the friends and neighbors of the departed come; and sometimes others who don't even know him arrive from miles away, wailing and crying till they fall exhausted. But mostly it is a time for communal entertainment, card games and the like, feasting and dancing. Although by law the corpse is supposed to be buried within 24 hours, decomposition is sometimes allowed to set in to insure that enemies or sorcerers won't dig it up and make a work-slave (*zombi*) of it. This widely-held superstition is based to some extent on an African practice of drugging people with the root of a certain tree, the effect of which is to turn the taster into an automaton. The extraordinarily heavy slabs of stone with which all Haitians cover graves is added insurance that the dead won't rise again.

THE *ÉLITE*

To the foreign visitor who, whatever he is, is not a peasant, peasants the world over seem more or less alike. Every ruling group, however, seems sharply distinguished by national peculiarities. This is particularly true in Haiti. I attended two dinner parties in Haiti some years ago. One was at the home of a very old family, its sons married to French or American women so that their children could not have been taken for Negroes anywhere; in fact, the daughters were now in finishing school in New England. The women—and this is true of the Mulatto aristocracy generally—would have been considered beautiful anywhere in the world: pale bronze or off-white, the eyes deep-set and incredibly clear but languorous under very long lashes, in carriage supple, feline 'like caged panthers dreaming.' The men were as typical of their caste and as striking: proud, fiery of mien, graceful in all their gestures but intensely masculine, relaxed and socially at ease.

The dinner itself was an elaborate affair of many courses and many wines. The dress was formal. The conversation was about subtleties in the acting of the Comédie Française. And after dinner in the drawing-room there was polite piano playing to which everyone listened politely. Then the men withdrew to discuss world politics and some pretty critical things were said about the current American effort to keep the Communists out of Asia. Our host, who insisted that the American State Department was "reactionary" and "imperialistic" was then well known for his opposition to the Haitian government's effort to impose a mild income-tax and permit the organization of labor unions.

The other party, given by a leading intellectual and attended by government officials as well as literary figures, was informal. There was as much a profusion of food, but the dishes were "peasant" plantains and dried fish, and the only drinks served were rhum-sodas and whiskey. The women, even more than at the other party, were relegated to the background, sat by themselves, and drank *kola-champagne*, a soft-drink. The conversation was much more animated and as the evening progressed became really brilliant. The men provided after-dinner entertainment by singing *vaudou* songs to the accompaniment of a guitar, and during one number a young officer of the Garde performed an impromptu *banda* dance climaxed by a feigned *crise de possession* which brought down the house. Very late in the evening some of the more adventurous youth departed to join the "Orthophonique," one of the largest Mardi Gras *bandes* with a special reputation for wildness; accompanying the revellers in old clothes and masks they would be sure to find plenty of excitement without being recognized.

At the first party the décor had been a little stuffy—academic still-lifes, Chinese vases and screens, heavy uncomfortable furniture of dark mahogany. The ladies fanned themselves and did not smoke. At the second, a Coca-Cola calendar, a photograph of a favorite soccer-star and a card-size reproduction of a Matisse were tacked haphazardly to the bare walls. The guests in shirt-sleeves sat cross-legged on the floor or steps, and they helped themselves. At both parties the American guests were treated with impeccable consideration—and just enough formality to make them sensible of the privilege they were being accorded.

In 1939 Leyburn was able to describe the *élite* as that 3% of the Haitian population which does not work with its hands. The percentage may have risen a point or two; and the employment of a well-born Haitian woman as a stenographer, hostess or curio-shop saleswoman, is no longer uncommon; but the definition still holds. Other criteria listed by Leyburn included education and the ability to speak French, an almost religious devotion to "culture," residence in the cities ("One must see and be seen by other members of one's caste"), formal marriage, and skin-color.

The last qualification has relaxed greatly under the administrations of the Negro presidents, Estimé and Magloire. The so-called "Two-Hundred Families," mostly very light in complexion and tracing their ancestry to Revolutionary times, are still the most important component of the *élite* socially speaking, but the bulk of the caste consists of the wealthy, the intellectually brilliant, and the more recently "arrived" among politicians and the military. It is from the latter that large accretions of dark-skinned Haitians have swelled the ranks of the *élite* under the last two administrations. And this, coupled with the rise of the small but aggressive urban middle-class, who now dispute even the sacrosanct Cabane Choucoune with the aristocracy, has led some Haitians to insist that the term *élite* itself has become anachronistic.

The *élite* established its character during the 72 years that followed Boyer's downfall, a period in which Mulattoes ruled for only nine. Adapting themselves to life under Negro (mostly military) presidents, the Mulattoes controlled business, monopolized the Law, became state secretaries and diplomats, valedictorians and poets. To the extent to which one may generalize, the *élite* then assumed such social-psychological traits as elegant deportment, fiery patriotism, conversational brilliance, a love of indirection and intrigue, mild anti-Americanism,[1] extreme Francophilism, indifference toward religion, cynicism in politics, *laissez faire* in economics. At the same time the *élite* was developing that social *savoir faire* for which it is renowned, its attitudes toward others were solidifying: a contempt for the benighted peasantry, a stern benevolence toward domestics, a double standard as regards women and a belief that children should be (if nothing else) *bien elevé*. Somewhere along the way, the *élite* acquired a marked taste for poetry and *belles lettres*, but little interest in any of the other arts—including interior decoration. "There are among the *élite*," Leyburn wrote, "broad-minded, tolerant and cultured persons. The average member of the caste, however, like the average American, is full of prejudices of all kinds. Travel produces a superficial polish; their patriotism consists of antagonism toward the outside world and an effort to secure position for themselves; they are sure that Haiti's laws are sounder, her culture superior, her schools more advanced, her civilization in general higher than those of most other nations (France generally excepted)." There used to be a saying that when somebody sneezes in France, they have whooping-cough in Haiti.

Times have changed since Leyburn wrote. France has lost prestige. Americans have abandoned much of their racial myopia, have come to Haiti to learn as well as to criticize. The common man everywhere has found champions. In the arts, primitivism and individualism have relegated academic standards to the dustbin. Haitian intellectuals have taken an interest in folklore, *vaudou*, Marxism, New Dealism. Poems and plays in the once-despised Creole have been publicly read and received with enthusiasm. The *élite* has not rendered Leyburn's description of them obsolete but it has given cause for sharp revisions. That ambivalence which on the one hand

[1] It is to the *élite*'s great credit and sense of proportion that they are not deeply anti-American, because it was under the Occupation that they were treated for the first time with social-racial contempt—and in their very homes. "It made many of us," a Haitian journalist says, "ashamed in our hearts of our own race, ashamed of our birth and of our families and of the blood that flows in our own veins. For not all of us are strong enough to laugh and say '*Je m'en fiche*' as I do . . . The general's wife often invites us to tea and finds us charming, but the sergeant's wife, or the captain's, who maybe did her own washing at home, was our social superior and would feel herself disgraced to shake hands with any nigger."—Chauvet, quoted in Seabrook, *op. cit.*

sought to emulate the Whites (even in coloration) and on the other regarded the "vulgar" foreign visitor as proof of the superiority of everything Haitian, has all but vanished. The *élite* Haitian of today may not be the most humble or self-critical of men, but he is one of the most hospitable and charming, and his ancient fear that widespread education would topple his eminence is rapidly giving way to a knowledge that his future and Haiti's are involved in the common weal.

POLITICS:

The Government and the Army

THE GOVERNMENT. According to the Constitution of 1950 which was drawn up at Gonaïves by a Constituent Assembly headed by Dantès Bellegarde, all Haitians are equal before the law without regard to sex, creed or color, save that women, though permitted to participate in municipal elections and to hold office, are temporarily not eligible to vote for national office.

The government is divided into legislative and executive branches. The former consists of a National Assembly comprising a Senate and a Chamber of Deputies. The Deputies, directly elected by the people for four-year terms, number 37 and are distributed according to the population. The Senators, numbering 21, are elected for six years by the primary assemblies of each department (provincial state). The chief executive, the President, is elected for six years and is not eligible for re-election. He is elected on the basis of a majority vote of communal electors, chosen by direct suffrage and secret ballot. He has the right to dissolve the Assembly, name all judges of courts and tribunals, and choose the members of his cabinet heading the various executive departments.

The President, in whose person and that of the Army which he commands, resides the real power in Haiti, receives a salary of $24,000 a year. He lives and works in the National Palace on the Champ-de-Mars in Port-au-Prince, adjoining the Cassernes Dessalines, which houses the Palace Guard. His cabinet consists of seven departmental secretaries (State and Religious Cults, Interior and Justice, Finance and National Economy, Foreign Affairs and National Education, Public Health and Work, Commerce and Agriculture, Public Works) each receiving a salary of $7200, and four Undersecretaries receiving $4800 each.

Almost one-fourth of the annual budget for 1953-4 (totaling

$25,839,379) was allocated to the most important of the ministries, that of the Interior, whose share was $6,040,620, but about $5,000,-000 of this sum covered the expenses of the Army, and $147,996 went to the Secret Police. Education and Public Health came next with budgets of about $3,000,000 each. $1,500,000 was allocated to Public Works. Foreign Affairs, Finance, and Commerce-Agriculture each received about $1,000,000; and the office of Secretary of State to the Presidency (which includes also support of the Catholic Church) $500,000. The sum total of these expenses, which includes the funding of the public debt and carrying forward of Haiti's share in the Artibonite Project, is paid out of customs duties ($17,513,-000), internal revenues ($6,733,000) and other taxes ($1,591,000).

In assessing the progress toward democracy in Haiti, two facts must always be remembered. Military dictatorships, of varying degrees of severity and efficiency, were the rule during the Nineteenth and early Twentieth Centuries. Even Pétion, though preserving the republican forms and never a tyrant, made the major decisions unassisted. The second fact is that no matter how democratic a constitution may be—and Bellegarde's contains many safeguards of people's rights—custom and usage are the ultimate arbiters; no more than 10% of the people participate in government even to the extent of voting, and it is inevitably in the interests of this minority that the lines are drawn and the laws enforced. The fact that the combined circulation of all newspapers is less than 50,-000 and that there are only a few thousand radio receiving sets in Haiti must also be taken into account.

THE GARDE D'HAITI. Haiti's small but well-disciplined Army, the Garde d'Haiti, consists of 400 officers and 4000-5000 enlisted men, and contains within itself the police force whose khaki uniforms are undifferentiated from the other services. Since policing is the main function of the Army in the country districts, a very large proportion of the Garde is delegated to this activity. Branches of the Army are the Coast Guard, whose half-dozen small launches and torpedo boats patrol the coast and give aid to navigation; the Air Force, which efficiently moves all passenger and air freight within the country in addition to its military duties; and the Artillery, a part of the ground forces, which is equipped with French 75s and American 105s and a few tanks. A battalion of the ground forces (40 officers and 500 men) constitutes the Palace Guard. The Army also maintains Haiti's prisons.

Qualifications for an enlisted man in the Garde are literacy and loyalty. A private gets $21 a month plus $6 for board and clothing,

Religion

The Catholic Church dominates Port-au-Prince as it dominates Haiti in terms of formal religion and educational influence. But *vaudou*, as portrayed in this painting of an offering to the gods of the sea by André Pierre, *houngan* Hyppolite's successor, remains the religion of the poor.

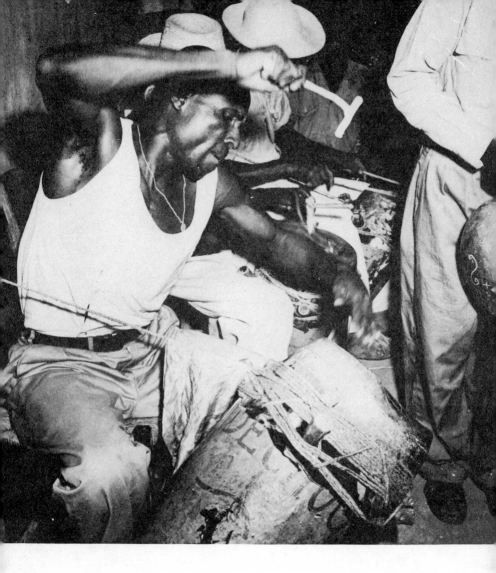

Vaudou: the Drummer

. . . must be a powerful man to make powerful music. This is especially true of the lead-drum in a *Rada* battery, shown here, for this instrument must signal the phases of the ceremony, keep the atmosphere charged, and carry the participants beyond their conscious selves.

Vaudou: the Vever

With the flour-drawing of these intricate symbols by the *houngan* around
the center-post, the ceremony begins. When the *loa* answer the summons,
the *vevers* have served their purpose and are danced away.

Vaudou: Possession

A participant who has not thus been "mounted" by the *loa* has not truly entered *vaudou*. In "possession," the possessed speaks strange tongues; assumes the character of the divinity invoked; afterwards remembers none of it.

Vaudou: Prayer
By far the largest part of a ceremony is devoted to prayer, the preparation
of offerings and sacrifices, the lighting of votive candles; in these phases of
vaudou the Catholic influence is strong.

Saut d'Eau: Ville-Bonheur

Site of a great Catholic fête July 15, attended by scores of thousands, the nearby waterfall serves as a perfect setting for *vaudou* baptismal rites which are observed simultaneously.

Vaudou: the Houmfor

Not every temple is as simple as this one depicted by Wilson Bigaud. The altar may be painted with *vevers*, decorated with everything from automobile headlamps to soft-drink calendars. The feathered dolls are *pacquets congo*, powerful charms carried on the head.

Black Magic: the Zombi

In Enguérrand Gourgue's dramatic presentation, one such unfortunate automation is being led back to his open grave by the sorcerer after a night's work in the fields.

Haitian Cemetery

This particular one, appropriately illuminated by a thunder-storm, is near St. Louis du Sud. But all are notable for their heavy above-ground tombstones, designed to keep *bocors* from making *zombis* of the dead.

A Mambo
This kindly priestess of *vaudou* from Bizoton posed for her picture with the *asson*, symbol of authority in one hand, and a sacrificial goat in the other.

Bazile's 'Triumph'

A symbolic painting of Christ and the Virgin by primitive painter Castera Bazile shows the *vaudou* influence in the 'mystery' on the altar and in its flat patterns. It was painted in 1949.

Protestant Apse

Painted by Catholic artists Bazile (right), Benoit (left), Levêque (vault), and Protestant Obin (center), this greatest of Haitian murals was commissioned for the Episcopal Cathedral of St.-Trinité.

and a mess allowance of $7 monthly. Qualifications for the officer corps are twelve years of school and a three-year course at the Military Academy at Frères where each year 15-20 second lieutenants are graduated. Competitive examinations, not membership in the *élite*, are the final basis of selection. More than 50% of the officers are dark-skinned. A few officers rise from the ranks.

Aids to the Garde in maintaining order in the rural areas, are the civilian *chefs de section* who wear blue denim, nickel badges and pith helmets. 550 in number, each is issued a carbine or revolver on a one-year signed contract with the Garde; their salary of $10 monthly is paid by the Garde, to whom (or to the local judge) they turn over malefactors. A bill is pending before the legislature to increase the salaries of the *chefs de section*, double their number and require literacy tests. The *chef* exerts his authority mainly by moral persuasion; the most respected man in the community is generally selected to be *chef*.

In 1959 the American Marines, who had controlled all of Haiti during the Occupation of 1915-34, were invited back as a strictly military mission to reorganize the Armée, demoralized by the demands of the successive regimes that had followed the overthrow of the Magloire government. A 40-man team was called in by President Duvalier to "stabilize" Haiti, threatened, in his view, by the Dominican Republic's militaristic regime on the Eastern frontier and Fidel Castro's pro-Soviet evangelism 70 miles across the Windward Passage from Môle St.-Nicholas.[1]

---

[1] The foregoing chapter has not been revised, except for the subsequent fate of the American Marine Mission, see pp. 30-31.

CHAPTER IV

RICH LAND, POOR LAND:

Physical Facts and Economic Theories

IN THE INTRODUCTION we had occasion to mention some of the paradoxes of Haiti's situation and the delight that amateur economists take in solving her age-old dilemmas—on paper. Some years ago one such benevolent visitor, who prided himself on his practicality, observed that the peasants near St. Marc were getting few vitamins. He therefore imported a whole shipload of cocoanuts and had them planted in neat rows. In a decade or two, he reasoned, there would be an abundance of milk and white meat for everyone. Returning to inspect the work a week later, he discovered that every one of the nuts had been dug up and eaten. He was outraged, but he need not have been. He had simply neglected to consider two basic factors. The community was wholly without education. And even if it had been educated to the point of appreciating long-range planning and conservation, it is doubtful whether its members would have been able to let the thought of tomorrow's plenty alleviate today's hunger. A similar thing happened in 1952 when reforestation technicians planted a hundred-thousand seedlings to preserve the capital's dangerously denuded watershed above Turgeau; every single seedling was pulled up and burnt for fuel.

To understand what is being done, and what can be done, to alleviate this pitiful necessity of living from hand to mouth, one must know a little about the land: what it provides and does not provide; what is being done to equip the peasant with a healthy body and an informed mind. The value of various approaches to a happier future can then be measured. But the reader who comes to Haiti to enjoy himself, or, as we suggested in the Introduction, to temporarily escape into a way of life utterly removed from his own, can be grateful that everything related to the "dismal science" of economics has been relegated to this one chapter—where he is at liberty to skip it.

44

GEOLOGY AND CLIMATE

We are not concerned with how Haiti took shape, geologically speaking, except to note that the island dates from the pre-Cretaceous period: sandstone and conglomerates overlaid with clays, limestone and chalk. Most of the soils derive from weathering of limestone in the mountains. On the plateaus there is red clay and clay loams. The alluvial soils on the coastal plains are fertile except in the dry areas where the earth tends to be alkaline. The sponge-like quality of the limestone underlying Haiti has prevented the formation of lakes in the mountains, but by the same token has favored the storage of fresh water underground.

There are no active volcanoes on the island. Earthquakes are fairly common, one such having toppled most of the houses in Anse-a-Veau on the South Peninsula as recently as 1952. Severe hurricanes, like the one that levelled the Dominican capital in 1930, are rare; but disastrous floods, resulting from torrential rains in the tree-stripped mountains, are frequent. As early as 1788 Baron de Wimpffen remarked sadly on the propensity of the planters to cut down every last tree within hundreds of yards of a settlement. Noticing one magnificent avocado that had been felled "for timber," he observed wryly that enough ordinary wood to rebuild the whole French Navy was available on an adjacent hill. It isn't any longer. Today a story is told of a flood in Jacmel where the rivers in the rainy season get completely out of hand. A *gros Nègre* had just returned from Port-au-Prince in his *dynaflow* and although warned by the Garde not to attempt to drive to his home up the river valley, persevered. The Jacmelians smiled and waited. In half an hour he was back. Five minutes later his car arrived. And five minutes after that his house . . .

Rainfall on most of the South Peninsula averages 60 inches but varies on the North Peninsula from as much as 60 inches around Port-de-Paix to less than 20 inches at Môle St. Nicholas. Rainfall along the semi-arid coast between the two peninsulas varies from 20 to 40 inches, but in the upper Artibonite Valley it reaches a maximum for all of Haiti of 122 inches at Mirebalais. Sheltered as it is by the high mountains along the Dominican border from the prevailing wind out of the East, Port-au-Prince is hotter than any of the other Haitian cities (all of which are seaports), temperatures ranging there in summer from 80 to 90 degrees Fahrenheit and in winter between 70 and 80 degrees. But due to its proximity to the mountains behind it, the capital's environs (Pétion-Ville, fifteen minutes away, 1500 feet above sea-level; and Kenscoff, thirty-five minutes away, 5000 feet) are cool the year round. The so-called "rainy season" varies greatly from one part of the country to another, but in Port-au-Prince it takes place between April and October, most of the rain falling in the evenings.

BIRDS, BEASTS AND FLOWERS

Visitors to Haiti have always been surprised that a country with a richness and variety of vegetation unsurpassed in the world should have so few animals. One can travel for days in Haiti without seeing a single wild creature, excepting the lizard and an occasional pigeon, guinea hen or waterfowl. No people, for all that, is more dependent on domestic creatures than the Haitian peasant and none treats them with as curious a mingling of blood-familiarity, superstition and downright cussedness. A whole volume, and an entertaining one, could be written about the ambivalent relationship of man and beast in Haiti, and it could begin with the three astonishing reasons given for cropping a cat's ears.[1] It would ask such questions as why a horse, even when confronting a loaded *camion* on a hairpin turn, is invariably held at the extreme end of a very long tether rather than by the bridle, and why an overloaded *bourique* that has fallen and can't get up is caned over the head instead of being relieved of its burden. It would include a stern lecture on the virtual extermination by slingshot of inedible (but ecologically indispensible) small birds. And it would certainly explore every fascinating facet of cockfighting, not excluding the under-the-wings baptism of a gladiator with a courage-bearing bath of rum and ginger-root sprayed through the teeth, and the advisability of an all-over "tasting" of your opponent's body before Round One to make sure his owner isn't the type who substitutes red pepper for ginger to give your bird the sneezes. It was the late Ralph Adams Cram who called Port-au-Prince "City of Ten-Million Roosters," but William Krauss, complaining that Cram had ignored "the packs of dogs that bay the moon and the uncounted burros that retch and whoop to make hideous the false dawn," found a better symbol of Haiti in the ponderous hush that accompanies the death of day: "A single dog, uncertain and tentative, will bark. On the instant, triumphantly, a thousand dogs will answer. You draw a breath. The stars appear. Life goes on. There is no death."

[1] To distinguish it from wildcats (are there any in Haiti?), to make it come in out of the rain (by tickling of the inner hairs) and to keep it home (by burying the ears, which, of course, it wouldn't want to be far from, in the yard).

The largest Haitian mammals, the agouti and the mongoose, are nocturnal. The iguana, or giant lizard, is almost extinct. Snakes, none of them venomous, are scarce. Crocodiles are still to be found near the mouths of some of the small rivers, and in the Étang Saumâtre, Haiti's one considerable lake. Wild cattle, horses, pigs, and dogs, descendents of those brought from Europe centuries ago, once roamed the less settled areas, are now rarities. The coastal waters teem with an abundance of tropical fish, but few are caught in the primitive straw traps and seines of the natives. The variety of insects that will congregate about a light bulb on a dry evening is as astonishing as the brilliance of their colors and markings; tarantulas, scorpions, centipedes and malarial mosquitoes are an infrequent menace. Bats are as common, and as harmless, as moths.

The Encyclopaedia Britannica does not exaggerate when it says of Haiti that "all tropical plants and trees grow in perfection, and nearly all vegetables and fruits of temperate climates may be successfully cultivated in the highlands." Cotton, rice, maize, tobacco, cocoa, ginger, native indigo, arrowroot, manioc (cassava), pimento, banana, plantain, pineapple, artichoke, yam and sweet-potato are indigenous to Haiti. Mango and breadfruit trees (both said to have been imported from the East Indies by Captain Bligh of "Bounty" fame) grow in every part of the country, along with cocoanuts, oranges and shaddock (the original and sweeter grapefruit), supplying that portion of the peasant diet for which he does not have to work. So rich are mangoes in food values that Revolutionary generals are said to have planned their campaigns to fall within the "Mango Season." Other important food products are coffee and sugar (Haiti's No. 1 and No. 3 exports), melons, cabbage, caimite (star apples), almonds, grapes, mulberry and fig. During an hour's walk behind Jacmel once the author counted no less than eighteen edible fruits growing wild, including such exotic items as carrasol, grenadine and guava.

Of the larger trees which do not bear edible fruit, the *acajou* (mahogany), rosewood, satinwood, manchineel and lignum vitae are most valuable—and in danger of total extirpation. The French colonists, as a matter of fact, made every effort to destroy the manchineel in their fear that the slaves would make effective use of the fruit whose juice is a deadly poison. This is the tree under which the lovers in Meyerbeer's *L'Africaine*, falling asleep in each other's arms while the dew sifts through the deadly branches, are found dead in the morning.

Mapous with buttressed roots (sacred to *vaudouists*), *sabliers* (whose fruit is poisonous) and Antillean Oak attain heights exceeding 100 feet. Most beautiful for their deeply scented blossoms are the *frangipani* (white), the constellated *immortelle* (red) and the leguminous *flamboyant* (orange). Twelve-hundred species of palm are to be found in Haiti but the spear-straight Royal and the wind-bent Coconut are the most common—and most beautiful. The calabash tree furnishes the peasant with a natural receptacle for carrying water. Occidental pine, Spanish cedar, eucalyptus and mimosa flourish in the higher mountain ranges. The bamboo, though it may be considered more a grass than a tree, sometimes attains a height of 100 feet. In the desert and brackish lowlands are to be found mangrove and logwood, cactus and mesquite, tamarind and tcha-tcha. Of shrubs to grace the porticos of the villas of the *élite*, one need only mention camellia and oleander, hibiscus and bougainvillaea, jasmin and poinsettia, the rose and the crape-myrtle. Cattails, tamarix and the rope-like *liane* with its lavender flower grow wild among the rocks. The *figier-maudit*, a fearsome parasite which grows from a seed deposited in a tiny flaw of the *mapou's* bark, embraces the mighty tree with its snake-like arms, eventually strangling it. And in the 6000-foot-high jungle of the South Peninsula are to be found the giant fern, the rose-apple and a dazzling variety of orchid.

WAYS OF MAKING A LIVING

With a population density of 300 per square mile, Haiti is more overpopulated than any country in the Western Hemisphere. Only one-third of Haiti's 10,000 square miles is tillable at all, which means that there is less than an acre per person to go around. Considering this, it is extraordinary that any cultivation at all beyond the primary needs of the peasants is possible. No less than 94% of the people gain their livelihood as small proprietors, lessees or tenant-farmers, from agriculture or such related occupations as charcoal and lime-burning, village handicrafts and fishing. Of the remaining 6% (182,240), 83,500 earn wages in agricultural industries, and 75,000 in domestic service, leaving a total of only 23,740 engaged in trade, government service and small industry. This fantastic disproportion may have altered somewhat since the United Nations made the foregoing survey in 1949,[1] but not substantially. The minimum industrial wage has risen from 30¢ a day in 1939 to 70¢ at the present time. But very few peasants are engaged in even part-time work for wages. Estimates of the average annual cash income of the Haitian

[1] See *Mission to Haiti*. Report of the United Nations Mission of Technical Assistance to the Republic of Haiti. Lake Success, New York.

run anywhere from $25 to $65—which may be compared with a $50 figure for the bulk of the world's population rather than with the $800 obtaining in England and $1600 in the United States.

During the fiscal year 1953 imports exceeded exports by $7,-360,830. As a result the Government, which depends upon export-import taxes for most of its revenue, ended the year with a deficit of $780,000, and this was a principal reason why a program of home industries was put into high gear. The budget for 1953-4 was $25,-839,379.

COFFEE. Coffee is and always has been (except during World War II when sisal and sugar temporarily displaced it) Haiti's most valuable export crop. 'Black Gold,' as it is sometimes called, was introduced into Saint-Domingue in 1739, and by 1791 production on 800 estates totaled 65,151,180 lbs., a figure not equalled for over a hundred years. In 1900, the record year of modern times, 700,000 bags of coffee were exported, as compared with a 1952-3 figure of 289,041. Three companies—Brandt, Wiener and Madsen—sort and ship more than half of the annual crop which is bought from the individual peasant (who generally decorticates the bean himself in a wooden mortar) at about 40¢ a pound.

It was the cutting off of the European market during the War that resulted in the impoverishment of such provincial towns as Cayes, Jacmel and Jérémie—a loss of prosperity from which they have not recovered. But another cause of the decline of Haiti's coffee trade has been the growing scarcity and high price of food, which has forced the peasant to turn some of the best coffee-growing slopes into vegetable gardens. Haitian coffee is of excellent quality, especially prized in France and Italy, but is produced by the peasant from a few bushes to which he gives little care. In consequence, the yield is small and the quality not what it could be. Composting, soil conservation and afforestation (coffee grows well only in shade) will be necessary before this industry ever regains its importance in Haiti and the world market.

SISAL. The low price of sisal, which enjoyed a boom during the War years in the absence of Manila hemp, contributed greatly to the decline of government revenues in 1952-3. Haiti's 35,000 tons annual production accounts for 12% of the world market. Sisal is now used largely for bailer and binder twine. The cactus plant from which it is extracted was introduced to Haiti by Captain Bligh (on the same voyage in which he brought breadfruit) from Central America.

Sisal is produced almost entirely by large privately-owned or government plantations on semi-desert land unfitted for other crops. The 30,000 acres on which the largest of these companies, the American-owned-and-managed Plantation Dauphin, operates in the Northeast, has a rainfall of only 25-30 inches a year. Before Dauphin started planting in 1927, these fields were covered with nothing but *mesquite*, although in Colonial times *campeche* (logwood [1]) provided a valuable export. 8000 workers at peak operation, 5000 in 1953-4, are employed by Dauphin, though double-row tractor cultivation and the introduction of automatic machines to process the waste, threaten soon to reduce this figure drastically. SHADA's government plantation is next in size with 12,000 acres; then Crooks' American company, also in the Northeast; and fourth, the very efficient all-Haitian company of Joseph Nadal with its 4000 acres northwest of Port-au-Prince.

SUGAR. Spaniards brought sugarcane from the Canaries to Hispaniola in 1506, but it was not until 1680 that French settlers first planted it in the western part of the island. Very soon sugar had supplanted indigo as Saint-Domingue's chief product. It was grown, for the most part, in four flat and fertile areas: the Plaine du Nord, surrounding Cap Haïtien; the Valley of the Artibonite; the Léogane plain; and the Cul-de-Sac. It is in the latter lowland, north and east of Port-au-Prince, that most sugar is now grown. In 1791 there were 792 sugar mills in operation producing 150,000,000 lbs. (67,-000 tons) of raw sugar annually. By 1826 production had fallen to 33,000 lbs., and thereafter disappeared entirely from the list of products exported from Haiti.

In 1919 the Haytian-American Sugar Company (HASCO) commenced operating. By 1951-2 it was producing 65,000 tons, more than 90% of the sugar processed in all of Haiti in that year of record output. A little more than half of HASCO's production is exported in raw form where it is sold on the world market, mostly to the United Kingdom, at the world price with no protection. The import quota for sugar from Haiti to be sold in the United States (where sugar brings the high price of $5 a hundred-pounds) is negligible—thanks to the power of the Cuban and Puerto Rican lobbies. 47% of HASCO's sugar is refined at the huge Port-au-Prince factory for the local market. Molasses, a by-product of the refining process, is shipped to the United States in tankers for cattle-feed. The Company's own fields supply 40% of the cane processed. The rest is bought from between 7000 and 9000 peasant pro-

1 The indigo dye extracted from logwood trees was Saint-Domingue's No. 3 export. Since 1918 indigo has been replaced by synthetic analynes.

ducers. There are 700 employees in HASCO's factory; its total staff of 5000 includes ox-cart drivers, stevedores and technicians who operate its sugar-railway running between Léogane in the South and St. Marc in the North. The Company paid the Haitian Government the sizable sum of $852,326 in taxes in 1953.

Haitian and Cuban-owned sugar "centrales" are getting under way at Cap Haïtien and Les Cayes. The small mills seen on country roads, in which the cane is ground between wooden rollers turned by a horse or mule, produce not sugar but sirup, molasses sticks (*rapadou*), and *tafia*, a potstilled raw rum. HASCO has facilities for producing raw rum, which it once distilled and sold by the millions of gallons, but does not at present because of unfavorable legislation. Haitian refined rum is not exported. The largest producer for the internal market is Jean Gardère & Co., whose Barbancourt distillery, not far from HASCO, uses sugarcane entirely from its own fields.

BANANAS. In 1947, Haiti's biggest banana year, peasants were getting $1.10 for a nine-hand stem which now brings 70¢; seven million stems were being exported as compared with half a million in 1953. Whatever the moral or political justifications may have been, the forced withdrawal of Standard Fruit Co.'s Haitian branch in 1952 constituted the major cause of this catastrophic decline. Standard Fruit came to Haiti in 1936. Its plantations were in the Artibonite Valley and it fertilized the land with nitrates and ammonium sulphate. It controlled "leaf-spot," the principal disease of the plant, with regular sprayings. It had the investment required to afford moving its plantations to new land at such times as three plantings (covering a fifteen year period) should exhaust the soil. In 1947, Standard Fruit's Haitian operations, in which the fifty-million dollar corporation had invested three million dollars, accounted for three-and-one-half million of the seven million stems exported, the rest having been shipped by six Haitian independents financed by small importers in Miami.

When Standard Fruit departed, the independents grouped together in a combine called HABANEX, headed by a Haitian business man who had been imprisoned under the Estimé regime for alleged monopolistic practices. Under the present government, he took up the claims of the six companies. HABANEX, with $700,-000 backing from the latter and $552,000 from the government, then began to push the development of new plantations. But the difficulty has been that Miami, out for a quick profit, has not been willing to make the long-term investment required for distribution of new plants to the peasants, fertilization of the ground, control of leaf-spot, and crop rotation. HABANEX now buys mostly from the individual peasant producer and most peasants prefer to grow non-exportable green plantains, a cousin of the yellow banana, which more readily resists diseases, requires less irrigation, and is more nutritious.

COCOA. Hopes that Haiti can regain her Colonial position as a leading exporter of cocoa have been revived by the establishment of a million-dollar American processing plant near Anse d'Hainault in the South. Even in the 1952-3 season cocoa ranked ahead of bananas as the fourth product on Haiti's export list. $1,155,940 worth of beans were shipped out in that year. The new company plans to dry the beans under cover and supply peasants with young cocoa trees as well as technical assistance.

COTTON, TEXTILES. Cotton, another crop suffering under independent peasant auspices from desultory cultivation and unchecked insect pests, is exported in very small quantities. Most current production is now absorbed by the new spinning and weaving plant constructed in 1950 by O. J. Brandt, a native Jamaican who is Haiti's largest coffee and textile merchant. Mills operated by Madsen and the Zephirin brothers will be in operation soon.

RICE. Haiti's production of rice in 1952-3 was estimated at 64,000,000 lbs., an increase of 15% over the previous fiscal year and of almost 100% over the previous decade. Most of it was cultivated in the paddies of the Artibonite Valley, a good part on land reclaimed by irrigation with American aid. If the reclamation continues, Haiti will soon become self-sufficient in this vital food staple.

INDUSTRIES, MINING. In 1954 the Government opened Haiti's first cement plant at Fond Mombin near Port-au-Prince, making the country at a stroke completely independent of this expensive import and providing cement to users at 20% less than before. The plant employs 300.

Rubber of excellent quality, free from South American "leaf-blight," can be grown in the rainy South where experiments under American technicians are now being made at Marfranc.

Three per cent of Haiti's exports consist of essential oils, 95% of which are distilled from the extensive and efficiently managed grass plantations of Senator Louis Déjoie at St. Michel de l'Atalaye and Ducis.

Bauxite—the natural base of aluminum—is mined in small quantities near Miragoâne and Gonaïves, and is to be found elsewhere. Firms have been given licenses to export manganese from Trouin;

this ore in Haiti analyzes at 61% as compared with 30% ore now being taken out of Cuban mines profitably.

FISHING. Between 4000 and 5000 Haitians are estimated to be engaged, at least part of the time, in marine fishing. Their equipment consists of small sailboats and dugout canoes, straw traps (often baited with no more than an orange) and seines. Almost no deep-water fish are caught, but marine turtles, shrimp, rock lobster (*langouste*), oysters and conch (*lambi*) make up part of the catch, most of which, in the absence of refrigeration, is sold and eaten within a few hours of the time it comes ashore. Partly because heavy trawling is not feasible in the coral reefs that surround Haiti, and partly because the fishermen have no seafaring tradition and rarely venture far from shore, attention has centered recently on means of increasing Haiti's fish diet by stocking streams and lakes with fresh-water varieties.

Under United Nations sponsorship, Javanese carp and African tilapia were introduced in 1953 as a supplementary source of food for the peasant. Simon Tal, the Israeli fish expert most recently in charge of this successful experiment, has also built a number of model artificial fish-ponds near Port-au-Prince; private enterprisers, he points out, may derive $1000 a year clear profit from a pond costing only $500 to construct, and thus supply the under-stocked city fish markets as well.

ELECTRIC POWER. The Haitian Government has a contract with the American-owned and operated Compagnie d'Éclairage Électrique des Villes de Port-au-Prince et du Cap Haïtien to supply power to these two largest Haitian cities and their environs until 1970. The company is frequently criticized by the Government for keeping its rates too high, and once it was actually attacked in the Senate for shifting over (1923) from wood-burning to diesel oil, "thus depriving the peasant of a valuable source of income"! The company's defense against the first charge is that its rates are lower than Westchester County's although the labor ratio (220) is actually higher in Haiti, the productivity of labor being so low and supervisory costs so high that labor costs more than fuel. In consequence of this, the company says, no dividends have been paid to stockholders since 1941, this in turn shutting off new investment and making plant increases to keep up with the growing number of consumers impossible.

Haitian consumers, who believe none of this, have their own way of beating the "imperialistic" power trust. Appropriately enough it was said to have been invented by an ingenious American named Cumberland, and bears his name to this day. A group of native "electricians," operating clandestinely, and of course for a fee, have a way of making the meter lie. If you don't pay *their* fee (and don't be surprised some day if you find a handful of fellows you have never seen before digging a small hole in your bedroom wall) they have an equally effective device for shutting off your power permanently.

Small government-operated diesel plants supply Gonaïves, Cayes, Jérémie, and Port-de-Paix. St. Marc has no electricity. Jacmel is supplied by Haiti's first hydroelectric plant, opened in 1920 and owned and operated by the Boucard family. A very small 100HP hydroelectric plant serves Belladère.

The great Péligre dam on the Artibonite is being constructed in such a way that generators can be added eventually at a cost of $6,000,000. These would be capable of supplying the Western provinces of the country, including Port-au-Prince. A wholly automatic plant there, costing considerably more, could take care of the entire Republic.

HEALTH

When the Marine Occupation ended Haiti's century of isolation in 1915, it was found that reputable physicians were few, hospital facilities were lacking and that an overwhelming proportion of the population were suffering from malaria, yaws, hookworm and a variety of intestinal diseases. 67% of the people were infected with malaria, 26% with hookworm, and 78% with yaws which had been brought over from Africa as early as 1509. Even before that, the Spaniards had introduced smallpox which wiped out thousands of the Indians, and the Indians themselves had unintentionally retaliated by infecting their conquerors with syphilis which shortly thereafter swept over Europe. The slaves, as we have seen, were largely immune to yellow fever, which gave the *coup de grâce* to the French.

All of these plagues, to which typhoid and tuberculosis were later added, flourished during the Nineteenth Century among a people who have always been susceptible in consequence of overcrowding, malnutrition, and lack of elementary sanitation. Camille Lhérisson, a contemporary Haitian doctor, says that the peasant diet has not improved substantially since slave days; but today Haiti's health problem is mainly a rural one, for three American health missions, in cooperation with Haitian health authorities, have succeeded in greatly improving sanitary facilities in the towns and in virtually wiping out yaws and malaria.

Yaws, Haiti's historic disease, eats away the flesh or cripples by ulcerating sores on the feet. It is transmitted by repeated contact, especially in districts where shoes are not worn and water is scarce. In 1924 the Rockefeller Foundation began attacking it with arsenic-bismuth injections. In 1942 a U.S. Sanitary Mission took over, using penicillin for the first time in 1945, and reducing the number infected to 55%. In 1950 the United Nations Childrens' Emergency Fund offered to pay for the expensive drug, and the Magloire Government, setting up injection centers, had needled 1,750,000 cases by April of 1953 at a cost of $500,000 to Haiti and $650,000 to UNICEF. The job was then taken over by the Service Cooperatif Inter-Americain de Santé Publique (SCISP), which had been operating successfully since 1948 in place of the American Sanitary Mission. With the Haitian Government contributing 60% and Point Four 40%, sixteen clinics were set up and SCISP is hopeful of holding yaws to a negligible phenomenon.

SCISP's general health work began in 1944. Water was the underlying problem and Port-au-Prince, where 125,000 people who required 12,000,000 gallons a day were getting only 3,000,000, came first on the agenda. Major Edwin Dudley, for seven years chief of the Mission, partially solved this problem by tapping underground reservoirs in the limestone ridges back of the city, increasing the flow of pure water to 8,000,000 gallons. The rural water supply situation, however, remains desperate, with thousands of peasant *cailles* five or more miles from water, the springs uncapped and polluted and in many regions drying up entirely.

Between 1942 and 1946 the Rockefeller Foundation carried out extensive drainage projects in Petit Goâve and Aquin, seaports suffering terribly from malaria. Other drainage systems were introduced later in Jacmel, Cayes, Léogane, Gonaïves, St. Marc and Cap Haïtien by the American Sanitary Mission in cooperation with the Haitian government. The projects were effective but malaria was not entirely wiped out from these coastal regions because upkeep on the drainage canals has not been sufficient to prevent them from periodically filling up.

Apart from the control of these prevalent diseases—to which may be added tuberculosis and hookworm which still flourish among the poorly housed and barefooted—Haiti's health dilemma comes down to a lack of trained doctors and rural clinics. In 1948 only fifteen doctors were graduated from Haiti's one medical school, and out of Haiti's total of 292 physicians in service, 17 were abroad for study, 150 were practicing in or near Port-au-Prince and 99 were established in provincial towns. In 1950, the General Hospital in Port-au-Prince, the ten provincial public hospitals, and the private clinics in the capital, employed between them a total of 76 doctors and had 1570 beds. This would take care, though far from adequately, of the few hundred thousand Haitians living in towns of more than 15,000 population. But the 3,000,000-odd other Haitians in smaller towns and rural areas had to get along as best they could with the services of just 26 additional physicians. The latter, on salaries of $60 to $160 a month, operated out of a scattering of poorly equipped clinics which could not supply them with even minimum transportation facilities. As the UN report stated wryly, "a civil service which does not provide means of transport or compensation for travelling expenses cannot reasonably order its officials to travel on duty."

The magnificent three-hundred-bed Albert Schweitzer Memorial Hospital at Deschapelle in the Artibonite Valley is one of the most modern and efficiently operated in the world. Conceived and administered by Dr. and Mrs. W. L. Mellon, Jr., of New Orleans it offers refuge to every Haitian who can reach it—and hope to the heretofore hopeless.

EDUCATION

A recent edition of the World Almanac contained, under Haiti, the sentence: "Education is free and compulsory; illiteracy is 90%." The percentage of the uneducated has fallen a few percentage points, but the paradox remains. To understand it, one must go back a long way.

Moreau de St.-Méry noted in 1797 that the French planters had been short on culture, that in fact they had created no schools in Saint-Domingue either for themselves or for the slaves. The Haitians were obliged to start from scratch. Under Toussaint there was little time for education. Dessalines had no use for it. Christophe educated strenuously during the dozen years of his reign. But Pétion and Boyer, who inherited a united country, were the first of a line of *élite* presidents who were aristocrats and governors precisely because they were educated. Not until Geffrard, in 1875, was any attempt made to extend the schools beyond *élite* ranks. By 1919 there was an enrollment or 61,313 pupils, and by 1946 this figure had risen to 103,310, or one child out of four or five. By 1953 the number had advanced to 181,638.

Breaking this last official government figure down, there were enrolled in all primary urban schools, public, religious and private, 79,839 students. Public and private secondary schools—corresponding roughly to American high schools and colleges, and going beyond the first four years—accounted for 6,827 more. There were 2042 enrollees in professional schools. The balance of 92,833 included all pupils participating in public and religious primary schools in the rural areas. Only 97 Haitians matriculated in schools preparatory to the teaching profession.

With a total educational budget of only $3,206,855, and with educated Haitians rarely willing to become teachers (especially in the rural areas) because of the low pay and isolated living conditions, it will be readily seen what the government's effort to reduce illiteracy is up against. It must be born in mind also that the primary reasons why three out of four rural children of school age do not attend schools at all, are: 1) because schoolbooks and uniforms must be supplied by the parents; 2) because the few rural schools themselves are often physically out of range; and 3) because the average peasant family depends on school-age children for a large share of the day-to-day work, and, even if it didn't, would be unconvinced of the practical value of reading, writing, arithmetic—and French.

Efforts have been made over the past decade to break down the barrier between the Creole-speaking peasantry and the fraction of the population which speaks French. Instruction in the primary schools, at least in the first grade, is now generally given first in French, then in Creole. Creole primary readers have been prepared by the UN Pilot Project at Marbial and by some of the Protestant missions, but have not received wide distribution. A difficulty in this regard was highlighted by a printing of parts of the Bible in Creole; it failed because people from the North objected that the dialect used was not *their* Creole and they couldn't understand it. French, taught in a simple phonetic system by teachers employing Creole may be the answer—at least until such time as the present effort of intellectuals to write some of their works in Creole has produced a body of printed literature.

Following the French system, education in the primary schools occupies four to five years; secondary education through the *lycées* and into the University another seven or eight. Standards and output in the Catholic *lycées* are higher than in government schools because the former tend to reject the slow and the stupid. Private schools maintained by the Church or by individual educators must follow the same course as those prescribed by the Government. Co-education is the exception, not the rule.

The University of Haiti, whose rector is also editor of the Catholic newspaper *La Phalange*, is divided into an engineering school (4 year course), a medical school (6 years), dentistry (5 years), agriculture (4 years) a normal school (3 years, with some scholarships available), a law school (3 years), and shorter courses in pharmacy, surveying and ethnology. Of these schools, that of Law has the largest attendance because in Haiti this profession has been traditionally the key to wealth through a government career. Of the 785 students enrolled in the University in 1953, about 300 were studying law and 200 medicine.

The J. B. Damier Trade School in Port-au-Prince, recently renovated and reopened by the Magloire Government, is providing Haiti's first student workshops to train mechanics and electricians. With financial assistance from the International Labor Organization, much machinery has been made available and courses in masonry, locksmithing and plumbing opened up. The school is named after an eminent Haitian Minister of Education whose father had been arrested and whipped by Christophe for failing to send his son to school.

A school unique in the Caribbean, for the training of hotel employees and bartenders, was opened in 1953 to cope with the expanding influx of visitors to Haiti.

Schools offering enrollment to the families of foreign residents, as well as the specialized Institute Français and Institute Haïtien-Americain, are described in the chapter on Port-au-Prince and in Appendix III.

Many schoolchildren in Port-au-Prince come from families whose homes are still without electricity. Visitors who have seen these kids doing their homework under the dim street lamps of the capital will never doubt that Haitians are eager for an education.

PROSPECTS

Three roads, if traveled upon simultaneously, promise to relieve Haiti of much of its burden. The first and most difficult to plot, but also the most vital, involves helping the peasant to help himself. The second, symbolized by the giant storage dam under construction on the upper Artibonite, has to do with reclaiming the land and establishing home industries. The third is tourism.

The Service Cooperatif Inter-Americain de Production Agricole (SCIPA) constitutes the latest approach to the first objective. It came into being in the 40's. Its first experiments were in the Artibonite Valley where it was demonstrated that rice cultivation on artificially irrigated land brought share-cropping peasants the unheard of yield of $80 per year per acre. It was on the basis of this experiment that the Export-Import Bank approved a $4,000,000 loan in 1949 to irrigate 70,000 reclaimable acres. Sharing in the same program, peasants at the "ghost-town" of Fond Parisien near the capital stood in the new irrigation ditch and screamed with delight when water flowed for the first time in forty years.

SCIPA operates at present with a staff of U.S. engineering, agricultural guidance and home economics experts, and a budget out of which every $2 supplied by Haiti is matched by $1 from Point Four (now F.A.O.). The home economics branch is trying to introduce wood-conserving smokeless stoves and get the peasants to eat regularly such foods as vitamin-rich mangoes and goats' milk. But its somewhat utopian approach, and the attempt of the agricultural guidance experts (*agronomes*) to impose advanced cultivation methods on the uneducated, are regarded by many Haitians as ridiculous.

A better approach, some of these critics of SCIPA feel, would be to have the government create semi-experimental farms with schools, stores and seed stations attached, as a means of ridding the peasant of the anarchic fluctuation of prices in the town markets; these eventually would become genuine producers' cooperatives, controlling their own funds to minimize graft, and with only the original government cost of setting them up to be amortized. Without some such system, it is felt, the hoped-for introduction and widespread use of hydroelectric power would only mean that city slickers would be in a position to buy out the poor peasants and operate big plantations with virtual slave labor.

The reason for the failure of UNESCO's Pilot Project (1949-53) to rehabilitate and educate the 30,000 illiterate and diseased peasants in the isolated Gosseline River Valley at Marbial was precisely because it was not part of a nation-wide program. The moment UNESCO funds cease, the hopeful valley, in which for a time Haitian and foreign experts had accomplished miracles, was permitted to "rejoin" the primitive economy surrounding it.

Infinitely sounder is the thinking behind the huge Artibonite project at Péligre. Its inception dates from 1949 when it was seen that the original $4,000,000 American loan to provide irrigation works in the lower valley would be vitiated by the alternating dry spells and floods from above. In 1951 the cost figure was revised to allow for more than $20,000,000, and in 1953 work started on the dam, a quarter of a mile wide and almost 200 feet high, behind which a deep lake 18-20 miles long would insure that enough water and never too much would be available the year round to make of Haiti's largest (and dryest) plain a farmers' paradise.

One serious objection has been raised to this project—an objection that highlights Haiti's Sword of Damocles. It was pointed out as early as 1950 that in thirty years, if the river continues to carry its present silt-load from the unforested slopes, the reservoir behind the dam will be filled up and useless. Whether this prediction is exaggerated or not, the acceleration of erosion in Haiti's mountains is something fearful to contemplate. At the present combined rate of birth and erosion, Haiti will have 7,000,000 people in the year 2000—and almost no cultivatable land. Except for the Pine Forest near Morne La Selle and a few almost inaccessible mountain slopes on the South Peninsula, Haiti's original forest cover is gone. As a result, the peasant fields, cultivated by the most destructive primitive methods and stripped of the surrounding bush which is burnt for firewood, charcoal and lime, is exposed to devastating floods which carry the vestiges of remaining topsoil—often together with the peasant's crop, and even his home—into the sea. Efforts by UN experts to plant seedlings, at least near threatened reservoirs and for shade on coffee plantations, have been poorly understood by the peasant and inadequately supported by the government.

Tourism, the third causeway to Haiti's salvation, offers the most immediate returns. Before the opening of the Bi-Centennial Exposition in 1949 tourists could be numbered by the hundreds, and hotels on the fingers of one hand. In 1952, 20,000 visitors came to Haiti and in the following year 34,439. By this time there were 21 hotels in Port-au-Prince and its environs and three in Cap Haïtien. The number of tourists was still a long way from the Bahamas' 68,000, Jamaica's 93,000 and Cuba's 216,000, but a country with potentially more to offer than any of those conventional island-resorts, seemed to have no limit to the expansion possible along this golden avenue. The $4,000,000 spent by tourists in Haiti in 1953 was already a source of revenue second only to coffee. Feasible development of good beaches near Cap Haïtien and Port-au-Prince, and the building of a direct road from the capital to Jacmel, a Caribbean port with just about everything to offer, could easily raise Haiti's tourist traffic over the 100,000 mark by the end of the decade. For recent developments see Appendix III.

CHAPTER V

MEN POSSESSED AND LIVING GODS:

The Religions of Haiti

THERE IS A SAYING in Haiti that ninety per cent of the people is Catholic and one hundred per cent *vaudou*. The saying is true only in the most general or symbolic sense—the sense that *vaudou* is the traditional popular belief, and that Catholicism, having been superimposed on it and widely accepted, is practiced by many Haitians concurrently and even interchangeably.

If one attempted to make a more accurate estimate of religious groupings in a situation where reliable statistics do not exist, it might be hazarded that ten per cent of the people are under the influence of various denominations of Protestants, which tend to immunize them more effectively against *vaudou* than does ritualistic Catholicism. Of the remaining ninety per cent, perhaps two-thirds are nominally Catholic and one-third more or less actively so. It is within the nominally Catholic segment—let us say sixty per cent of the total population of the country—that the active *vaudouists* are to be found. Another ten per cent of the people—Catholics, Protestants and Indifferents—may attend a *vaudou* ceremony from time to time, for some special reason or out of curiosity.

If a disproportionate share of this chapter seems to be devoted to *vaudou* that is because *vaudou* beliefs and practises are found in their purest form in Haiti; being exotic, they will naturally interest the foreign visitor more than those creeds with which he is familiar. The Catholic Church is dealt with briefly because (with the exceptions to be noted) its program and practise are the same everywhere. The Episcopal experience is singled out for specific description because its members are the most active of the Protestant sects, and to describe each separately would be tiresome and repetitive.

CATHOLICISM

The early religious history of Haiti is extremely revealing. The French planters treated the Church with indifference or in-

61

solence. France itself, though still officially recognizing Rome, was entering the Enlightenment, and the colonists of Saint-Domingue were too busy making fortunes and spending them to give much thought to another world. Priests who showed interest in the souls of the slaves were regarded as subversive; in fact the Jesuits were expelled for precisely this in 1764. "The safety of the Whites," a Governor wrote home at the time, "demands that the Negroes be kept in profound ignorance." In such an atmosphere it is not surprising that the priests accommodated themselves to local mores. A report to the Vatican charged some of them with leading lives "so indecent . . . that the citizens and Negroes have lost all the sentiments of religion which the Jesuits gave them." The free Mulattoes, for their part, are reported to have been as licentious as the Whites. What the slaves believed in, at least until the Ceremony at Bois Caïman brought their secret ambitions into the open, is not recorded.

Toussaint's Constitution of May 9, 1801, while granting freedom of conscience and worship, declared that "the Roman Catholic Apostolic religion is the only one publicly professed in Haiti." But Dessalines' Constitution of 1805 ("The law admits no dominant religion") separated Church and State and made marriage a purely civil compact. For the next fifty-five years an open schism existed during which the Vatican refused to allow any of its priests to enter the country. The consequence of this was that while Catholicism persisted in Haiti, it became confused with folk practices. By the time of Soulouque (who openly served *vaudou*) the rites of the heretical Church were scarcely distinguishable from the African ones. And by the time President Geffrard signed the Concordat of March 28, 1860 with Rome (a treaty which has been re-affirmed by every Haitian government to this day) *vaudou* was much too firmly entrenched to be eradicated.

Faced with a competitive religion that accepted everything visible in Catholicism, these first priests of Rome must have been baffled. The *élite* in revulsion against the pre-Concordat clergy who, it is said, would bless a boat or even a privy for a fee, had become open unbelievers. It is little wonder that the missionaries feared to open their ranks to native membership. And it is understandable that when they went among the peasants they took advantage of the already existing confusion of identities between the Saints and the *Mystères*.

By 1930 there were 205 priests in Haiti of whom only eight were Haitians. Today there are about 300 of whom eighty are

Haitians. Few of the 220 French priests speak Creole. Each of them receives a monthly salary of $18.75, plus expenses, out of the $230,-923 which the Haitian government sets aside yearly for the "cultes." The Archbishop's salary is $372.50. Although a school for the preparation of a native clergy was established in 1918, almost all of the French priests are Bretons, graduates of the St. Jacques Seminary maintained by the Haitian government at Finisterre, France. The first Negro Bishop, Monseigneur Augustin, assistant to Archbishop Joseph Le Gouaze, was consecrated in 1953, at which time the Pope is said to have promised informally that the first native Haitian to become Archbishop would be made a Cardinal.

Five teaching and charitable institutions exercise their ministry in Haiti with government support. The Fathers of the Holy Ghost conduct the important institution of secondary education known as the College of St. Martial. The Brothers of Christian Instruction established the seminary of higher learning known as St. Louis de Gonzague, which includes the best library in Haiti; many government elementary schools are also under their jurisdiction. The Nuns of St. Joseph de Cluny have a large high school for girls and are in charge of many public schools. The Daughters of Wisdom conduct hospitals as well as schools in the provinces. The Belgian Sisters of Mercy manage several vocational schools for young women, including the École Professionelle Élie Dubois in the capital. The important work being done by the Oblate Fathers in the South is discussed in Chapter VII.

Such questions as the resources of the Church in Haiti, its influence over the people, and how it handles its chief rival, the priest of *vaudou*, are difficult to determine. Church spokesmen say the Church owns no property to speak of. On the other hand a semi-official government paper once charged, in an anti-clerical lapse, that the Church had $80,000,000 stashed away in real estate and foreign banks. One thing can be said with certainty; although the Church is rich in terms of Haiti, compared with the Church in most countries the Haitian branch is very poor indeed. If its influence, notwithstanding, is proportionately far greater in Haiti than, say, in the United States, that is because the Haitian Church is not only financed by the government but controls, through the same alliance, the key positions in education.

How deeply the teachings of the Church penetrate, and the extent to which it is winning its cold war with *vaudou* will be examined in the next section of this chapter. Here it remains to be said that while the Churches are generally full at service-times, Masses are said in Latin or French and the peasant regards the typical priest exactly as the priest regards himself—as a member in good standing of the *élite* caste. The *élite*, whose philosophical scepticism remains strong, exert no social pressure to attend Mass, but neither do most of them neglect to set what they consider a good example.

VAUDOU

Voodoo in Haiti is a profound and vitally alive *religion*—alive as Christianity was in its beginnings and in the early Middle Ages when miracles and mystical illuminations were common everyday occurrences . . . The high gods enter by the back door and abide in the servants' lodge. It has been a habit of all gods from immemorial days. They have shown themselves singularly indifferent to polite company, high-sounding titles, parlors and fine houses . . . indifferent indeed to all worldly pride and splendor. We have built domed temples and vast cathedrals, baited with glories of polychrome and marble to trap them, but when the gods come uninvited of their own volition, or send their messengers, or drop their flame-script cards of visit from the skies, it is not often these gilded temples or the proud of the earth they seek, but rather some road-weary humble family asleep in a wayside stable, some illiterate peasant girl dreaming in an orchard as she tends her sheep, some cobbler in his hut among the Alps.—William Seabrook in *The Magic Island*, 1929.

The reason the Catholic Church finds itself in the often helpless position of trying to convert the already converted, is that *vaudou*, an adaptable cult without written codes or any country-wide hierarchy of its own, has managed to integrate into its own structure almost all the symbols, ceremonies and outward forms of the Roman Church. The Saints have been melded with the African deities (*loa*), who were also once human beings. The Cross of Christ doubles for the sign of *Baron Samedi*, and also for the symbol of the treacherous crossroads, guarded over by the African *Legba*. Baptism is an old African tradition pre-dating Christianity. And no one who has seen in Haiti the once-Catholic observances of Ash Wednesday (*Mardi Gras*) and Lent (*Ra-Ra*) will deny that it is the *serviteurs* of *vaudou* who have adapted them to their own ends. The Holy Trinity is thought by some students to correspond roughly to the three primitive powers invoked at all *vaudou* rites, "les Mystères, les Morts, les Marassas" (the Spirits, the Dead, the Twins). And even God himself (*le Bon Dieu, le Grand Maître*), is recognized as having precedence over the *loa* and is paid at least lip service at all ceremonies:

> Don't the Catholic and the Vodun worshipper believe in the existence of a supreme God? Don't they both believe in His unceasing intervention in the course of human life as well as in the realm of universal phenomena? Don't they believe Him sensitive to offense, terrible in vengeance and yet merciful, responsive to prayer and to the offerings of his poor creatures lost in misery and sin? Don't they both believe in supernatural beings—saints, angels and demons—who stand between man and his Creator and are ever disposed to concern themselves with the affairs of this world? [1]

The differences between Catholicism and *vaudou* are fundamental, of course—but not so easy to define. *Vaudou* is a living religion, and where still practiced devoutly is as integrated a governor of a man's whole life as any religion in the world today. Those, as Leyburn observes, who conceive of religion in terms of orthodoxy, monotheism, sin, moral law, eternal rewards or punishments won't understand it at all because, for one thing, "its conception of spirits is anthropomorphic. No man is wholly good or wholly evil, nor is any god." Failing to recognize the Occidental dualism between spirit and matter, and therefore placing no premium on asceticism, the *vaudouist* regards the sensual body and the aspiring soul as one; and like the Oriental, as Maya Deren points out, he predicates his faith "on the notion that truth can be apprehended only when every cell of brain and body—the totality of a human being—is engaged in that pursuit." Far from making a primary virtue, as we do, of self-restraint, the *vaudouist's* whole drive is toward *participation* in his religion, and therefore the man who becomes "possessed" (or, as they say, "mounted" by the *loa* that then speaks through his temporarily unhoused body) has achieved the final aim of his faith: communication with the gods.

Stanley Reser, one of the very few foreigners who has been accepted as a devotee himself, defines *vaudou's* hold in terms rather of the *vaudouist's* well-known ability to handle live coals or to effect surprising medical cures. "Nothing in this world," he likes to say, "is supernatural, but many things are inexplicable or 'abnormal.' The Haitian peasant is simply closer to nature, and has been for hundreds of years, than we are; so empirically he is in close touch with the laws of nature, many of which are still beyond our comprehension."

[1] Quoted from *Ainsi parla l'oncle* by Dr. Jean Price-Mars, Haiti's leading ethnologist.

Since one never sees the same *vaudou* ceremony twice, since practices vary from place to place and from time to time, and since "authorities" seldom agree on the meaning of any specific symbol or ceremonial object, the difficulties involved in attempting to describe the rites succinctly are manifest. Not every aspect will be of equal interest to every reader. Nor would a description of any one, or two, or three ceremonies be likely to coincide with any one, two or three that the reader is likely to witness. To overcome some of the difficulties inherent in a narrative, therefore, the remainder of this section will consist of a number of hypothetical questions and answers.

QUESTION: What is the meaning of the word "voodoo"?

ANSWER: "Voodoo" (or "vodun," or "vaudou" as we prefer to spell it here), although traced by some scholars to a corruption of the French *Vaudois* (a Waldensian) is probably synonymous with the identical African word for spirit.

QUESTION: Where did it originate?

ANSWER: *Vaudou* is first mentioned by Moreau de St.-Méry, a French savant who had spent ten years in the Colony just before the Revolution of 1791. If one discounts the patronizing tone taken by all Europeans of the period to anything non-European, his description is acute as well as prophetic:

> It is logical to believe that *Vaudoux* owes its origin to the cult of the serpent to which the people of Juida are particularly given. They say it originated in the kingdom of Ardra on the slave-coast; and after reading to what a pitch these Africans pushed their superstition for this animal it is easy to recognize it again in what I have just reported. (The Malabar Indians also worship the snake; they call it *Nalle Pambou*: Good Snake.)
>
> What is very real and at the same time very remarkable in *Vaudoux* is a sort of magnetic power which compels the participants to dance until they lose consciousness. The contagion is so strong that Whites found spying on the mysteries of this sect and touched by one of the cultists discovering them, have sometimes started to dance and have eventually had to go so far as to pay the *Vaudoux* Queen to put an end to their torment. However, I cannot help but observe that no member of the police force—sworn to combat *Vaudoux*— has ever felt this compulsion to dance, which (if exerted) would no doubt have saved the dancers themselves from the necessity of taking flight.
>
> Doubtless to soft-pedal the alarm that this mysterious cult of *Vaudoux* has aroused in the Colony, they (the slaves) pretend to dance it in public, to the sound of drums and handclapping; they even

follow it with a meal at which nothing but fowl is eaten. But I am certain that this is merely a further device to circumvent the vigilance of the magistrates and to assure the success of those shadowy secret assemblies which are not held for amusement or pleasure but rather as a sort of school where the weak souls surrender to a domination which a thousand circumstances can render disastrous.

It is hard to imagine in what complete subjection the *Vaudoux* chiefs are able to hold the other members of the sect. Not one among them but would prefer anything to the horrors that threaten him if he does not go assiduously to the meetings and blindly obey what *Vaudoux* demands of him. We have seen some so seized with terror they lost all reason; who, in attacks of frenzy, uttered shrieks and howls, lost any resemblance to the human and aroused one's pity. In a word, nothing is more dangerous on every score than this *Vaudoux* cult, founded on an absurdity, yet capable, because of its belief, of being turned into a terrible weapon . . .

Early *vaudou* was indeed based on the serpent cult of Dahomey, and snakes, though no longer actually introduced into the ritual, continue to play a symbolic and decorative role. We have seen how Boukman, a *papaloi* or priest (the word *houngan* is now used) employed *vaudou* in its most aggressive (*Pétro*) form to summon the slaves to revolt. Toussaint, Christophe and Dessalines prohibited *vaudou* entirely, the latter with the bayonet; it prevented regimentation for work and posed too great a threat to absolute power. Pétion tolerated *vaudou* as he tolerated most things; and during the seventy years of the Catholic exclusion, the beliefs assumed their characteristic shape.

QUESTION: Does *vaudou* involve human sacrifice?

ANSWER: Whether or not human sacrifices occasionally were made during this period of Haiti's reversion to African patterns, *vaudou* acquired a bad name when Sir Spencer St. John, an English traveller of anti-Negro persuasion and sensationalist tendencies, reported the so-called Affair of Bizoton in 1863. A peasant in that year had been brought to trial at Port-au-Prince for allegedly sacrificing a child, and Sir Spencer promptly indicted the Haitian people as cannibals. His phrase for the sacrifice, "a goat without horns," was in turn taken over by such later American sensation-seekers as William Seabrook (*Magic Island*, 1929), and it was some time before any serious reporting and effort to understand *vaudou* was made.

QUESTION: Is the practice of *vaudou* legal or illegal?

ANSWER: Ever since Dessalines' Constitution of 1805 a law has been on the Haitian statute books prohibiting the practice of *vau-*

dou. Only rarely, however, has it been invoked. One such period was the time when the American Marines occupied Haiti. So rigorously was it enforced during those twenty-five years, in fact, that when Seabrook pled with Dr. Price-Mars to show him a ceremony, the Haitian scholar had to get special permission from the Commandant to "stage" one, engage a venerable *houngan* who couldn't find any drums, pay him $80—and finally be informed that it couldn't be managed! Seabrook's subsequent descriptions, Price-Mars says, were based entirely on notes he showed him covering ceremonies that took place before the Occupation.

Under Lescot attempts were made to re-apply the ban, and the Church was encouraged to wage a vigorous extermination campaign, burning ceremonial objects and drums, and cutting down sacred Mapou trees—but to little avail. The present method of controlling *vaudou* is to charge a fee of $30 for any ceremony involving religious sacrifices (cocks, goats, pigs, bulls and the like) but considerably less for ceremonial dances alone. Clandestine ceremonies are hard to hide from the police and the *chefs-de-section*, since drumming is an essential part of all rites and the type of ceremony being held is clearly indicated by the particular rhythms used. The principal effect of this policy has been to strengthen *vaudou* in and around the capital where politicians find it expedient to remain on good terms with the influential *houngans*, while weakening it in the provinces, at least in the provincial towns, where the Church is strong.

QUESTION: When are *vaudou* ceremonies held, and where?

ANSWER: Ceremonies may be held at any time, if an individual *serviteur* or community is in need of assistance or consolation and is willing to pay for the ritual ingredients required. However ceremonies are almost certain to take place on the major religious holidays and saints' days, especially around Christmas; ceremonies during Lent are rare.

The "temple" in which the rites are held consists of an outer gathering-place and one or two smaller inner chambers. The gathering-place, the *peristyle* or *tonelle*, is covered with thatching or a tin roof; its center pole (the *poteau-mitan*), sometimes banded to resemble a serpent, is the "staircase" by which the *loa* enters and leaves, and around which the invocational designs (*vevers*) are drawn. Benches or chairs along the walls accommodate those not actively involved. Sometimes there is a bed to one side for the children, though any child old enough to keep awake chants and dances with its elders. The inner chamber, the *houmfor* proper, contains the altar, the drums and other ceremonial objects (though the baptised ceremonial drums are sometimes suspended when not in use from the ceiling of the *tonelle*), the earthenware jars (*govis*) or pre-Columbian stones (*pierres loa*) in which the ancestral spirits reside, the *houngan's* symbols of authority, the sequined flags of the *societé*, etc.

QUESTION: What is the best way to see a ceremony?

ANSWER: If you do not know a Haitian who can take you to an authentic rite, the best way is to wander about the poorer quarters of Port-au-Prince or its environs on a Saturday or Sunday evening. Listen for the cadence of drums and follow them. If you are not conspicuously dressed, enter the *tonelle* unobtrusively, say '*Bon soir*' casually to those nearest you, and behave with respect, the chances are that you will be ignored or treated courteously; and that if you wait patiently (perhaps for several hours) you *may* see something interesting. The ceremonies to which tourist agencies conduct foreigners are generally staged for that purpose. If you are on your own, and the "plate" is passed, give a *gourde* or two; if the requests are repeated, politely refuse or leave.

QUESTION: What do the ceremonies signify, and which ones is one likely to see?

ANSWER: The ceremonies are a series of graphic demonstrations [1] of the forces of nature, symbolized by the various *loa* and of the participator's capacity to integrate himself with them. Every ceremony begins with a salutation to the *mystères*, following which the *houngan* lights a candle and draws a *vever* (by dribbling flour or ashes through his fingers) appropriate to the *loa* or *loas* being summoned. It is supposed that the *vevers*, since they are uncommon in African rites and somewhat resemble Indian sand-drawings, were introduced into *vaudou* by the aboriginals; intricate and very beautiful when skillfully drawn, the *vevers* serve no purpose once they are completed and are therefore danced on until they vanish. *Hounsis*, the priest's female attendants and dancing chorus, now enter, dressed in white, and perform gestures and prayers designed to adjust the relationships of the various participants. The prayer, some-

[1] "The serviteur learns love and beauty in the presence and person of Erzulie, experiences the ways of power in the diverse aspects of Ogoun, becomes familiar with the aspects of death in the attitudes of Ghédé. He sings in the chorus, and feels in his own person that surge of security which is harmonious collective action. He witnesses the wisdom of ancestral and divine counsel, and learns the advantages of accepting such counsel, with its history and experience, for his own guidance in action. In effect, he understands the principles because he sees them function."— Maya Deren in *Divine Horsemen: The Living Gods of Haiti*.

times in Creole and sometimes in *langage* (a vestigial African tongue understood only by the *loas* themselves), may last for hours. The sacrifice, the climax of the ceremony, which follows, depends for its character on circumstances.

The *mangé loa*, at which the deity is renewed with food and drink, is the most frequently performed, and may take anywhere from a matter of hours to days. Baptismal ceremonies are closely related to the *mangé loa*. But the next stage of a *serviteur's* progress, in terms of the hierarchy of the *houmfor*, is the series of rites known as *canzo* (or initiation); once graduated, a *canzo* initiate is thereafter a full-fledged participator in all ceremonies, only outranked by the *houngan* and his immediate assistants. *Canzo* ceremonies, and their ultimate stage, the *brulé-zin*, or trial by fire, are akin to death-and-resurrection rites in their symbolism; the initiate is covered with a sheet during his ordeal which involves handling hot meal or walking over live coals.

QUESTION: Which are the principal *loa* and what are their attributes?

ANSWER: The principal *loa* of the *Rada* family are *Damballah* and *Ayda Weydo; Erzulie; Legba; Agwé Woyo* and *Maîtresse La Sirène; Guédé; (Baron Samedi); Loco* and *Aïzan; Papa 'Zaca;* and *Ogoun Feraille*.

Damballah Weydo, the ancient Dahomean rain god and his wife *Ayda Weydo* are characterized respectively by a heavy constrictor and a narrow green snake. *Ayda* is also seen in the form of the rainbow. Chickens are sacrificed to both gods, both control fertility, and both are represented as of white color in Haiti. *Damballah* is sometimes identified with St. Patrick whose symbol is also a serpent.

Erzulie Fréda Dahomey, goddess of the home, of purity and of love, is invoked by a chequered heart symbol, and is identified in Haiti with the Virgin Mary. She is not to be confused with *Erzulie Jérouge* (red eyes) a malevolent goddess of the *Pétro* pantheon.

Legba, well-known in Africa as a seducer of women and mischief-maker, is known in Haiti as a kindly old man, but he still has to do with fertility and likes sacrifices of goats and cocks. Ceremonies begin with a song to *Legba* and the sprinkling of a few drops of rum on the ground in his honor. *Legba's* Catholic equivalent is St. Peter. He opens the way from the material to the spiritual world.

Agwé Woyo and his wife *La Sirène* are gods of the sea and the islands therein. *Agwé* is symbolized by a boat-drawing and sacrifices to him are often loaded on small barques and set adrift at sea. His wife takes the shape of a mermaid. Fishermen are naturally much concerned with propitiating these *loa*.

Guédé Nimbo, sometimes known as *Baron Samedi*, personifies death itself. Dressed in black, always hungry, carrying a cross, smoking a cigar or cigarette and wearing dark glasses, *Guédé* is one of the most powerful and dreaded of *loas*.

Loco Attiso, the master of the *houmfor*, and *Aïzan*, his wife, are related to *Legba*. Both are major healers, and protectors against Black Magic.

Papa 'Zaca, or *Azzaca*, the deity of agriculture, is a crude fellow with a big appetite and the voice and proclivities of a goat. He wears a peasant's blue denim jacket and carries a *macoute* (market basket).

Ogoun Feraille, one of several powerful Ogouns, is the ancient patron of warriors and iron-makers and carries a sword (or *machete*) as his symbol; his color is red. He still wears a Revolutionary uniform but is now inclined to concern himself with politics rather than war.

QUESTION: What is the difference between *Rada* and *Pétro*?

ANSWER: All of the deities listed above are of the *Rada* family, the *loas* most commonly invoked in Haiti. *Rada* is a corruption of Arada, a West African tribe that supplied many slaves to Haiti. On the whole, *Rada* gods are benevolent, or at least malleable.

Pétro deities, on the other hand, while not necessarily malevolent, are definitely aggressive. Unlike the *Rada* family, they are of Haitian not African origin, and their rites (at which pigs are most often sacrificed and which are characterized by frenzy and sometimes violence) are said to have originated with a certain Dom Pédro of Petit-Goâve, a Spanish *houngan* of early Colonial times. Some see a distinct influence of Indian rites in *Pétro* ceremonies. It was at a *Pétro* ceremony, incidentally, that Boukman issued the call to insurrection.

Other families of *loas* such as Ibo, Congo, etc. are less frequently served.

QUESTION: What is "possession" and when does it occur?

ANSWER: Leyburn defines possession as "something more than the elation of the Holy Roller, and less than the mystical exaltation of the enraptured saints, yet partaking of elements of both." The thing to be noted is that possession occurs according to rules; participants succumbing at inappropriate times are "out of order" and are not treated with respect, but those seized with the *loa* being invoked, whether during the drawing of the *vever*, or at the climactic sacrifice, or during the dance that follows both, are handled with great gentleness. J. C. Dorsainvil, an *élite* ethnologist, regards the *crise de possession* as "abnormal," resulting in part from an historical tradition making it respectable and in part from neurotic tendencies in the family of the person seized. But Herskovits, and most other authorities, regard possession as normal in the pattern of Haitian culture.

The *loa* for whom the ceremony is given makes known his modest desires through the mouth of the person possessed. The latter, retaining afterwards no memory of what he has gone through, is relieved of his anxieties by becoming the mouthpiece of a force outside himself. What happens to the personality during possession is conveyed in the following fine description by Maya Deren of two simultaneous seizures during a ceremony for *Agwé Woyo:*

> The initial convulsive movement occurred so suddenly that almost no one had remarked it, and now their faces, which had been normally feminine, planed off, imperceptibly, into a masculine nobility. Water was drawn up from the sea in a pail and poured over them, since normally *Agwé*, being a water divinity, would have immediately immersed himself in the *bassin*. Those who were near saluted the arrival of the divinity, and, through each of the women, *Agwé* spoke a few words of greeting in a voice which gurgled as if with rising air bubbles, and seemed truly to come from the waters. His mood was not displeased, but it was sober. The *Houngan*, conscience-stricken, began to explain that he, too, would soon make a ceremony. The two *Agwés* listened to him, their eyes at once forgiving and somehow detached. And, with the same air of noble, gentle sadness, they looked slowly from person to person, from the barque of food, to the *mambo*. There was something in their regard that stilled everyone. One had seen it in the faces of those who prepare to leave and wish to remember that to which they will no longer return. They met each other's eyes, and as a way was cleared for them, approached each other, and crouched down in an embrace of mutual consolation, their arms about each other's shoulders, their foreheads lowered, each on the other's shoulder. So mirrored, they wept.

QUESTION: What is the function of the *houngan*?

ANSWER: The *houngan* (or *mambo* if the priest is a woman) generally inherits his calling, but to become active he must serve an apprenticeship (as *La Place* or *Houngenikon* to another *houngan*), and to become influential he must both demonstrate his leadership in the community by his superior wisdom and be able to ef-

72

fect cures. His symbol of authority is the *asson*, a gourde rattle webbed with beads and snake vertebrae to which a small bell is attached.

The *houngan's* business does not stop with knowledge of the many complex rituals he must conduct, of how to make *vevers*, of how to impart magnetism to the various participants and style to the ritual, though all of these are important. His equally vital function is as medical advisor to a community generally without doctors. In this capacity the *houngan's* knowledge of herbal remedies must be profound. He must know how to cure colds with infusions, shock with salt, bleeding with spider-web applications, infections with garlic; there is even a case of a *houngan* on La Tortue who is said to have cured yaws with poultices of mould—the basis of penicillin. When the illness is beyond his capacity, if he is a reputable *houngan* (it is the disreputable ones who have given this aspect of *vaudou* a bad name) he will send the patient to a licensed physician. But many of the *houngan's* cures are in the realm of psychology. He is apt to be trusted by peasants to whom an *élite* doctor is as a visitor from some hostile planet. Moreover he insists on the patient "putting himself right" with the offended *loas* thus often contributing to the patient's peace of mind and his psychic capacity to recuperate.

QUESTION: Is the average houngan cynical or sincere?

ANSWER: Fifteen or twenty years ago the odds were overwhelmingly in the *houngan's* favor. Today, driven out of many provincial areas by the Church,[1] and concentrated in the Port-au-Prince-Léogane region where tourism is heaviest, the temptations for a *houngan* to exploit his powers commercially are enormous. When a notorious *houngan* like the late 'Ti Cousin of Carrefour Dufour exploits his office, traffics in Black Magic, operates distilleries and a fleet of *camions*, and rides to the capital in a Cadillac limousine, enemies of *vaudou* are naturally quick to take advantage of such a conspicuous break. But an effective deterrent on the average *houngan's* capacity to go astray is *vaudou's* very lack of civil sanctions; any communicant is free to change *houngans*.

[1] In some areas, such as the North Peninsula, where the Army has cooperated actively with the Catholic priests, persecution best describes the situation. On Tortuga Island, drumming, even for *coumbites*, has been proscribed. In Cape Haïtien most ceremonies now take place far out of town and are not easy to see. The same applies to most provincial towns. Only during great festivals, such as the mass *Ra-Ra* conclave at Carrefour Dufour on Good Friday and the July 15 baptismal rites at Saut d'Eau-Mirebalais, is sufficient safety provided by numbers to make secrecy unnecessary.

QUESTION: What part do sex and liquor play in the rites?

ANSWER: The first part of this question is difficult to answer, so different are "primitive" and "civilized" notions of what constitutes sex. In circumstances where sex is regarded as a wholly normal and unsinful activity, where no conversational inhibitions exist, and where each of the gods is presumed to have an active marital and extra-marital sex life, it is not surprising that even the least Calvinistic of Christian observers regard *vaudou* ceremonies as licentious. On the other hand, though occasional fertility rites are accompanied by overtly sexual acts, most ceremonies are marked by too much discipline, solemnity, and time-honored translation of act into symbol, to permit of anything approaching orgies. Even the dance, it will be noted, does not permit bodily contact; copulative movements are acted out by the dancers' hips and shoulders but never in close proximity as, say, during a "civilized" tango or rhumba.

As to liquor, the Haitian peasant drinks fiery *clairin* in and out of ceremonies without any sense of restraint, but drunkenness is virtually unknown. The author, in twenty visits to Haiti, has never seen an intoxicated Haitian.

QUESTION: What is Black Magic?

ANSWER: *Magie Noire* is the use by a *houngan* or sorcerer (*bocor*) of supernatural powers to encompass evil ends, such as the death of an enemy, the destruction of a neighbor's crops or the alienation of his wife. Every *houngan* knows how Black Magic is made, but no reputable one will have anything to do with it. To practice it, for one thing, a deadly bargain must be made with the evil spirits (*baka*) or the *loups-garou* (werewolves). For this the sorcerer himself will ultimately have to pay. This is not to say that the *houngan* will not provide appropriate *gardes* against *ouangas* (objects obtained from a sorcerer designed to cast a spell over someone), but the *houngan's* work is done in public, and like the work of any other priest's is designed less to bring immediate results than to put the worshipper in tune with the gods and with himself. "In religion the *serviteur* is changed; in magic the world is changed" (Deren).

QUESTION: What is the attitude of the educated Haitian to *vaudou*?

ANSWER: There are many stories of educated Haitians, including even a President or two, holding private *vaudou* rites in their homes. In general, however, with the exception of a handful of intellectuals who regard *vaudou* as an interesting curiosity from the

Folk Art

The decorative paintings sometimes found on the walls and doors of peasant *cailles* are related to the *vever* but indicate an aesthetic verve independent of religion. The one at the top was found near Moron (1946), the door was not far from the Carrefour on the main road out of Port-au-Prince (1954).

Mardi Gras

. . . gives play to folk talent in sculpture and painting as well as in dancing and music. The bat-man is standing in front of Jacmel's Hotel Excelsior (1947). The clown with a bottle was photographed from the steps of the National Palace (1954).

Popular Music

. . . is here supplied by a *Ra-Ra* band playing *vaccines* and tin horns. The *Pétro* drum is responding to the masterful hands (and calloused heel) of 'Ti Ro-Ro, Haiti's foremost concert drummer.

The Déjean Choir

The famous male chorus is here shown at the end of a number which involves costumed dancing and acting as well as singing.

Lambi Soloist

Music of a more primitive sort is being produced by this peasant on a conch-shell.

Dancing

. . . predominates in the *Ra-Ra*, two of whose "kings" are here shown in a complicated number which involves twirling their batons and keeping them in the air. The candelabra of kerosene lamps will provide illumination on the country lanes far into the night.

Sculpture in Tin and Tree-root
André Liautaud's "Sea Goddess," hammered from a discarded Esso drum, and
André Dimanche's "Politician," carved from the root of a disprized tree, are
alike in their original, mordant fantasy.

Sculpture in Wood and Clay

The wooden figure, perhaps symbolizing the sadness of the peasant's isolation, is by Odilon Duperier. The memorial panel to Hector Hyppolite is part of Jasmin Joseph's choir-screen for the Cathedral St.-Trinité. Both pieces were executed in 1954.

Port-au-Prince Chateau
This magical *élite* mansion in a style made popular at the
turn of the century is in Bois Verna, Port-au-Prince.

Painters of Genius

The late Hector Hyppolite, *vaudou* priest, is here shown in the last year of his life, with several uncompleted pictures of Black Magic in the background. Wilson Bigaud's big canvas, behind its creator, documents such various items as a haircut, a dice-game, the Centre d'Art jeep, a cock-fight, cock thieves and a *Ra-Ra* procession.

Obin, Normil

The 'Funeral of Charlemagne Peralte,' generally regarded as Philomé Obin's masterpiece was painted in 1946. More than twenty years later another primitive realist, André Normil, summed up the life of the capital's streets.

guste, Valcin ... lam and Eve,' ... nted in 1949 ... ved as the pro- ... ype for one of ... ussaint Augus- ... murals in the ... thedral St.- ... inité. Gerard ... lcin's 'Hospi- ... is by a former ... -setter who ... st have loved ... t profession.

Cathedral Murals

These details are from tempera murals painted in the transepts of the Cathedral St.-Trinité in 1951. The 'Last Supper' is by Obin, the 'Baptism of Christ' by Bazile.

point of view of "folklore," the *élite* Haitian and the middle classes (in conversation at least) characterize the religion of the peasants as "superstition" or "nonsense," a disgrace to the country and a deterrent to progress. Georges Sylvain, a well-known author, writes that "Today *Vodun* is nothing more than a mixture of quackery and superstition and it has no other raison d'etre than to provide a subsistence for the *houngans* . . . who minister to popular credulousness." Léon Audain, another Haitian man of letters, insists that "*Vodun*, at least in its present form, is a pastime. One day I was curious enough to attend a *Vodun* dance . . . The truth is that the ceremony preceding the sacrifice of unfortunate and docile animals is out of proportion with the objective: to partake of a good meal." [1]

If few of the *élite* have gone further into *vaudou* than these misinformed comments would seem to indicate, the reason in part is because the educational background of the intellectuals is exclusively French; Africanisms, in any form, are deplored or carefully concealed from the foreigner who would presumably receive a bad impression of the country from anything primitive. It might be pointed out, however, that the net effect of suppressing *vaudou* in such areas as the *élite* (including the clergy and the military) have found it possible to do so, has been to drive it underground where, inevitably, as in Colonial times, it tends to be practiced in the more aggressive *Pétro* forms.

Discussion of dancing and drumming, two essential ingredients of *vaudou*, is reserved for the chapter on the arts that follows this one.

PROTESTANTISM

In 1939-40 when Professor Leyburn was making his penetrating study of the culture of Haiti, he was able accurately to dismiss the non-Catholic Christian elements with a single sentence. "No Protestant sect," he wrote, "has ever gained a real foothold in Haiti." Today, several sects, the Baptists, Wesleyans, Methodists, Jehovah's Witnesses, and others, have managed to gain footholds in Haiti, accounting in their combined influence for perhaps as many

[1] Parts of the animals sacrificed are never eaten, but in any event a more complicated means of obtaining a "good meal" would be hard to imagine. Both of these hostile comments are taken from the chapter on *vaudou* in *Haiti*, a compendium of writings by Haitian authors published by the Pan-American Union.

as 400,000 out of Haiti's 4,000,000 people; and one of them, the Protestant Episcopal Church, with 53,362 baptised members and 14,478 additional communicants, has made enough of an impact in several spheres of Haitian life to warrant describing its activities in some detail.

The Episcopal Church came to Haiti in 1861 when a group of 110 American Negroes decided, because of racial problems at home, to emigrate to an all-Negro country. One-third died, another third returned to escape tropical diseases, but among the third that remained was the Rev. James Theodore Holly of Detroit, Michigan, who proposed to improve "corrupting influences of society here where neither the public morality nor religion have yet firmly taken root," and established the Holy Trinity Parish in Port-au-Prince. In 1874, after Holly had established branches of the Church elsewhere, he was consecrated Bishop and continued his work until his death in 1911. The Rev. Harry Roberts Carson was ordained the first Missionary Bishop of Haiti in 1923. He completed the building of St.-Trinité Cathedral in 1928. By the time of his retirement in 1943 the Church had 62 missions, 13 schools, and 18 members of the clergy in Haiti. The present Bishop, C. Alfred Voegeli, a native of Morristown, New Jersey, was consecrated the same year, and under his vigorous regime the number of organized missions has grown to 79, and the number of active clergy to 31, all of whom (excepting the Bishop and the Dean of the Seminary) are native Haitians.

The Protestant Episcopal Church operates on a total annual budget of only $75,000, out of which $10,000 is devoted to the educational work of such institutions as the Grace Merritt Stewart School for Girls and the Seminary at Mont Rouis, where all the clergy receive their four-year training, and where a Boy Scout camp is maintained. Another $10,000 goes to the St. Vincent School for Handicapped Children, the only school in Haiti taking care of and training blind, deaf and crippled children. The Church's budget is made up mostly of funds contributed in the United States.

Although the Episcopalians feel that the Roman Catholics waver between stamping out *vaudou* and attempting to play along with it, the attitudes of the two Churches vary little in their hostility to the cult. Bishop Voegeli, who spends a very large part of his time visiting remote missions, such as one on La Gonave Island which requires a journey of two days in a fisherman's sailboat and twelve hours on horseback, claims to preserve wherever possible the folklore and musical aspects of *vaudou*, but he asks: "How can you reason with or explain such distinctions to a primitive people? *Vaudou* is their temporary opiate, as we see it, giving them the same kind of release from their poverty and misery as would a drunken binge. *Vaudou*, far from doing away with anxiety or fear, encourages both."[1]

The principal cultural contribution of the Episcopal Church has been its sponsorship of the murals by primitive painters in the Cathedral St.-Trinité, a phenomenon which will be described in the next chapter.

The Baptist Mission under the dynamic leadership of Wallace Turnbull was now the fastest growing of the Protestant sects, its spacious center (Mountain Maid/L'Artisane) for folk arts and crafts on the Kenscoff Road externalizing the roots it had begun to tap among the mountain folk.

[1] It is improbable that Monseigneur Luc Garnier, Bishop Voegeli's Haitian successor, would speak of *vaudou* so scornfully. For one thing, the Haitian government's attitude toward the cult altered drastically under the first Duvalier. Whether because of political considerations—the *houngans*, in return for unofficial sanction of their ceremonies by the police, helped the government maintain control in some regions—or because this ethnologist had written about the cult sympathetically in the past, the President was popularly regarded as a friend of *vaudouisme*.

But attitudes to primitive religions have changed drastically throughout the world, too. It is the organized religions that now find themselves on the defensive, hard pressed to justify their prohibitions and material wealth in comparison with cults enlisting the worshipper's whole being as Christianity did in its first centuries.

CHAPTER VI

RENAISSANCE OF THE SEVEN ARTS

THE RECENT WORLD-WIDE interest in Haitian 'popular' painters has completely overshadowed concurrent developments in sculpture and architecture and has obscured the fact that a literary revival was in full cry a decade earlier. It has served, however, to focus attention on those enduring manifestations of the peasants' aesthetic vitality which survived every hazard of Haiti's history: folklore, music and the dance.

FOLK ARTS

The aspect of life which distinguishes Haiti most sharply from its Caribbean neighbors is the richness of its folklore. Whatever blessings colonialism may have brought to the other islands in the Nineteenth Century, its persistence there faded and "civilized" native traditions if it did not actually sterilize them. The Haitian peasant was not given the amenities of plumbing nor was he made conversant in a European language; but neither was he subjected to the levelling blight of middle-class provincial taste. For entertainment he had to entertain himself. What music he heard, he made. And if he ever had time to indulge in a carved or painted decoration, the design he used was something that pleased him or seemed appropriate to its use, not something he had seen and repeated.

Tourists who look in Haiti for the equivalent of Navajo rugs or old Dutch tobacco boxes will be disappointed. The peasant has been content to dance over his finest drawings; he has been too poor and too hard-pressed to search for imperishable mediums. The buyers' market has been a recent phenomenon, and leisure has never existed except for those who made a principle of indulging their taste for luxuries abroad.

The tourist will have to look more closely at a few humble objects whose great beauty is a function of their simplicity. For example: the colored paper kites of children (*cerf-volants*); the painted swagger-sticks (*coco-macaques*) of Jacmel; the scooped-log washtubs and canoes and the laundry paddles employed wherever there is water; the brick-red paper trunks, striped with gold; the mortar-and-pestle used for grinding grain; the superbly designed straw saddles, baskets, conical hats and shoulder-bags; the earthenware coffee-pots and lidded jars; the tooled-leather scabbard of the peasant's ever-present *machete;* the elaborately embossed *Ra-Ra* candelabra made of ordinary American oil funnels and tin cans; and last but not least the painted drums, ceremonial calabashes and Mardi Gras masks whose variety of invention defies description.

If he looks from such simple objects to the more subtle questions of why Haitian women choose head-bandanas of primary flaming hues, and how intricately they knot their wiry hair; and why their carriage as they walk is so freely noble; and the unerring way Haitians have of composing themselves in groups, standing or cross-legged, to harangue each other or to laugh—then he will be prepared to enter into their more elaborate rituals with an understanding that with these people (as with all artists) the grace of doing anything is as important as the thing done.

With a religion as pervasive and as intimately related to every aspect of life as *vaudou*, it is inevitable that most aspects of folklore and peasant art will be colored by it to some degree. We have already, in the last chapter, noted the aesthetic nature of the rituals themselves. In most instances, it is the *societé*, grouped together in the *houmfor*, that also organizes whatever is organized in Mardi Gras, *Ra-Ra* and other fêtes.

During Mardi Gras, for example, there is a band of young men who get together every year in Port-au-Prince and put on Indian costumes. These costumes include suits of the most gorgeously painted feathers and a headdress of superbly interlocking golden horns. Each Indian makes his own costume but its style, I am told, goes back to a certain *houngan* who once headed the club. It is not unlikely that this *houngan* inherited his particular skill from another *houngan*, and that still farther back there was a slave-*houngan* who knew Indians with similar headgear, or was an Indian himself.

Not all the fêtes are connected with *vaudou*. The Judas Hunt which is celebrated in some parts of Haiti the Saturday before Easter Sunday is an ancient Holy Week ceremonial. In effigy, Monsieur Judas comes to visit a peasant as one of the Twelve Apostles and an honored guest, but as soon as the death of Christ is announced on Good Friday, the symbolic traitor flees, and, dressed in the hides and mask of a bull, is chased through the streets by a laughing mob that beats him (except when he turns and threatens to gore them) with whips and barrel-staves. In the capital Judas used to be burned in effigy by children, but this led to so many fires that the police put a stop to it.

Most of the designs that are used on ceremonial drums, calabashes, altars, etc., are derived from the *vever*. But occasionally, as when they are used to decorate the exterior wall of a *caille*, they deviate so freely as to approach pure abstraction.

MUSIC

It may have been precisely because the slaves were deprived of the wooden and cast-bronze effigies of their gods in Saint-Domingue, that the compulsion to memorialize everything African in song became so powerful. At all *vaudou* ceremonies, singing is as important as drumming and dancing, and it is performed by the participants themselves, and for the most part by the *hounsis*, the priest's female "chorus." Most of the songs sung are in the nature of chants, but they are not sung in harmony. The melodic statement appealing to the god is brief. It is the repetitions of the refrain that intensify the emotional effect. The musical forms, Herskovits[1] asserts, "are almost entirely African in their rhythmic structure, but European influence is traceable in their melodic line, which varies from unchanged European folk-melodies to purely African songs. In the use of the falsetto, however; in the statement of a theme by a leader and its repetition by a chorus; and in the countless modulations introduced into the song, the singing is entirely African, as are the postures struck by those singing."

Most of the songs are very old, handed down with variations from generation to generation, but there is no injunction against creating new ones, and once they catch on they become part of the tradition. Hardly any music in Haiti has been written down, much less copyrighted, but valuable work in preserving and collecting the songs has been done by Professor Werner Jaegerhuber, Mme. Lina Mathon-Blanchet, Harold Courlander and Issa El Saieh.

There are songs to every *loa* and for every conceivable occasion, but they may be roughly divided into those that are associated

[1] See *Life in a Haitian Valley* by Melville J. Herskovits. Knopf, 1937.

with the *vaudou* subdivisions—*Rada, Pétro, Ibo, Congo, Nago, Yenvalo,* etc.—and those that accompany secular activities such as *Ra-Ra,* a *coumbite* or a simple party (*bamboche*). Songs of the sea are inspired by the rhythms of waves and oars. Songs of the plain are "plaintive," long-drawn out. But in the "party" songs, like the mimicking *bal* or the elegant *meringue,* we pass from *vaudou* and Africanism into the world of the *élite.*

After the invocation at a ceremony, and while the ritual drawing is being made, the *hounsis* chant:

> *Aprés Dieu houngan vever moin!*

But after that the choice of songs will depend on the "family" being "served" and the particular *loa* invoked. If the *serviteurs* are fishermen such a song to *Agwé* as the following may be sung:

> *Lans la mer m't'allé m'té pèché Agué Woyo!* etc.[1]

To the sea I went, I went fishing, Agué Woyo!
I lost the hook of my *loa!*
I lost the hook of my *loa!*
I ask you, what am I going to eat for supper?
Little Conch in the Sea, what am I going to eat?

One of the countless songs to *Guédé* is the famous '*Papa Guédé bel gaçon*' which is supposed to have originated in a demonstration making fun of the Mulatto President Louis Borno. Another takes the familiar form of reproach:

> *Gédé Nimbo Papa!*

That which you do makes you no good.
When I am present you speak well of me.
Behind my back you speak badly of me . . .
Saud jamais, I say *saud!*

A song may be anecdotal, referring to some long-forgotten event, but it is always pointed and often poetic, as in this memorial to a priestess:

[1] According to Harold Courlander, whose authoritative *Haiti Singing*, University of North Carolina Press, 1939, I am quoting in this section, without choral repetitions, for both Creole first-lines and translations, this song belongs to the *Nago* cycle, the two that follow to *Rada*, the fourth to *Pétro*, the last to *Congo*.

Mambo Mésiré manqué noyé, etc.

Mambo Mésiré saves herself from drowning.
The day a leaf falls in the water
Is not the day it sinks.

Tijean Pétro is a bad actor among the *loa*, feared especially by children, but this song seems to dispel his fearsomeness by reducing it to round numbers:

Tijean Pétro, combien ti mounes ou mangé? etc.

Tijean Pétro, how many little men have you eaten?
I have eaten two-hundred-eighty,
I have just begun to make it two-hundred-ninety-two,
I have just begun!

Finally there is the love song, bawdy and jocular, with none of our romanticism:

Vin prend leçon nans main moin, ya ya! etc.

Come take your lessons in my arms, *ya ya!*
My mother is not here, come take your lessons in my arms!
My mother has gone looking for wood,
Come take your lessons in my arms!
My mother has gone away for water,
Come take your lessons in my arms!

Some of these folk songs have been tidied up a bit and are now to be heard in the salons of the *élite*, and even on phonograph records. Such are the great invocation to *Erzulie* of Revolutionary times '*Moin tandé oun canon qui tiré*' and the immensely moving ceremonial chants '*Damballah, Damballah, Damballah!*' and '*Ministre Azaca.*' The rousing, ever-popular *congo* of Jacmel, '*Panama'm tombé*,' has already been mentioned. Romantic *meringues* like '*Carolin Acao*' and '*Angélico*,' although of fairly recent date, are of unknown origin and should be considered genuine folk songs, however hopped-up and manhandled by ballroom orchestras. The nostalgic, fabulously hypnotic '*Haïti Chérie*,' the Haitian's paean of love to his homeland, where no one is in a hurry and women are not the same monotonous color, is the masterpiece of Othelo Bayard of Cayes.

Haïti chérie, pi bel pé, passé ou nan poin, etc.

Haïti chérie, loveliest country, compared to which there's none,
Compared to which . . . One has to leave to sense what you
   have cost;
One has to leave you, Haiti, to know what one has lost,
To feel the truth of what you mean, of all that you have done.

In countries of the white man, all faces look the same:
No *mulatresse,* no Creole *griffe,* no lovely *marabou,*
No dress-bewitching and sweet-scented girls come up to you,
No beautiful young Negresses whose wit is never tame . . .

Only with the organization of the superbly trained male choir
of Michele Déjean in 1952 has any effort been made in Haiti to
present this corpus of magnificent music with sophistication and
style.[1]

Musical instruments in Haiti run the gamut from the four-note
bamboo flute, the African *marimba,* the conch-shell (*lambi*) and
the papaya-stem (*piston*) to the enormous bamboo base-*vaccine,*
five inches in diameter and more than four feet long, whose thun-
derous one-note accompanies the singing, tapping and stamping
of a *Ra-Ra* band during Lent. But everything begins and ends with
the drum. The mosquito-drum, with its single plucked string an-
chored in the earth, is for children. The tambourine and flat *basse*
are used in *coumbites.* The giant *assator,* sometimes played from
the branch of a tree, is employed in the rarest of ceremonies and is
"baptized" in a ritual having dances of its own. All *Rada* rites are
accompanied by a "battery" of three cowhide pegged drums. The
largest, the *mamam,* is played with a mallet and one hand and does
the "talking"; the middle drum is played with one hand and a
bowed stick called a *baguette;* while the smallest drum, the *bula,*
conveys an unvarying rhythmic tatoo with thin sticks held in both
hands. Sometimes a fourth musician, an *ogantiér,* beats a piece of
iron with a small rod. In *Pétro* ceremonies, two drums whose goat-
skin hides are held to the body of the instrument by laced cords,
are used, and it is this drum which is most frequently employed by
soloists, accompanists and ballroom ensembles in Port-au-Prince.
   During a *vaudou* ceremony it is the drummers, seldom pos-

[1] Available recordings of Haitian folk music, including one by the Déjean Choir,
are listed in the last paragraphs of Appendix III, following which the score of *Haïti
Chérie* is printed in its entirety.

sessed themselves, who bring on possessions through the excitement and insistence of their drumming. It is they who signal the passage from one phase of the ceremony to the next and who are empowered to break the almost unbearable tension their percussion has created, when a break is called for.

> Instead of being able to move in the long balanced strides of relaxation [writes Maya Deren] the defenseless person is buffeted by each great stroke, as the drummer sets out to 'beat the loa into his head.' The person cringes with each large beat, as if the drum mallet descended upon his very skull; he ricochets about the peristyle, clutching blindly at the arms which are extended to support him, pirouettes wildly on one leg, recaptures balance for a brief moment, only to be hurtled forward again by another great blow on the drum. The drummer, apparently impervious to the embattled anguish of the person, persists relentlessly; until, suddenly, the violence ceases, the head of the person lifts, and one recognizes the strangely abstracted eyes of a being who seems to see beyond whatever he looks at, as if into or from another world. The loa, which the song had been invoking, has arrived.

Virtuoso drumming is something else again, and to hear it one must hear (and also see) the now celebrated 'Ti Roro.[1]

DANCING

The Haitian peasant, whether he is participating in a ceremony or in a purely social affair following, let us say, a *coumbite*, or in a *Ra-Ra* procession, never dances "with" anyone. The man dances, and the woman dances. Sometimes they are facing each other and sometimes not, but the emphasis is on self-expression or bodily release, disciplined within bounds by what the rite or the musical accompaniment calls for. To a foreigner, observing this for the first time, the general impression is usually summed up in such epithets as "disorganized," "anarchic," "sex-crazed" or "orgiastic." None of them is a correct description.

In a people physically uninhibited, sexuality enters into every

[1] This individualistic *marron* of the *houmforts* whose improvisations and variety of tone have become legendary, arrived once at the Miami airport, en route to a booking with the Katherine Dunham troupe, sans passport, sans identification of any kind, and sans money save for seven dollar-bills. Frankly amazed to be asked who he was, he replied "Everybody knows 'Ti Roro," and followed this statement with a classical demonstration of drumming. While the authorities were making arrangements to conduct him to an asylum, Roro, who had already stated that his $7 would take him to New York—"and Paris"—characteristically stepped over to a drug counter and bought himself a pair of $5 sun-glasses.

dance, by overt suggestion (as in the *banda*, which frankly imitates copulative movements) or by implication, but it is never stimulated by bodily contact as in Western ballroom dancing. Freedom and relaxation are the keynotes. Shoulders and hips are as active as feet, often more so. In a ceremony the dancers (who are also, of course, the singers) move counter-clockwise around the central post, making approximately identical movements to the accompaniment of the drums. In a *Rada* dance, Courlander says, "the foot movement is a step to the side, left and then right, to a one, two, three, rest count; the shoulders move forward and backward, and the arms are in position to retain balance. Dancers pirouette as they please, sometimes moving forward rapidly, sometimes slowly." *Pétro* dances are governed by the rhythm of the second drum, bring the feet more into play, and involve a lot of pairing off. "Women sometimes use a Congo pose, with the left hand on the hip and the right arm held outward, a gesture which lends a good deal of grace to what might otherwise be rather violent aesthetics." Maya Deren describes a dance in honor of *Agwé* as appropriately suggesting water:

> Before me the bodies of the dancers undulate with a wave-like motion, which begins at the shoulders, divides itself to run separately along the arms and down the spine, is once more unified where the palms rest upon the bent knees, and finally flows down the legs into the earth, while already the shoulders have initiated the wave which follows.

With the acceleration of tourism to Haiti in the late 40's, numerous attempts have been made to stage Haitian dances and to exploit them commercially at home and abroad. Most of the well-meaning attempts to "clean it up" have resulted only in vulgarization, and the efforts to "give it style" in banality. As early as the late 30's, Katherine Dunham spent some time in Haiti and introduced versions of "voodoo" on the New York stage with questionable taste and almost complete loss of authenticity. One of her star performers, the Haitian dancer Jean Léon Destiné, had already (under Mme. Mathon-Blanchet's direction) organized Haiti's first folklore troupe which participated in 1941 in the National Folk Festival at Washington. A dancer of sincerity and talent, Destiné sought dancers among the peasants, learning from them as he trained them in professional ensemble. His great success as a solo interpreter of Haitian dancing on the New York stage led to Destiné's recall to Port-au-Prince in 1950 to direct the Troupe Nationale Folklorique in its regular performances on the stage of the Bicentennial Exposition's new Théatre de Verdure. This troupe, and others, such as the one later organized by the Haitian singer, Emerante de Pradines, have performed abroad as well as at home with skill and dignity.

POETRY AND THE NOVEL

With the arts of writing we shift, inevitably, to the world of the *élite*. Poetry is a part of the daily life of the peasant, as we have seen, but it is a physical and verbal poetry. The nearest it comes to being literary is in the story-telling sessions that take place on a rainy night in a *caille* where one peasant asks "Cric?" and if the answer is "Crac!" tells a fable of 'Ti Malice, the foxy urchin who plays tricks on the credulous Bouqui.

Until the late 20's Haitian *élite* writers devoted themselves to the production of *belles lettres* in the strictest and narrowest sense. About the turn of the century the poet Massilon Coicou introduced Creole words and phrases into such writings for the first time, but this bold gesture did not bear fruit. "From independence to our day," wrote Jacques Antoine, "our constant preoccupation has been to produce favorable evidence of the Negro's intellectual capacity before the tribunal of white opinion"—and this defensive psychology inevitably produced works that writers thought would be well received rather than works generated by an inner necessity.

The coming-of-age of Haitian literature coincided with Haiti's occupation by the Marines. "We were children when the Americans arrived in Haiti," Réné Piquion writes, "and we grew up enraged in the presence of a flag that symbolized a military occupation." This national and racial self-consciousness was part of the impetus behind the founding of the Révue Indigène in 1927. Edited by the poet Émile Roumère, and numbering among its co-founders the now-famous novelists, Jacques Roumain and Philippe Thoby-Marcelin, this short-lived magazine broke the first lances for symbolism and Africanism. But it owed the later part of its emphasis to the pioneer work in the study of native folklore contributed by such *élite* ethnologists as J. C. Dorsainvil, who devoted his life to the study of *vaudou*, and Jean Price-Mars, who had set for himself the task of answering in the affirmative the questions: "Does Haitian society have a background of oral tradition, legends, tales, songs, riddles, customs, observances and beliefs? . . . And if this folklore exists, what is its value from the literary and scientific point of view?"

The answers to these questions may now seem ridiculously obvious, but in 1927 they appear to have hit the intellectuals of the *élite* like a blockbuster. The poet Carl Brouard was so disturbed by it that he moved from his parents' home in aristocratic Bois Verna to live in the slums. With Lorimer Denis and François Duvalier, who also believed that *vaudou* must provide the inspiration of the new literature, he founded a society to combine African ideas and socialist economic principles. Roussan Camille, in a sheaf of free-verses entitled *Assaut à la Nuit*, prefaced by Piquion, attempted to bridge the gulf between past and future. The tone was nostalgic, but militant:

Your fires this evening
are as fine
as the fires of mystery and hope
that burned at Bois Caïman.

The Mambo repeats the sacred sign
before the persistent flame.
Is the wind too soiled
with satisfied sighs
and cynical laughs
to recall
to the priestess those ancient promises?

O surely the gods
who know that our sorrows
are as long as the way
from Africa to here—
our black gods—now
can foretell again
the victorious colors
of tomorrow's dawn!

So these fires are as fine
as the fires of mystery and hope,
and your dances,
painful, triumphant,
remind me
of the nights (unforgotten)
of battle.

Camille is now a diplomat and government counsellor. Roumain went into politics and became a Communist just before he died. Jean Brierre, another poet, emerged as the leader of a student strike and author of fiery dramatic pieces honoring Macandel and Toussaint. Roumère himself wrote poems entirely in Creole. It was recognized suddenly that the most effective poem by the respected elder poet Oswald Durand, who had written volumes of indifferent verse in French, was the Creole lyric he had contributed to a popular song about Choucoune, a lovely *marabout* who falls for a French-speaking stranger with a red beard and forgets about her fiancé.

Roumère, not to be outdone, treated the theme of a similar country wench from his native Jérémie with a more unconventionally realistic symbolism:

Marabout de mon coeur . . .

Black bird of my heart, whose breasts are oranges,
More savory than eggplant-stuffed-with-crab, you please
My taste better than tripe in the pepper-pot;
Dumpling in peas and araomatic tea are not more hot.
You are the corned-beef in my heart's custom-house;
The meal-in-syrup in my throat; the grouse
Smoking on the platter, stuffed with rice.
Crisper than sweet potatoes, browner than fish-fries,
My hunger follows you—no wonder crude,
You whose buttocks are so rich in food!

Still more recently (1952-3) Franck Fouché and F. Morisseau-Leroy took it upon themselves to render into Creole two plays of Sophocles, the *Oedipus Rex* and the *Antigone*, and both were produced with brilliant effect at the Théatre de Verdure. A poem from the latter poet's *Diacoute* addresses a tourist in the peasant tongue, grimly:

Tourist, don't take my picture
Tourist, don't put me in.
I'm too ugly.
I'm too dirty.
I'm much, much too thin.
Don't take my picture, white man.

For Mr. Eastman's sake
Don't take it: he wouldn't like it.
I'm too dirty. I'm too ugly.
Your Kodak, I'm sure, will break.

I'm too black, tourist.
Leave me alone, White.
Don't take the picture of my donkey;
This animal's overloaded,
Feeble and small of limb;
He hasn't eaten, this donkey
Don't take a picture of him.

Tourist, don't snap my dwelling,
Neither the one of straw
Nor the one of mud and guinea-grass:
Both are falling apart.
Go take a shot of the Palace
Or the Bicentennial's art.

Don't take a picture of my garden.
I haven't got any plough.
I haven't got a tractor.
I haven't any machine.
My trees are worthless. My bare feet
Are too dirty to be seen.

My clothes? Nothing left to tear . . .
The poor Negro doesn't look a White
In the face, tourist. Look at my hair;
Your Kodak isn't used to that color and grit;
Your barber wouldn't dare
To even try straightening it.

Tourist, don't take my picture.
You don't understand my pose.
You don't understand a thing.
It's none of your business, I say.
Gimme five cents, tourist,
And then—be on your way!

It would be a mistake, nevertheless, to conclude that Haiti's poets have "gone native" or that the use of Creole offers any permanent solution of their dilemma. That dilemma is: how to establish or retain roots in the rich soil of the peasantry while at the same time leading the sophisticated and sometimes irresponsible life of an *élite* intellectual—and the dilemma has led more than one of Haiti's many talented poets to cynicism, drink, or silence. As late as 1947 when Jean Brierre dedicated his *Black Soul* "au nègre Dumarsais Estimé qui nous souhaitons rencontrer toujours dans le sillage de l'Empereur" and called upon Joe Louis to

> frappe à chaque victoire
> le gong sonore des revendications de la race

the answer seemed clear. But Brierre and his comrades, including Camille, have come to realize that poetry is not the by-product of attitudes but is the distillation of a man's capacity to become involved in and reflect his world. The symbolist poet Magloire St. Aude, who has never deviated from the ambiguities of style that are true to his nature, but who has turned his back (like Brouard) on polite society, is becoming more and more the idol of a less-illusioned generation.[1]

In the field of the novel, this same dilemma remains unresolved. Roumain's *Masters of the Dew* broke virgin soil by entering into the hard life of the peasant community and has not been surpassed for the realism of its presentation and the angry power of its prose; but its weakness stems from the artificial and propagandistic nature of its conclusions—the Marxist assumption that class-conscious rebellion will resolve the individual's personal problems. The brothers Pierre Marcelin and Philippe Thoby-Marcelin, equally well-known abroad for the translations of their novels, *Canapé Verte*, *The Beast of the Haitian Hills*, and *The Pencil of God*, seem even more removed in spirit from the peasants whose superstitions and quaint gaucheries they describe with such amused detachment. The Marcelins have been praised for the "objectivity" of their reporting and for creating "a basic tension between the primitive material and the sophistication with which it is presented," and for this they deserve praise; but again, the younger generation would like to escape from this dualism and create works that do not "look down"

---

[1] For a penetrating study of this poet and of some of the others mentioned in this section, see "Land of Poets" by William Jay Smith in the November 1953 issue of *Américas*, monthly publication of the Pan-American Union.

on their subject matter, regardless of whether this deals with the peasants or the *élite*.

It remains to be said that literature in Haiti, to a greater extent than in the case of any of the other arts, suffers from provincialism. This is inevitable. Writing is a sophisticated business. Emotion and craft suffice to carry conviction in most of the other arts, but not in writing. The poet can make use of primitive material but he cannot be a primitive unless he chooses to ignore ideas, and the very nature of language makes this difficult. Ideas are rooted in civilizations, and the Haitian writer who goes far afield in their pursuit is in danger not only of alienating himself from his own milieu but of assimilating imperfectly another country's. In Haiti itself, whether they write in French or in Creole, authors are writing for a very small audience. Worse still, they may be writing only for their friends who can hardly be unappreciative. Criticism, as we know it, is non-existent. Freedom of expression is limited. There is no private publishing house in Haiti. There are no positions for professional writers as such, and no scholarships as there are for engineers, painters, etc. Under the circumstances the variety and vitality of Haitian writing is remarkable.

ARCHITECTURE

Involving as it does the expenditure of large sums of money, a high degree of technical training, and an almost complete subordination of the artist to his employer, it would be surprising if architecture had developed in Haiti any characteristic forms of its own. It hasn't. Yet the three styles that it has borrowed from abroad—the African thatched hut, the ginger-bread *élite* mansion of the early Twentieth Century, and the modernistic villa of to-day—have all assumed typically Haitian guises.

The *caille*, as shelter for the bulk of the population, has already been described. Part of its charm is in the hand-hewn construction that causes it to lean, sometimes precariously, off center. But a better part is in the carved woodwork, brilliantly painted shutters and doors, and incidental decoration that is to be found where money and time permit.

Aside from its tremendous natural setting, the visual glory of Port-au-Prince is in its *fin-de-siècle* architecture. Those peaked, half-timbered castles of sheer invention, with their stately hinged doors and cuckoo-clock dormers, their elegance, their mystery and their obscure provenience, have been a source of wonder and delight to visiting art-lovers. Unfortunately, the *élite*, who built them and own them, no longer like them, and there is a real danger that in a decade or two they will have vanished. The Vieux mansion on Lalue now stands in almost solitary splendor. And in the Champs de Mars only the Hotels Mon Rêve and Excelsior and the Café Savoy-Vincent remain to reproach the iron reviewing stand with its hideous Coca-Cola sign. But Bois Verna and the section of the city lying between it and the Hotel Oloffson are still virtually intact.

Where this architecture came from is disputed. The likeliest theory is that it grew out of the Paris Colonial Exposition of 1900 where East Indian pavilions and pagodas nudged Mohammedan mosques. It is found, with local variations, in the provinces. The imposing iron balconies of Jacmel were imported from Germany in the '80's where, presumably, they were cast to grace that country's short-lived overseas empire. Cap Haïtien's high shuttered doors, red-tiled roofs and projecting cornices are Haiti's most noticeable Spanish heritage; but the indescribably beautiful pastel colors with which this city's dwellings are painted are unique.

Most of the villas built in Port-au-Prince since the War are no better and no worse, architecturally speaking, than similar unimaginative piles of masonry in Kingston, Havana or Miami. But Haiti has produced at least two modern architects of taste, and though they haven't been lavished with commissions, their work may be seen. Older and more traditional of the two is Robert Baussan, who had already (1937) experimented with the adaptation of African materials and forms in Pétion-Ville's conical thatched night-club, Cabane Choucoune, when he became Haiti's first Minister of Tourism. Baussan had meanwhile built himself a luxurious villa overlooking the residential suburb, and in 1949, deciding to move where the view would be less spectacularly distracting, he transformed it, with a few deft alterations, into one of the Caribbean's loveliest hotels, the Ibo Lélé.

Of a younger generation, Albert Mangonés, a graduate of Cornell and a cousin of the novelist, Jacques Roumain, has to his credit a similar transformation: the present Villa Créole Hotel, with its terraces, outbuildings and pool. Mangonés also designed the Théatre de Verdure and Cockfight Arena in the Exposition grounds, but his masterpiece is probably the Diquini home of an American, Mrs. Anne Kennedy. Built of yellow limestone beside a natural waterfall, its tropically planted interior patio gives the spacious living-room open perspectives of Haiti's natural beauty on both sides.

SCULPTURE

The failure we have already noted of the African tribesmen imported into Saint-Domingue as slaves to resume and carry on the arts of sculpture in which many of them must have been skilled, has never been adequately explained. For a hundred and fifty years following independence, no carving of any originality was produced in Haiti. Then, suddenly, it began to reappear! One would have to subscribe to Jung's theory of the persistence of a "racial subconscious" to account for it. Unless, of course, one were to assume that there were always sculptors but never an audience that considered their pieces worth mentioning.

That may well be the case. Two circumstances support it. One is that as soon as tourists in the late 30's and early 40's, aroused by the world-wide interest in primitivism, began to make inquiries, peasants came into town from the hills carrying now a crudely carved but powerful figure in mahogany, now a strange bird or lizard chipped from a block of limestone. The second circumstance is that although both of Haiti's sculptors of genius, Odilon Duperier and Jasmin Joseph, were discovered by the American sculptor, Jason Seley, neither of them worked in a style in any way resembling his own.

Jasmin tried to, when he saw Seley's terra-cotta figures being fired at the Le Baudry brick-kiln, near which he lived; but when Seley saw these imitations standing in a *caille* beside the boy's own startlingly original work, he was quick to tell him in which direction his future lay. Jasmin had begun by modelling small figurines in clay—dancers, horsemen, athletes, lions, dogs. In the beginning he had to be restrained from giving these pieces away, so appreciative was he of recognition and the chance to work night and day at his craft. Then, as his work began to sell at the Centre d'Art, and his paintings also attracted attention, he discovered a startling way of endowing the figurines with monumentality. He fired them in the form of open-work bricks, the figures silhouetted against space and surrounded by foliage. A window made up of 23 such terra-cotta bricks whose piercings permit the light to play among the figures and cast shadows on the floor, was executed for the Kennedy home in 1952-3. Two small windows, less successful because more crowded in composition, were then designed for the transept of

St.-Trinité Cathedral. But the choir-screen for that church on which Jasmin is now engaged promises to be his masterpiece and the most original, deeply-felt sculpture ever to come from the West Indies.

Jasmin's innovation undoubtedly owes something to the wood-carvings of Duperier, who was already established at the art center when Jasmin arrived, and whose favorite theme was a man in a tree, or under one, enveloped in foliage. Duperier was a young carpenter's assistant who had come to Seley and begged for wood and some tools. Duperier worked for years on an elaborate Ark of the Covenant which was to contain scores of saints and demons in its wooden niches, but the project cut him off from the other artists, interfered with his ability to make a living, and ended in disaster. Now on his own for several years, Duperier has carved masks and standing figures for the curio shops, some magnificent, some derivative of African pieces he has been asked to imitate.

Another woodcarver of outstanding talent is André Dimanche, a native of Jérémie, whose large figures have achieved surprising vogue among discriminating members of the *élite*. Dimanche chisels his figures out of *sucrin* (horsewood, a shade-tree for mahogany), often employing the root itself for serpents, twined limbs, hair, etc. in a most imaginative style.

André Liotaud, an unlettered man of 60 from Croix-des-Bouquets and a blacksmith all his life, is the only one of the sculptors to draw upon *vaudou* for his inspiration. Having forged iron grave crosses and the like, he now uses *vevers* as the basis for his open-work iron figures and fantasies. His work is handled by the Centre d'Art.

PAINTING

Haitians who have visited every part of the country have been heard to confess that they never have seen a painted design on a peasant *caille*. One sees what one is prepared to see. Travellers criss-crossed Africa for centuries without one of them noting the existence of one of the world's great sculptural styles. There were signs, before 1944, that Haitians painted. The decoration of drums, the stippling of center-posts and the depiction of the life of the *loa* over the altars of *houmfors* has already been cited. The paintings on *cailles* were related to these. But painted *cailles* are rare. To bring the painters themselves into the open, a demand had to be created. It was created when the Centre d'Art opened its doors and began to offer 'primitives' for sale.

The establishment of this market was not, in its initial phase, an attempt to mobilize the latent visual-talents of the *vaudou*-worshippers. On the contrary its director, DeWitt Peters, himself a painter who had taken a wartime English-teaching assignment in Port-au-Prince, states that his only intention had been to set up classes at which educated Haitians might learn the fundamentals of traditional draftsmanship and oil technique. In so far as Peters had any stylistic prejudices, these may be deduced from his invitations, as late as 1947, to contemporary Cubans practicing a neo-Parisian cubistic simplification, to give demonstrations and teach gifted students at the Centre. By this time, however, the primitives were beginning to establish themselves, and Peters was encouraging them to work in their own homes. It had been the fortuitous discoveries of Hector Hyppolite and Philomé Obin several years before that had opened Peters' eyes to the possibilities of a 'popular' movement, and at the same time turned the Centre into a rallying point for a variety of part-time native artists and talented youths who would probably otherwise had "died on the vine" for lack of a market.

This element of "opportunity" in the Haitian experience cannot be overstressed. Hyppolite and Obin, whose arts came to form the two poles of Haitian painting—the vatic and the descriptive—were in their late 'forties when the Centre opened its doors to them. Both of them had been painting, off and on, for twenty-five years. Without an audience, without the stimulus of even a single sale, there had been nothing in their world to confirm any intuitive sense they may have had of the importance of art. To survive and continue to paint in such an atmosphere requires a kind of genius in itself. The by-ways and back-ways of this earth have their Hyppolites and Obins; but by the same token the score of competent, imaginative men who developed into fine painters once the Centre made art a worthwhile occupation in Haiti, indicates the enormous number of potential artists who range the world disguised as taxi-drivers, day-laborers and tramps.

The Artist as Priest: Hector Hyppolite. The discovery of Hyppolite came first. Hyppolite was a *vaudou* priest who appears to have practiced his duties with only a perfunctory attention. This is unlike *vaudou* priests; but it was the measure of Hyppolite's genius. So completely, in fact, was the expressive artist enthroned in Hyppolite's frail body that his *vevers* were notable for their uninspired rote and imprecision. It was his decoration of the doors at a roadside bar in the village of Mont Rouis that led to Hyppolite's discovery. Intricate floral patterns and gaily colored birds had been painted there with a brush of chicken-feathers. A sign overhanging the porch announced grandiloquently "ICI LA RENAISSANCE." By the time Peters and Philippe Thoby-Marcelin (the Haitian novelist whom Hyppolite thereafter identified with John the Baptist, his patron saint) had located the artist, the Centre d'Art was in business. Wifredo Lam and André Breton bought his first pictures, and it was the theoretician of French Surrealism who introduced Hyppolite's work to Paris where it caused a sensation in the international painting exhibit staged there by UNESCO in 1947. In 1948, the last year of his life and only the third of his fame, Hyppolite remarked: "I haven't practiced *vaudou* for a while. I asked the spirits' permission to suspend my work as a *houngan*, because of my painting. Also, you know, there are so many false priests around today that it saddens me. The spirits agreed that I should stop for a while. I've always been a priest, just like my father and my grandfather, but now I'm more an artist than a priest. When people ask me now what I am, I say that I am an artist . . . Both *Maîtresse La Sirène* and St. John help me. *La Sirène* helps me to earn money and St. John gives me ideas for my paintings." [1]

It was probably the artificial division of his life into the priest who occasionally painted and the painter who occasionally conducted religious rites that gave Hyppolite's work its uneven quality. His technique was never wholly adequate to translating his visions into effective plastic images, and as his life as a medium gave way to his life as an artist, he tended deliberately to forsake the central content of *vaudou* for the peripheral subject-matter of folklore, *zombis* and Black Magic which seemed to offer material for a freer exercise of his fantastic imagination. But Hyppolite enjoyed one triumph that probably no painter since the early Italian Renaissance has experienced: he lived to see one of his religious canvases born aloft through the streets of Port-au-Prince by a cheering mob.

[1] Quoted from *Renaissance in Haiti* by Selden Rodman, Pellegrini & Cudahy, 1948. In writing this section the author has drawn on this book, which is now out of print, as well as the following of his more recent articles on Haitian painting: "The Christ of the Haitian Primitives," *Harper's Bazaar*, December 1950; "A Mural by Wilson Bigaud," *Magazine of Art*, October 1951; and "Murals for Haiti: From the Centre d'Art Jeep to the Miracle at Cana," *Art in America*, December 1951.

Provincial Master: Philomé Obin. The more restrained and disciplined genius of Philomé Obin never encountered the distraction of divided loyalty. Obin has been fortunate, from the point of view of his art, in his habitat. His is the art, par excellence, of the provincial master. Cap Haïtien, where he was born and where he still lives, is less than 200 miles from Port-au-Prince with its art center and visiting celebrities, but it might be a thousand. In Cap Haïtien "nothing happens." Before Obin, no one had ever given the city's life and appearance artistic expression. Years before he sent a picture to Peters in 1944, Obin had regarded himself as a professional painter, accepting his neglect philosophically, so that fame when it did come to him changed neither his way of life [1] nor his style. He painted many more pictures, since he was released by their sale from the necessity of making a living by other means, and he painted with increasing skill, but his meticulous rendering of detail and his documentary approach to subject matter remained the same.

The primitivism of Obin, like that of Henri Rousseau, is a regressive phenomenon. Rousseau admired the academician Bouguereau and believed he was painting like him. Obin had some academic art training in his youth and asserts that his pictures are no more than the most accurate record of what he has seen, transcribed "according to the classical laws of perspective." Neither painter was aware that the charm of his work was precisely in the extent to which both failed to understand and carry out "the rules." The subtle distortions that result from this failure are what give their paintings their resemblance to the work of such "true primitives" as Sasetta and Piero di Cosimo—and also, in frequent in-

[1] The simple one-room shack in which he lives out by the gate leading to the Plaine du Nord is put together of an assortment of old crates, cylinder blocks and boards bearing such legends as 'Engine Soap' and 'Hazlehurst & Sons, Ltd., London.' It contains a cot, an *armoire*, two chairs and a table. The walls are papered with Chesterfield Cigarette ads and faded copies of *La Guerre Illustrée:* planes, Sherman tanks in echelon, and rows of crosses with the caption *"Le Prix de la Victoire."* On the table stands a bizarre triumphal arch constructed entirely of matchboxes, each drawer containing a single treasured object—a collar button, a safety pin, a feather, a smooth stone. Refreshments in the form of a sweet liqueur in tiny glasses, are served to the artist's guests by a black hand which passes a tray through a slot in the wall leading to an adjoining stable. On the cot is a fine pencil draft of the artist's next picture, a melancholy but lovely girl seated on a rock: she appeared to Obin in a dream the night before, giving him a message which is too intimate to reveal. The blackboard now bears the motto: *No. 14: Que 1948 soit pour moi une année de reconnaissance et de remerciement à Jésus mon Sauveur.* —Renaissance in Haiti.

stances, to the *deliberate* distortions of those moderns who seek to recapture a lost innocence, a more "direct" graphic shorthand.

Obin's masterpiece, "The Funeral of Charlemagne Péralte," is a picture of medium size containing no less than 750 individual figures. He worked on it, he says, six hours a day for forty-five days. The emotional content of the subject-matter is rare in Obin's work; in fact this picture, and a related one of the guerrilla leader "crucified" to a door by the Marines, are unique in dealing with subjects in which the painter could be personally involved. In the "Funeral," the impact of the central scene is conveyed by the fact that the street fails to recede to a vanishing-point. It stops abruptly —like a man's life. The eye is not carried into the irrelevant background but returns perforce to the massed mourners for whom the rows of tiny Haitian houses are but a frame. The *size* of the marchers is depicted in terms of their actual importance rather than in the usual diminishing scale that a true academic artist would consider important. We will return to Obin when we discuss the murals of St.-Trinité which are the crowning achievement of Haitian art.

DuFaut of Jacmel. Still a third type of Haitian painter is manifested in the person of Préfète DuFaut, a peasant living near provincial Jacmel who decorated the walls of his hut with pictograms of somewhat geometrical design. DuFaut perfected his style, after receiving paints and masonite from William Krauss, an American journalist then living in Jacmel, without seeing the work of the other primitives in the capital. This style he lavishes on three and only three subjects. The first is a maplike vision of the streets of Jacmel zigzagging from upper right to lower left across a landscape of conelike mountains or waves; every building, street-lamp and power-line is exposed frontally without any attempt to simulate depth. The second, equally flat in pattern, shows a huge spider-web with a golden spider at its center hung between trees or buildings. The third, less formalistic and presumably expressing DuFaut's debt to a spiritual protectress, represents *Maîtresse Erzulie* standing in a shrine or on the pinnacle of a temple. DuFaut cannot explain what conscious meaning, if any, these subjects have for him. But the third, especially, is often invested with a wealth of subconscious (and possibly racial-subconscious) detail.

The Primitive as Realist: Wilson Bigaud. As in the early Renaissance in Italy, the intense religious life of Haiti provides an atmosphere and a symbolism that is helpful even to painters without strong religious convictions of their own. Thus Wilson Bigaud, now the most brilliant and technically advanced of the self-taught artists, elects to paint realistic dramatizations of native life—dice games, cockfights, murders, thefts, wakes and the like. But when called upon to paint such a subject as his great Marriage at Cana mural in the Cathedral, he was able to do so with sincere reverence and conviction of the reality of miracles, and without sacrificing any of the illustrative flavor of native life for which he was already renowned. I asked Bigaud at the time whether he believed in the divinity of Christ. "They say," he replied, "that He was divine. Who knows? I believe in Him. The priests of *vaudou* perform miracles too; I've seen them; but that's diabolic. Christ's miracles were to teach lessons, not to arouse fear.[1] Yes, I still go to *vaudou* ceremonies—more often than to church, perhaps, because the ceremonies are more interesting and intimate and certainly more colorful—but I don't believe in the *loas* anymore."

Bigaud's subsequent development as a painter has been astonishing. Only 14 at the time Hyppolite discovered him in 1947, Bigaud showed a precocious facility, not only for reflecting the Haitian scene—he appears to have overcome a dangerous tendency to dramatize with overly-moondrenched highlights—but in being able to assimilate the technical innovations of sophisticated painters, as do none of the other primitives, without sacrificing his unmistakable style. This ability to grow has never diminished; nor has Bigaud's capacity for feeling, his pictures of 1953-4 indicating a tragic sense generally associated with the late periods of schools of painting.

Bigaud says of his style "I began like Hyppolite. Hyppolite's style was very strong but it had no nuances. I was never influenced by Obin, whose pictures are flat, to my taste, though beautiful. Besides, all Obin's pupils paint like him. If I have pupils I shall see that they paint in their own way, not in mine. Today I use only white Sapolin[2]; the other colors are oils in tubes. I begin a picture with the background of hills, trees, houses, and so forth; I do the clothes and faces last, so that the figures will detach themselves from the background. I never paint from nature . . . My memory is enough."

[1] Bigaud, of course, was here echoing the Church's position on *vaudou*.
[2] The furniture enamel employed by all the primitives, at least in the early days of the Centre d'Art.

Gourgue and the Racial Memory. Still another step removed from direct mystical experience, yet capable of existing nowhere but in an atmosphere of belief, are the pictures of Enguérrand Gourgue. Gourgue paints for the most part not *vaudou* but *magie noire*. He has never had traffic with Black Magic, but like most Haitians he knows all about it, and unlike most he has visualized its cosmos down to the smallest cloven hoof. As an infernal world, it bears striking resemblance to a psychoanalyst's well-equipped dream house. It is complete with all the props and accessories of the racial subconscious. Yet withal, too evenly lighted and gaily colored and orderly to be exactly frightening. One has the feeling, though, that one has been in a room like this before—perhaps in a nightmare. And the sexual symbols accord well with the popular Creole song:

> Mother, dear Mother,
> A snake is after me!
>> Suzanne, my child, when I was young
>> The same thing happened to me . . .

In a picture that Gourgue painted when he was only 17 (it is now in the permanent collection of the Museum of Modern Art) a small table with a tablecloth supports a gigantic bull's-head; white light fans out from the eye-sockets and between the bull's horns reposes the fanged head of a very large python. Attendant devils in a doorway to the right carry (by one foot) a tiny naked man with blood spurting from his heart; this blood, conveniently, is being caught by another serpent. The properties resemble something out of Dali, yet the over-all effect is more in the style of the "Guernica" by Picasso—two painters that Gourgue, of course, had never heard of.

Gourgue's painting today, with its low color-key, eerie lighting, dazzlingly smooth technique and sinister atmosphere is utterly unlike that of any of the other painters; and in fact Gourgue from the beginning of his career has been a lone wolf. He has been in and out of the Centre. Like Bigaud, he can be called a primitive only in terms of his origins and lack of formal training. If, as he now tells clients, Gourgue was tormented by demons until he painted them, he has a good and very convincing memory.

Other Painters. Outstanding among the other self-taught painters are Castera Bazile, an artist with an innate sense of the monumental who has carried his sensitive style to a high degree of refinement; Rigaud Benoit, another artist of originality, whose work has been uneven; Toussaint Auguste, a painter of childlike pastorals rendered with the utmost delicacy and directness; Senêque Obin, whose fierce visions are as revealing an expression of the North as the meticulous documents of his more famous brother; Antonio Joseph, a water-colorist and mural painter of surprising sophistication; and Robert St.-Brice, a middle-class *serviteur* of the *loas*, who defies all classification with his crude but compelling fetishes reminiscent of Dubuffet.

Among the group of artists who broke with the Centre in 1950 to form their own gallery, the Foyer des Artes Plastiques, Max Pinchinat, Roland Dorcély and Luce Tournier have gone furthest. Pinchinat has worked in the post-Cubist tradition with daring and taste. Dorcély, whose hotel murals have been much sought after, is perhaps too prolific for his own good but handles figures as patterns with engaging assurance. Mlle. Tournier, the most sensitive of the trio, has tried to relate primitive subject matter to the modern tradition.

Christ Reborn in Haiti. During the winter of 1949, in my capacity as Co-Director of the Centre d'Art, I had invited William Calfee, then head of the Art Department at American University in Washington, D.C., to come to Port-au-Prince and give the painters instruction in tempera technique. For the trial run in the Centre, five of the leading "sophisticated" painters of Haiti were given an upstairs chamber. The primitives took over the stairwell and basement. Obin, in solitary grandeur, barricaded himself in the library. For a while chaos reigned. The gesso failed to dry. The glue refused to dissolve. The eggs would be broken (or eaten) before the basket got to the refrigerator. Brushes would mysteriously disappear. A painter would vanish into the hills for a week. Another (Benoit), who much preferred driving to painting, would have to be forcibly removed from the wheel of the Centre d'Art jeep.[1] It was fascinating to watch the differences in approach upstairs and downstairs. One of the "advanced painters," as they were called, worked with the help of a projection machine. Another erased his initial drawing five times; finally gave up. Another would descend from his ladder and ascend to correct with dizzying regularity. And all of this group—though three of them finally turned out creditable

[1] Before this period the hood and fenders of this Jeep provided the only target for the ambitious painters-without-walls.

exercises—leaned heavily on Calfee for technical advice and moral support. Downstairs, in contrast, the primitives, once coaxed into an initial effort, attacked their wall-spaces with abandon. The briefest of charcoal sketches—then on with the paint! Talent, not trial and error, separated the sheep from the goats. The untalented produced some real horrors. But Benoit, Levêque, Bigaud, Bazile and Obin simply translated to the dimensions of the wall-space (we had deliberately given an eccentric area to each painter to prepare him for later work) the image of the easel picture that had always been monumental in its simplicity. That month there appeared on the door of the Centre d'Art privy a derisive pencil-scrawl in a primitive hand: *"Les artistes de l'étage qui se disent des avancés ne sont pas même des préliminaires primitives."*

Hardly had fixitive been sprayed on the completed murals when the attack began. With some notable exceptions, the *élite* had been unhappy about the Centre d'Art from the start; primitive painting was said to give people abroad a dim view of Haitian culture—that culture which they would like to have people believe has nothing at all of Africanism in it. The Catholic press published a series of articles charging that "paganism" was being encouraged. Inspired by fear that primitive murals would be commissioned for the forthcoming Exposition or by Pan American for its new airport building, the academic painters published a pamphlet purporting to prove that the trial paintings would crumble from the walls and that only true fresco should be used in future murals. But the net result of this offensive was that the Exposition imported second-rate talent to vulgarize the facades of its buildings; Pan American stalled until the zero hour before finally employing primitives in a makeshift program; and the Roman Catholic Church lost the opportunity of filling its bare churches with unrivalled Catholic painting.

The only gainer, paradoxically, was the small Protestant Episcopal movement whose enterprising bishop at once determined to appropriate the talents of the painters for his new cathedral. Bishop Voegeli's remark to a visiting archdeacon who had been unable to understand his confidence in unschooled painters was typical of the man. "It only shows," he said, "that it sometimes pays to be a little crazy!" As it happened the bishop was called away from Haiti just before the charcoal sketches went on the walls of the apse and didn't return to Haiti until the work had been completed; his remark on entering the cathedral revealed how much wisdom lay behind his apparent madness: "Thank God," he exclaimed, "they painted Haitians!"

That, as a matter of fact, was the one stylistic injunction I, as director of the project, had given them. The 900-odd-square-foot area of the apse divided naturally into three 21-foot-high vertical panels and a fourth area surrounding the windows up under the vault. The widely differing styles of the artists, without artificial demarcation, would provide natural divisions. Unity would be achieved by merging the skies and the horizontal axes of principal interest. The angels above would be carrying flowers, some of which might drop into the panels beneath to avoid a sharp break below the windows.

All of the four men in their different ways were devout, though Benoit least so. He alone would not kneel in prayer before beginning to paint. His essentially decorative genius took more interest in what the Virgin would wear than in her face, a conventional Byzantine mask. He would devote more time to the concentric eyes of the animals and the veining of exotic leaves than to the perfunctory image of the Child. Once when I inquired why he was devoting so much time to a bamboo drainpipe in the roof of a tiny *caille* thirty feet from the floor of the cathedral (from which it was not visible) Benoit replied tolerantly: "How long would thatching last in the rainy season without a drain?" Asked why one of the attendant women had an arm cut off above the elbow, he replied laconically "Yaws." But Benoit for all that was not so sure of himself as Bazile and Obin. He was troubled one day when an American tourist asked him why the Virgin's hands were so tiny, out of all proportion to her body, and asked me whether I thought he should alter them. I said: "Do you think that woman knows more about painting than you do? Would you ask her to come up here on the scaffold and finish the mural her way?"

Bazile had known exactly what he wanted to do from the time he painted his first picture—a recognizable Bazile. He never deviated from that style except in the direction of a greater monumentality. He is a natural mural painter. Though he can paint a hand or a foot in perspective, his instinct tells him in a work of great scale to distort so that the fingers and toes are exposed *flat*. Though the other artists took the full twenty-eight days to finish their panels, Bazile was through with his in a little over two weeks. He had other pictures to get back to and wasted no time.

Obin, like Bazile and Levêque, would invariably kneel in prayer before painting but his religion seemed to express less of piety than of proud participation in the Lord's work. As he began to advance with the figure of Christ he would sing in a muted falsetto voice a Protestant hymn with many stanzas which began:

> Mon Sauveur mourit sur la Croix.
> Gloire à l'Agneau de Dieu . . .

In the hope that he would put into Christ's face some of that proud strength with which he had endowed the martyred Péralte, I suggested that he paint Him without the traditional beard. He was shocked at first but then took to the idea. I was surprised one day to hear him remark to a deacon, who objected, that Christ had died young and that besides "He was a Man, not a Symbol." Obin would often tell me about the laws of perspective while actually engaged in painting a figure in the foreground half the size of one behind it. His Eye of God, looking down out of a cloud, he borrowed from the masonic symbol in his early "Apotheosis of Franklin D. Roosevelt." The wonderfully expressive clasped hands of the Virgin would remind later visitors of Gruenewald. That crowd of respectable women behind the Cross, who contemplate the tragedy with about as much interest as spectators at a horse-show would devote to the apprehension of a pickpocket, recalls many of Obin's early pictures. But it recalls, too, that atmosphere of everyday life going on amid the spectacular events of history which has permeated the work of so many of the great narrative painters from Breughel and Piero della Francesca to Ben Shahn.

The huge "Miracle at Cana" which the 22-year old Bigaud painted on the wall of the south trancept the following winter differed markedly from the murals in the apse both in color-key and in the episodic realism of its content. The Miracle, while by no means Bigaud's first mural, was his first successful one. His acceptance of the principle that a mural should synthesize the elements of a painter's most successful easel pictures led to the realization of his potentialities. Though the space assigned to him, a wall measuring 528 square feet and pierced by two windows, was by far the largest and presented the most problems, the artist never wavered in his execution. The charcoal drawing on the wall itself, which established the iconography in its final form, took almost two weeks. The actual painting, though interrupted by sabateurs who broke into the Cathedral one night and smeared it with black oil, was accomplished in twenty-five days.

Although the spirit of the St.-Trinité murals probably couldn't be reproduced anywhere else on earth—for what other country has remained so insulated against the ravages of visual propaganda, photography and scepticism as Haiti?—developments over the next two decades proved conclusively that Haiti's "renaissance" had deep roots. Discounting the proliferation of galleries, boutiques and street vendors whose merchandise—especially in pseudo-African mahogany pieces—tended to overwhelm the genuine product, it could still be said that more *good* painting and sculpture were being created in 1973 than ever before. Not only were the Old Masters like Obin, Benoit and Liautaud continuing to produce masterpieces but artists of the same stature such as André Pierre, Gerard Valcin, Seresier and Janvier Louisjuste, and Murat Brierre, had joined their select company. And artists only slightly less original—Philippe-Auguste, Merisier, Normil, Casimir, Antoine, Chéry, Domond, Gerard Paul, Pauléus Vital, H. J. Laurent, Raymond, Ducasse, Arbelroi Bazile, Damien Paul, and the talented progeny of the elder Obins in Cap Haïtien—were knocking on the door.

Nor could painters based abroad like Tournier, Pinchinat and Dorcely any longer be considered monopolists of talent among the sophisticated, for the mature styles of Antonio Joseph, R. Olivier and Jacques Gabriel had begun to fuse quite skillfully such modern developments as cubism with Haitian subject-matter.

In the 1940's the only painted vehicle in Haiti was the Centre d'Art jeep, and its appearance sometimes evoked derision. In the 1970's the driver of any *camion* or *camionette* the length and breadth of Haiti whose hood, side-boards and tailgate boasted no painting would be regarded as pitifully impoverished or a victim of cultural lag.

Into the Fifth Decade. By 1978, the four successful auctions of Haitian art, mounted by Sotheby Parke Bernet in New York, had begun to stabilize the prestige—and high prices—of the Old Masters in the international market. But at the same time younger artists with as much talent were beginning to make their marks in Haiti. A young metal sculptor with astonishing technical bravura, Serge Jolimeau, opened vistas of erotic symbolism undreamed of in Haiti hitherto. Among the brilliant new painters of the Seventies not already mentioned, Roland Blain, Cameau Rameau, Etienne Chavannes, Smith Blanchard, Arnold Etienne, Ismael of Deschapelle and Pierre Augustin were outstanding. The extraordinary stone carver of the capital, La Ratte, was in a class by himself. And among the nonprimitives, Bernard Séjourné and Simil were most prized among the growing band of knowledgeable Haitian collectors.

CHAPTER VII

WHAT TO SEE:

The Capital, The Provinces, The Islands

PORT-AU-PRINCE

AN ENGLISH VISITOR to Haiti in the year 1842 described the Port-au-Prince of Boyer's time as a city of "wooden buildings, with the pavement dislocated or broken up, the drains neglected, filth and stable dung interrupting your steps in every direction." With all its matchless advantages of situation, this disappointed tourist added, "with every inherent capability of being made and kept delightfully clean, it is perhaps the filthiest capital in the world." An American visitor thirty years later reported Port-au-Prince to be a breeding place for malaria and yellow fever, without sanitary codes of any kind, where in the open squares "sick animals are taken and left to die and rot without hindrance from anyone." [1] Even as recently as 1939, Leyburn described the capital as having "hardly half a dozen buildings which would detain the lover of architecture," and he concluded that while as a whole "the city is not a blemish; yet not to have seen it is to have missed no great aesthetic experience."

None of these three passages describe accurately the Port-au-Prince of today. There are still wooden buildings and broken pavements and unsanitary conditions in parts of the city, founded in 1749 and now having an estimated population of 150,000. But a visitor would have to be jaundiced indeed to deny that the present-day capital—from its magnificent bayside esplanade, through the bustling but orderly shopping-center, to the spacious Champ de Mars with its imposing government buildings, and on into the necklace of wooded hills the city then so gracefully climbs, enfolding as it goes the elegant shrub-shrouded villas of past and present—is one

[1] The first quotation is from John Candler's *Brief Notices of Hayti*, London, 1842, and the second is from *Santo Domingo Past and Present: With a Glance at Hayti* by Samuel Hazzard, New York, 1873.

Port-au-Prince—and out!

The capital reaches into the foothills. The airport is left, the Exposition right. Light patches center and right-center are the Champ de Mars and the Cemetery. The *camion*, as always, is loaded, defiant and dusty. The rich man's car often provides the poor man's entertainment.

Anywhere along the Road
... wherever fresh water is to be found, women will be seen (as here in Lake Miragoâne) washing, doing the laundry, filling their calabashes and loading their *bouriques*.

Miragoâne

Fringing a spacious blue bay, Miragoâne, with its little Catholic cathedral, is one of the loveliest of coastal towns.

Jacmel: Cathedral, Waterfront

The tiled roofs to the right of the church are part of Jacmel's iron market; the building to the left is a typical balconied town-house.

Jacmel: Bassin Bleu, Pueblo

This turquoise pool is the second of Bassin Bleu's three wonderful waterfalls. The houses with gardens on each other's roofs face the picturesque hilltown's harbor.

Cayes, Jérémie

East of Camp Perrin, in the heart of the South Peninsula, Saut Mathurin's mighty cascade offers fine swimming in the deep green pool at its base. Jérémie's architecture has the reckless, improvised look one would expect at the end of the earth.

Cap Haïtien: Ruins and Streets
French plantation gateposts, the mighty ruins at Milot, and the houses and bridges built on the foundations of forts surround the pastel-colored streets whose iron balconies and hinged doors recall Spain.

Islands, Beaches, Boats, Mountains

Fisherman's wife at the Arcadins. The beach at St. Marc. Boatmen between Port-de-Paix and Tortuga. The peasants at Furcy were given a *gourde* to pose; the grinning one is about to abscond with all of it.

Surprise!—Bassin Zim

The peasant woman in the Pine Forest was cooking when the camera caught her. The Bassin Zim near Hinche was also caught by the camera—in such a way that its falls could be mistaken for marble.

Luxury and Overpopulation

. . . co-exist in Haiti. The terrace at Ibo Lélé overlooking the Cul-de-Sac plain, the capital and the bay; peasants at Villebonheur assembled to worship.

Haitian Sports

Cockfighting in the Exposition's *gaguère*. Spearfishing does not necessarily mean tangling with a shark; shallow submarine gardens abound with multi-colored small fish.

Art Dominates the Scene

In Haiti, as nowhere else in the world, art is the most profitable way of making an honest living, and the one product (from the sublime to the ephemeral) every tourist wants to take home with him.

of the most beautiful cities in the world. Only Naples, crowned by Vesuvius, or Rio with its Sugar Loaf, can boast a comparable background. And neither city can offer as breath-taking a reverse view, the panorama that unfolds from vantage-points high above the city. From one such, Le Perchoir, the capital itself lies directly below, dazzling in daylight or sparkling by night, the burnished sheet of mountain-banded bay focusing the sky's deep blue like a giant reflector; and Gonave Island, cloud-capped, misty, hugely mysterious, provides just enough punctuation to keep the picture within its frame and the eye from roving uncontrollably.

Nor is this all. From here, or better still from one of the crows-nests above Pétion-Ville, you were looking *west*. Now turn to your right and look *north* and *east* into the Cul-de-Sac. Instead of the bay's cerulean plate, you look down upon a perfectly flat carpet of intensest green, a gridded geometry of sugarcane dotted with barely distinguishable clusters of *cailles* stretching as far as one can see—except on the clearest of days, when this most pastoral of perspectives is capped at its misty verge by the great salt lake of Saumâtre shimmering with the ghostly unreality of a mirage on the distant Dominican border.

Come down to earth again, and out of the city's murderous noon drive south and west under a canopy of almonds, flamboyants and palms, to Carrefour. Turn left, and when you have gone as far as the road goes follow on foot the rushing Rivière Froide along a narrow jungle path where you will never be alone—nor ever want to be. If you prefer mountains and the long view, the longest you may ever see lies beyond Pétion-Ville, beyond Kenscoff, beyond Furcy, and still less than an hour from the Palace's glittering domes. There the tradewind howls in the pines and La Selle's eight-thousand feet tower less than two-thousand above you though across chasms dwarfing the craters of the moon. Or, if it's desert you prefer—but wait! there is that, too, but the city itself deserves at least a perfunctory promenade . . .

STREETS; BUILDINGS, PUBLIC AND PRIVATE

Let us consider three approaches to the city. Supposing you have come by ship and want to visit first the white pavilions of the Presidential Palace that dominated your view once you had sailed past La Gonave. Clearing customs, you walk to the Rue du Quai, turn right a block and then left on the Rue Roux which crosses the Grand Rue (Haiti's Main Street and axis of its shopping center), leading directly to the Roman Catholic Cathedral. Started in 1884 and completed in 1915, this pink-and-white stone structure in Romanesque style capped by twin towers resembling Moslem minarets is visually more rewarding outside than in, but yields in architectural interest to the buildings on either side of it. To the left, as you approach, is the Old Cathedral, built in colonial times but largely restored under the administration of President Vincent. To the right is a half-timbered dwelling with a long sloping slate roof said to have been the home of Comte d'Estaing, a colonial governor of Port-au-Prince, and perhaps the only wholly intact building in the capital pre-dating the Revolution.

There are two ways, at this juncture, of getting to the Champ de Mars. The shortest involves turning right and following the Rue Monseigneur Guilloux past the Cathedral St.-Trinité (whose murals have already been described) into the Place Dessalines, where a left fork leads into the eastern part of the great square and a continuation straight ahead passes the Ministries of Finance and Justice with the Palace and the adjoining Casernes Dessalines to your left. The Palace faces the lower portion of the Champ, the Place Louverture.

The other way of getting there from the Cathedral is longer but more interesting. Continue along the Rue Roux, which becomes the Rue Borgella behind the Cathedral and starts climbing uphill. At the next intersection, two streets go off to the left; one continues straight up past the National Archives to old Fort National; and two lead back into the Champ de Mars. Take the narrow uphill one, the Rue Poste Marchand (Bel Air), because this is in many ways the most picturesque street in the capital. The one-and two-story wooden houses that overhang it are very old. Most of them include small *boutiques* in which everything from clay pipes to *kola-champagne* is sold. At the end of the street turn sharp right at the small post-office sub-station and descend into the Champ de Mars by any one of several streets. The lowest passes the headquarters of the Garde d'Haiti, a handsome two-story collonaded building of gleaming white with orange and black doors. The highest and nearest, the Rue Capois, runs along the top of the Champ de Mars, passing the Café Savoy-Vincent, the Hotel Excelsior, the Rex Theatre, the American Embassy, and (on the far corner) the Cercle Port-au-Princien, one of Haiti's two most exclusive *élite* clubs.

If you turn sharp left at the Savoy-Vincent and mount the Rue Magny you will come to the so-called Rond Point des Cinq-

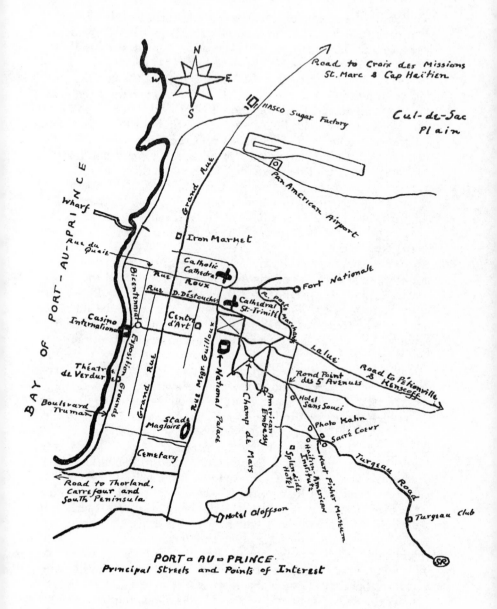

PORT = AU = PRINCE
Principal Streets and Points of Interest

Avenues in the middle of which stands a vigilant traffic policeman. The street crossing it at right angles to Magny, if followed left, leads back to the main Pétion-Ville road just above the postal sub-station where you crossed it; if followed *right* (but not in a car, un-less you want a ticket) it passes the Restaurant "Aux Cosaques" and continues into the suburb of the city dominated by the Cita-delle, Splendide and Oloffson Hotels. The fork bearing uphill to the right passes the Sans Souci Hotel, the studio of Photo S. Kahn, and the *lycée* Odeïde to the Church of Sacré Coeur where, in turn, a left fork leads to the residential heights of Turgeau, and a right, doubling back, descends past the Haitian-American Institute and over a bridge to the Rue Capois. Returning for a last time to the "Five Avenues" where that policeman is still standing, the remain-ing fork, up the hill and almost straight ahead, is known as Bois Verna, and is bordered by some of the finest gingerbread chateaux in the Republic.

Now, suppose that on debarking at the wharf you decide to put off seeing the heart of the city, and inspect instead the Bicen-tennial Exposition grounds stretching along the seawall to your right. Starting at the illuminated fountain in front of the Post Of-fice, a short boulevard, closest to the sea at this point, passes the Ministry of Foreign Affairs and the Bar d'Italie on the left and the Venezuelan Building and the French Institute on the right, before becoming the main Exposition thoroughfare, the Boulevard Harry Truman, at a traffic circle. Two other short avenues, containing shops, newspaper offices and United Nations bureaus parallel it to the circle. At the circle, on the sea side, is the Casino Internationale, for gamblers, and the adjoining Café Sorrento, beyond which lies a pier from which spear-fishing tours take off. But following the Boulevard Truman south, a succession of Exposition buildings have been converted into: the Cafés Rendezvous, Pigalle and Vert Ga-lant, the Hotel Beau Rivage, the Museums of Ethnology and Fine Arts, the Théatre de Verdure, the Foyer des Arts Plastiques and the Cockfight Arena behind which a fine stand of palms once pro-vided the perfect setting for a night-club but is now unaccountably abandoned. Just before leaving the Exposition there is a two-foot-high bump in the road that has caused at least one cracked skull, and that appears to be permanent; if you're in a taxi, hold tight!

At the end of the park, the road forks. Doubling back behind the gas filling station, you come to the Portail Léogane on the Grand Rue, where one right fork leads around the vast and fasci-nating National Cemetery and another to the Stade Magloire, where international soccer matches are held, and the Port-au-Prince Tennis Club where the best Haitian tennis is played. Continuing *right* along the main shoreline drive, however, you pass Captain Ace's Ki-Pi nightclub on your right, the Hotels Simbi and Riviera on your left, the Coast Guard Headquarters, the Thorland Club Hotel and Mon Repos on your right, arriving finally at Carrefour, and beyond that the South Peninsula.

But one other entrance to Port-au-Prince remains to be described. Should you arrive by plane, the airport lies *north* of the city and you would therefore be entering by the main highway to Cap Haïtien which is but an extension of the Grand Rue. Bowen Field lies at precisely the point where Dessalines met his death in 1806 and there is a modest monument west of the runway to mark the spot. Turning right, the highway to the Cape first passes the HASCO sugar factory on the left, and a mile or two further out the Agricultural College of Damien and the Barbancourt rum distillery behind it. A little further on is the sugar village of Croix des Missions, where *vaudou* ceremonies are at their liveliest. And beyond that, the flat plain of the Cul-de-Sac ends and the cactus desert begins. Turning *left* on Grand Rue after leaving the airport, and passing on your right the long sheds of the Régie de Tabac, you come to the gates of the celebrated Iron Market. The following description of it by William Krauss, since it cannot be improved on, is reprinted in its entirety:

> It is the source of racy odors—of sweat, blood, chickens, and very dried fish; source too of the perfumes of every known tropical fruit that anyone would care to eat. It is not clean. Why should it be? Only the washed dead are clean. The Iron Market is more vitally alive, more crowded, more clamoring, than the deck of a sinking commuter's ferry. You get the impression that somebody has just shouted 'Last boat to shore.' Foodstuffs are dumped and stacked and scattered everywhere, on the floor overflowing into narrow aisles, on crazy counters, in baskets on the backs and under the rumps of cooing, crying, pipe-smoking, gesticulating, coal-black peasants from five to ninety-five. Few sales are consummated without the exchange of withering insults. *Nobody* ever had more fun. (And, for the housewife on the serious side, nowhere on any island is a wider range of supplies availables: everything tropical, much that is temperate, oranges to cauliflowers, bananas to beets, hens' eggs with a real bite, twenty-five cents a dozen.) [1]

[1] *Holiday*, March 1949.

It might be added that the Iron Market, quite apart from its sunless atmosphere, is *not* a good place to take photographs. Save them for what follows, because it is an axiom that the further you get from Port-au-Prince the friendlier are the people. They have seen less of the people who take pictures . . .

The following buildings and institutions mentioned in the foregoing paragraphs, together with one or two not previously referred to, are worthy of some description:

The National Palace is distinguished in style and impressively simple in its furnishings. Its two predecessors on the same acre of the Champ de Mars were destroyed by revolutions in 1869 and 1912. The present edifice was designed and built by Georges Baussan in 1918. Its south wing contains the offices and living quarters of the President and his family. The Chapel and the Hall of Busts of the Presidents are open to visitors.

The National Archives, back of the Cathedral and near the modern green building of the College St. Martial, contains 32,000 civil registry volumes dating back to Dessalines' time and 120,000 manuscript records, but is seriously endangered by inadequate weather-protection, fire-prevention and filing facilities. The Director, who operates on a yearly budget of less than $25,000, is glad to show visitors his treasures.

The National Library stands on the Rue Hammerton Killick paralleling the Grand Rue to the east. It contains 12,000 volumes. The Magloire government has provided funds for construction of stacks to house 10,000 more books in the rear. The general collection is spotty, but the 4000 volumes in the Haitian collection, built up over the past decade, is exceeded only by that of the Christian Brothers of St. Louis de Gonzague (whose 7000 volumes are encased directly across the street) and by the private collections of Menthor Laurent, Edmond Mangonés and Kurt Fisher.

The National Museum, on a lower corner of the Champ de Mars, suffers from the same budgetary and technical deficiencies as the Library and the Archives. Interesting exhibits are: the 8-foot-high anchor of the *Santa Maria*; a primitive painting of Sans Souci Palace said to date from 1812 and, if accurate, a conclusive argument against its much-discussed restoration; an impressive embossed cannon from the Citadelle; and the manuscript of Sonthonax' proclamation of the Abolition of Slavery. Less interesting items include President Estimé's Parker fountain pen; General Nord-Alexis' bread-knife; the bronze feet of Katherine Dunham donated by Miss Dunham; and a handsome bronze bell bearing the provocative label in English: BELL OF THE SPANISH PEOPLE IN THAT COUNTRY.

The Musée de l'Art Häitien on the Champ de Mars shares with the Cathedral Ste. Trinité the distinction of being Haiti's greatest man-made attraction. Its unrivaled permanent collection and current exhibits are presided over by the Centre d'Art's Pierre Monosiet.

The Centre d'Art, on the Rue de la Revolution, the street above the Rue Hammerton Killick, is open to visitors mornings and afternoons and sells paintings, painted boxes, ceramics and sculpture. The trial murals of 1949 and the current exhibits are worth seeing.

The Museum of the Haitian People and the *Museum of Fine Arts* are both on the Boulevard Truman, adjoining each other at the end of a shallow reflecting pool with ornamental figures in plaster by Jason Seley. The former contains some interesting exhibits of folk-craft, once well displayed but now in a sad state of preservation. The latter does not contain a single first-rate picture or sculpture.

The Agricultural College at Damiens, also open to visitors on week-days, is divided into the school proper (15 professors and 40 students); an agricultural extension service; laboratories for experimentation with plants and seeds; a herd of 30 cows which provide some of the milk for the city; and a library of 8000 volumes.

The Barbancourt Distillery, behind the above and surrounded by its own cane fields, will impress visitors with the up-to-dateness of its American machinery and the spotlessness of its huge French vats. 500,000 bottles of the famous rum are produced and bottled here annually by Jean Gardère & Cie. Drinks are on the house.

HASCO's Sugar Mill, described in Chapter IV, is well worth visiting. So efficient is this plant that the cane wastage provides the fuel for the furnaces, and even the ash is used as fertilizer.

The French Institute maintains a permanent staff of six professors who also teach at the University. Founded as a result of an agreement signed in 1945 between Haiti and France, it is influential through the lectures, social affairs and field trips it conducts.

Haitian-American Institute (unlike the French Institute, which is generously supported by its government and whose position of leadership is taken for granted by the *élite*) has to sell itself, figuratively and literally. It offers courses in English for adults, a film and record library, and a social-cultural program. It has managed to hold its head above water solely through the character and enterprise of an able series of Directors who have been sympathetic to Haiti and well-liked by the Haitians.

The American Club, on the Pétion-Ville Road behind the American Embassy Residence, has a swimming pool, tennis courts and the only (completed) nine hole golf course in Haiti—though a second is being developed at Kyona Beach on the main road to Cap Haïtien.

The Cercle Bellevue, closer to Port-au-Prince on the same side of the same road, is an exclusive *élite* club whose hospitality to foreigners is most generous. It has two floodlit clay courts, a swimming pool and a handsome modern clubhouse designed by Camille Tesserot.

Kurt Fisher Museum (private, by arrangement with Kurt Fisher) is on the Avenue Charles Sumner above the Odeïde school. This collection, richer in pre-Columbian treasures than the national museums and in Haitian books than the National Library, is organized, safeguarded and displayed with typical Germanic thoroughness by its scholarly owner. (Now moved to new home on Kenscoff road.)

PÉTION-VILLE, KENSCOFF, PINE FOREST, LAKE SAUMÂTRE, LÉOGANE

From Port-au-Prince every part of Haiti is accessible in a day —if a day is taken to have 24 hours, and you enjoy killing yourself. But three excursions from the capital can be accomplished without hardship in much less than the time between dawn and dusk, and are so thoroughly worth the slight strain on the car which is involved as to come within range of a description of Port-au-Prince itself.

The first, easiest, and most rewarding, is the trip mentioned in the Introduction to Furcy via Pétion-Ville and Kenscoff. 1500 feet above the city, and pleasant the year round, Pétion-Ville is the home par excellence of the *élite*. It is reached by taking the Rue Dantès Destouches (also called Rue Pavée), a street that crosses the Grand Rue two blocks south of Rue Roux and that passes the Cathedral St.-Trinité on the left and the Champ de Mars on the right. Then it becomes the Avenue John Brown, or Lalue, or simply the Pétion-Ville Road. It is narrow and it has many blind curves. It is crowded with passenger station-wagons (*camionettes*) whose drivers are almost always in a high state of excitement, pressing the horn more frequently than the foot-brake. All night long market-women, their heads loaded with vegetables and fruit, file down one side of the road in order to be in town for the dawn market; what little sleep they get they take like refugees on the pavements under the

114

Rue du Quai's arcades. And most of the afternoon the other side of
the road is choked with the same (but wearier) women starting the
long, long tramp homeward.

The square at Pétion-Ville, aristocratic with cypresses, is
flanked by a church on the left and the Cabane Choucoune night-
club and Hotel Choucoune on the right. At its end is the local headquarters of the Garde d'Haiti and the offices of HABANEX, the
banana trust. Leaving the far end of the square, the street to the
left passes the Hotel Quisqueya, crosses a small bridge and winds up
the steep hill passing Haiti's finest restaurant, La Lanterne, to the
Hotel Ibo Lélé. This hotel overlooking the city, the bay, and the Cul
de Sac Plain as far as the salt lakes on the Dominican border, is
rivalled for its view and extra-attractions only by Cap Haïtien's
Mont-Joli. Extra attractions in this case give guests the option of
spending their time at Ibo Beach, a jewel of an island in the bay with
two salt-water pools, day and night tennis, miniature golf, shuffleboard, snorkeling and water skiing.

Returning to Pétion-Ville's Square, the street top-right is the
paved and poinsettia-lined highway to Kenscoff.

BOUTILLIERS, FURCY, CARREFOUR
DUFORT, ÇA-IRA

3000 feet above Port-au-Prince and fifteen minutes from Pétion-Ville, a right turn off this highway leads to Boutilliers, where
the restaurant "Le Perchoir" affords the view of the city, the bay
and the plain already described. It is intended that this road, which
was started in 1948, will eventually gird the slopes of Morne l'Ho-
pital as far as Carrefour. Why it was not built a few feet higher,
with a view from the ridge of *both* slopes, is one of the unanswer-
able Haitian puzzles.

Two thousand feet higher still on the main highway is Kenscoff, and another thousand beyond that (6000 feet) Furcy. The
legend is that these two towns were named after French counts who
owned estates there in colonial times and who used to meet at the
"Rendezvous" for protection against the *marrons* on the long ride
down to Port-au-Prince. Kenscoff today is an *élite* summer-resort
and Furcy is rapidly becoming one. At present the projected mountain road to Jacmel is completed to only a mile or so beyond Furcy
and its termination provides a most spectacular view of the mountain wilderness beyond. This region is known as Fond de Trou
Cou-cou. Across its rich red-earth ravines to cloud-capped La Selle,

Haiti's highest peak, floats the mystery of a world at work and at peace. The wild, high, heart-rending strains of a *coumbite* song rise from time to time out of the smoky vastness, seeming to come from a race untouchable, integrated with itself and God.

A somewhat longer but equally rewarding drive has as its objective the Forêt des Pins which covers the lower slopes of La Selle and Morne des Commissaires, and where in the winter the temperature falls as low as 32°, covering the chrysanthemums and wild strawberries with frost. From Croix des Missions on the main Cap Haitien highway a right turn leads through Croix des Bouquets and Gantier in the Cul-de-Sac to Fond Parisien where the road divides. First follow the left fork along the southern shore of Étang Saumâtre. This 40-square-mile lake shows by the shells and coral on its beaches how recently it has risen from the sea. It lies in a sparsely inhabited desert region; it is brackish, but not too brackish, I have been told, for extensive irrigation. At present it supports only a few small fish, ducks and egrets, and crocodiles up to fourteen feet in length. The beaches are pebbly, but the swimming is good, and the sailing, if the lake had a single sailboat, would be magnificent. Just beyond the Garde d'Haiti post of Malepas lies the Dominican border, and indeed the high buildings of Jimani can be glimpsed from the tip of the lake.

Returning to Fond Parisien and continuing along the south fork, the main road mounts constantly, and deteriorates as it mounts. The valley of Fond Verettes is a lush oasis between the desert and the pines. A village called Refuge marks the top elevation, and Savanne Zombi, a few miles beyond, the red-clay vegetable country along the slopes that descend to the Caribbean. Further than Savanne Zombi the road is impassable without 4-wheel drive. Saltrou, well-named, is its terminus on the south shore. But anywhere between Verettes and Refuge is the loveliest spot for a picnic in Haiti because it is almost the only place where the population is sufficiently sparse or occupied with its own business to let you eat without feeling a little guilty. It is also one of the few places where you will be almost certain to hear the *musicien*, the smallest, rarest and most elusive of songsters whose voice sounds like a chord played on three silver flutes.

The third and shortest (in time) of the recommended excursions from Port-au-Prince follows the southern highway through Carrefour and Gressier to Léogane. Just beyond the first of these towns is a stretch of coast (Mariani, Mère-Frappé) where sea-bathing and coral-reef exploration are possible—though rapidly the accessible spots are being staked out as private cabanas by the *élite*. Beyond Léogane a few miles is the village of Carrefour Dufort where on Easter Sunday all the *Ra-Ra* bands of Haiti (or so it seems) gather to really whoop it up; the street is crowded and noisy enough then to make Times Square on New Year's Eve seem like a Sunday School picnic. Through and on out of the town of Léogane itself a narrow but passable track leads from the far-right corner of the Cathedral square two miles to Ça-Ira. A handsome bronze bell hanging outside the chapel of this tiny fishing village bears the inscription IOANNES SPECHT ROTTERDAM 1754. Hugging the beach to the right it is possible to drive past Léogane's "airport" on which goats graze to a tiny black-sand beach amid mangroves where a thriving local boat-building industry is to be seen. Excellent fat *langoustes* may be bought here for $1 the pair, but if you buy fish be sure the bones aren't blue: water with iron in it can give one a bad case of ptomaine poisoning. Ça Ira cannot be called a fine beach, or even a good place to bathe, but it has something—just what, the reader will discover for himself.

ISLAND-HOPPING

A round trip of the Bay of Port-au-Prince—if you are lucky enough to have a boat, or find one willing to take you—would include stops at Sand Cay, Cabrit, the Arcadins and La Gonave.

Sand Cay, also called "Iroquois," is a coral reef with a sandy bottom varying in depth from two to six feet, five miles out in the bay from the main wharf of the capital. Presently shiploads of stone are being transported there for the purpose of building a bathing pavilion and bar. The bathing is good, and safe. Through goggles a fine view can be had of the coral formations and small fish. The large fish have long since sought less populated places. Another series of reefs, the Pelicans, lie to the north of Sand Cay. One of them, called Black Angel on U. S. Hydrographic Office Chart 2656, has a depth of only three feet and a truly spectacular display of the principal corals, elkhorn (white) and brain (yellow), with purple and crimson gorgonias waving between them.

Approaching the north shore of the Bay, Ile-à-Cabrits (Goats' Island; it is called Carenage on the charts and most maps) emerges into view. It is separated from the coast (near Sources Puantes on the main Port-au-Prince-Cap Haïtien highway) by a channel less than a half-mile wide and navigable for ships drawing no more than twelve feet.[1] Cabrits has no fresh water, little vegetation besides cactus, and no life but the lizard and the humming-bird. It has several good beaches, however, and (though combed and re-combed by amateur archeologists) a wealth of pottery and figurines left there by the Arawaks who must have used it as a burial ground.

The three uninhabited Arcadin Islands lie midway in the channel between the north shore of the Bay and Gonave Island, twenty-five miles northwest of Port-au-Prince. The central island, bare and shaped like a bone, carries an automatic lighthouse visible for nine miles. The northernmost and smallest is round and wooded and surrounded by viscious reefs. The southern island is also wooded but is accessible to sailing craft. It has fine beaches of sugary coral sand and is used as a temporary base by fishermen out for conch.

> Mounted in turquoise, armored by the shark,
> Collared in coral to the ocean's bed,
> Each holds the secret in its perfect park
> Of harmony: uninhabited.[2]

Gonave Island is the size of Martinique or a third the size of Long Island. It rises to 2500 feet along its central spine which, resembling in one place a recumbent dog, is called Mon Chien Content. There are no roads. The peasant population is estimated to be 10,000. Many of these isolated Haitians are engaged in fishing and most of the villages are on the coast. On the heights are a few springs, one waterfall, and many caves, but there are very few trees left on La Gonave and most of the island is barren. Gonave made the news in the 20's when an ex-Marine Sergeant named Faustin Wirkus published his memoires covering the time when he was in charge of the big island and its *vaudou*-worshipping inhabitants "crowned" him King in appreciation of his sympathy and kindness. The chief villages today are Anse-à-Galets and Les Étroits on the north shore, Picmi on the south, and Nan Café inland between them. Off Pointe Fantasque, facing Port-au-Prince thirty miles to the east, lies the tiny island of Petit-Gonave with a fishing village in the channel; its pitted limestone surface is (or

[1] For this and other sailing information, see "Blue Water in the Black Republic" by William A. Krauss. *Yachting*. April-May 1946. Having covered the same territory with its author in the same year, I can attest his accuracy and seamanship.
[2] Quoted from *The Amazing Year* by Selden Rodman, Charles Scribner Sons, 1947. All other unidentified verse quotations in the text are from the same source.

was) inhabited by giant iguanas. A mile to the west of Pointe Fantasque is Parc Bay with one of the finest small white-sand beaches in Haiti. A mile off the point to the east are several curious almost square islands; they appear to be built up out of discarded conch shells and are covered with fishermen's *cailles*. In the channel between Gonave and the South Peninsula are the Rochelois Banks on which the famous ghost-ship *Mary Celeste* foundered on January 3, 1885.

JACMEL

It would be the rankest hypocrisy to pretend that I could be objective about Jacmel. Twenty-five years before I joined two friends in buying a house in Haiti's Caribbean port, I had decided that this was the place I wanted to live. If anyone had asked me why at the time, I would have been hard-pressed for logical reasons.

Jacmel had long since seen its glory days. Its iron mansions were rusting and its wooden ones were collapsing. Its nearest usable bathing beach was then ten miles away over a rutted road, and the highway connecting it to "civilization" (Port-au-Prince) was a river bed filled with boulders and rapids and no other visible signposts. Sophisticated Jacmelians (meaning those who had abandoned it for the capital) called Jacmel a ghost town. And until my move there in 1972, anyone contemplating the investment of so much as a *gourde* in the place would have been looked at askance and possibly referred to a psychiatrist or local *houngan*.

Which is not to say that Jacmel ever lacked admirers. Poets, artists, publicity-tired executives and beachcombers had always been enthusiastic about it. For them, its unspoiled beauty exerted an almost hypnotic attraction, and they were careful to keep silent, emphasizing only the hazards of getting there. The fact that the river road provided high adventure (and that peasants along the way delighted in changing tires or lifting stalled vehicles out of high water when flash floods occasionally turned the lazy Gosselines into a torrent) was a well-kept secret. And initiates were careful to stress the negative aspects of the place: the chronic shortage of water at Jacmel's only pension, or the difficulties of sleeping soundly amidst stentorian snorers, all-night bell ringers, dawn buglers and insomniac roosters; they played down the overall sense of communal good fellowship—hitherto experienced for the most part only second-hand in the paintings of such Jacmelian master painters as Castera Bazile or Wilmino Domond—where animals fluttered underfoot or overhead during dinner and the village barber shaved the mayor on an adjacent pool table. If they mentioned the great white-sand beaches, extending in an unbroken chain from Carrefour Raymond to the Dominican border, it would be to enumerate the potholes in the coastal road. And if they disclosed the proximity of the three turquoise blue pools formed by the waterfalls of Bassin Bleu, it would be to complain about the uncomfortable gaits of the tiny horses rented to reach the place, or an alarming appearance of Maîtresse La Sirène, reputed to guard the sacred grotto from which the topmost cascade tumbles.

Jacmel today happily has not changed, except for the ease of accessibility and the comfort of accommodations. Daily plane service from the capital is safe, inexpensive and quick (15 minutes). A new road over the mountains, with magnificent vistas of the lush countryside, has cut the driving time to little more than two hours. Two pensions, that can hardly be improved upon for taste and efficiency, are run by Jacmelians. The Craft on the town square, presided over by Eric Danise and his American wife, Marlene, is for people who like fun, music at night, and gourmet food. The Alexandra, quieter but with food as memorable, doubles as the home of Mme. Alexandre Vital, and has balconies overlooking her "hanging gardens" and the sea. A luxury hotel projected to rise in the coconut grove fringing Jacmel's black-sand beach is expected to open in 1977. Nightclubs and restaurants are already in business. Coquitte's Couture turns out the finest hand-embroidered dresses and men's shirts in Haiti, and there are two art galleries, Selden Rodman's "Renaissance II" and a branch of George Nader's capital emporium, both a block from the water. Transportation to the more distant beaches, like Cyvadier and 'Ti Mouillage, are provided by "Maurice," "Bidot" and others, and good horses and guides for the Bassin Bleu excursion by "Geoffroi" of Edith's Boutique a block from the Iron Market.

Anyone living in Jacmel is bound to have ambivalent feelings about broadcasting its charms. When my friend Axel Madsen, the local coffee czar and tireless promoter of the town's progress, took me to see one of the prototypes of all steam engines and talked of installing it in a museum, I looked at him in horror. He was right, of course. This venerable relic, dated 1818, with its pendulum-like counterpoise suspended in an iron pavilion of fluted Doric columns, was pleasing no one but us in its clandestine jungle shade.

But Jacmel's architectural charms are already accessible to everyone who wanders through the hillside streets between the Cathedral and the wharf, some so narrow and steep that steps protect them forever from any traffic but the unshod foot and the *bourique*'s vagaries. Jacmel's glory is its dozen or so "coffee palaces" built in the 1880s and 1890s out of cast iron columns, balconies and doors shipped from France and Germany as ballast for the incoming freighters. This ironwork—slender Corinthian-type columns with fluted bases; ornamental brackets swirling from capital to capital to form shallow arches; railings with interlocking circles, crosses and arabesques; massive doors set in Romanesque or Gothic portals—combines in such a way as to give an effect of grace rather than weight. Decorative foot-square tiles in many colors, imported in the same epoch, floor the piazzas, courtyards, fountains, or provide a frieze above the doors. When the doors double as windows they are generally provided with hinged shutters opening down the middle. But cast iron swirling in floral billows under every step of every staircase, blooming as banisters and window grills, light poles and garden gates, is Jacmel's trademark.

Where did it originate? Albert Mangones, Haiti's leading contemporary architect, thinks that the country's Victorian Gothic, in its iron as well as wooden manifestations, owes more to New Orleans than to Paris. Much as I would prefer to see the credit go to America, I am inclined to think the style came to Haiti from France —by way of Jacmel. The Renaissance II structure carries the date 1888. It was in that year that Alexandre Gustave Eiffel was completing the famous tower that bears his name; three years before, he had designed the skeletal structure of the Statue of Liberty. But this was engineering. The *art* of wrought iron, freed of its hitherto almost exclusive dependence on ivy and acanthus motifs, was being perfected in the workshops of such master craftsmen as the Moreau brothers, Émile Robert and Edgar Brandt. Iron was "in." Art Nouveau was just around the corner. And Jacmel, perhaps without being conscious of it, became a repository for some of the fanciest experimentation in forged filigree and cast columns.

The days of Jacmel's glory can be traced in the yellowing ledgers of J. B. Vital & Sons, coffee merchants. The grandfather of the three Vital sons who presently run the business (from Port-au-Prince) and constitute, with the Boucards, Turniers, Madsens, Cadets and one or two other families Jacmel's *élite*, came to Haiti from France in the 1870s. In 1894 the total Jacmel coffee crop was 110,936 bags, almost half the amount exported from the entire island today. In 1900, 700,000 bags were exported from Haiti—which then had a population of only 1,500,000. Ground coffee the year *grand-père* Vital arrived could be bought from the peasant for 9¢ a pound;

today the peasant gets 40¢ or more. And he is growing less and less as his land shrinks, its productivity falls, and his family grows.

It is clear that a revival of Jacmel's prosperity lies not in coffee but in tourism—a revival that has already begun. It is evident in the boom in real estate, in the fresh coats of paint that cover gaily the once drab houses, and it will be compete when the filled-in channel is dredged anew to permit the steamship pier to receive those cruise ships that account for half of Cap Haïtien's prosperity. For as Jacmel and Le Cap go, so will go Haiti. Port-au-Prince is already becoming unbearably overcrowded.

MIRAGOÂNE, LES CAYES, JÉRÉMIE

We left the main South Peninsula highway at Carrefour Fauché to visit Jacmel. Returning to it there, we pass through Petit Goâve twelve miles east. A fairly prosperous coffee-port with a lively bay-side market and an imposing church, Petit Goâve lies midway between Léogane and Miragoâne. The latter, although it has nothing to offer in the way of beaches or hotels, is one of the most attractive of Haitian towns, with a fine harbor, a beautiful little Cathedral in the Gothic style, and a hillside situation that invites photography. The two sizeable fresh-water lakes southwest of Miragoâne are hard to get to but offer the best duck-hunting in Haiti. Bauxite is being taken out of the hills to the southwest by an American company.

Forsaking the main road to Cayes for a while, and continuing due west along the Gulf of Gonave, the next village of any size is Petite-Rivière-de-Nippes, where the spearfishing is good and where horses may be obtained for a 2½-hour ride to one of Haiti's four great waterfalls, Saut de Baril. There is an impressive view of the upper falls, creasing the distant profile of the mountain from which it emerges in two motionless white ribbons, as one crosses the interminable ridges that intervene. The falls themselves are a roaring five-acres of water gone wild, flowing in every direction, torn from their original channel, it is said, by the same earthquake that struck Anse-à-Veau in 1952. Petit-Trou-de-Nippes, beyond Anse-à-Veau, is the end of the line as far as the coastal road is concerned.

Returning to Miragoâne, the highway turns abruptly south and one passes through St. Michel-du-Sud, Fond-des-Nègres, Vieux-Bourg-d'Aquin, Aquin, St. Louis-du-Sud and Cavaillon before reaching Les Cayes, 120 miles from the capital. It is a good eight hours trip in the present (unpaved) state of the roads. The spot to stop for lunch and a swim is where the highway dips down to the beach—and a fine beach it is, with white sand, and six small wooded islands offshore—between Aquin and St. Louis-du-Sud. (When passing through Vieux-Bourg-d'Aquin you can buy a gallon of clear honey for 50¢ and fifteen juicy mangoes for a penny.)

Les Cayes is the capital of the South, Haiti's third city, and a good base for excursions to Jérémie, Ile-à-Vache and Saut Mathurin. Its situation is too flat and swampy, and the streets too wide and dominated by powerlines running down their centers, to make Cayes exactly picturesque; moreover the city has an air of faded grandeur that is a little depressing. One of its lovely *élite* ladies confided to the author proudly that "We may come after Le Cap in population, but we're *much* lighter"; she admitted in the next breath, however, that she lived only to escape to the more "civilized air" of the capital. Cayes has no good beach, and this, coupled with its remoteness from Port-au-Prince, has made it even more insulated against the blessings and ravages of tourism than Jacmel. Its claim to international fame is in the supposed derivation of the universally accepted assent "O.K.," the legend being that U. S. trading ships in the Nineteenth Century, picking up cargoes of rum there, dispelled doubts as to its quality by mispronouncing "Aux Cayes!"

From the attractive bayside section of the city known as Islet there is a little park on the site of an old English fort, graced with a bandstand and some Revolutionary cannon. Here Bolivar landed and received aid to liberate his homeland. And from here the large island of Ile-à-Vache may be clearly seen. A trip across from the nearby wharf may be arranged by applying to the director of the Douane, who has a motorboat. Vache is an island about 20 miles long and three or four across, and visiting it—from the moment one transfers to a rowboat the size of a washtub and from that to the back of an island fisherman—is a memorable experience.

It also has a history, one incident of which is not to our credit. "On December 31, 1862, Abraham Lincoln signed a contract engaging the United States to pay one Bernard Kock $250,000 for settling five thousand freedmen at Ile-à-Vache . . . The contract was signed against the advice of the Attorney General, who for over a month had been denouncing Kock as an impostor . . ." According to Ludwell Lee Montague, who relates this version of the story in his *Haiti and the United States: 1714-1938*, Lincoln realized his mistake in time to rescind the order, but Kock actually managed to collect from several hundred deluded ex-slaves, take ship, and land them on the then-uninhabited island where most of them perished of thirst.

The island is rich in Indian remains and has a population estimated to be 5000. There are still many trees, though it is said they are being rapidly depleted to stoke the ovens of Louis Déjoie's Anacoana Aromatics Co. at Ducis on the mainland. The Caribbean shore of Vache has some good beaches near La Hatte, the capital. A chapel at the town of Madame-Bernard, near Ca-Coq on the Cayes-side, has a painting of a converted *houngan* telling his beads while drums and fetishes whirl about his dazed head. It tells a story of what has happened around Cayes where the Catholic Church is exceptionally strong and where *vaudou*, if it survives at all, has gone underground. The Bishop of Cayes, John Louis Collignon, came from Boston in 1943, and his brotherhood, the Oblate Fathers, have done a remarkable job, establishing dispensaries and clinics, opening schools and seminaries, making marriage the rule rather than the exception, and distributing (over the decade) $500,000 in charities among a people who are by temperament, in the Bishop's words, "calm and uncombative."

Ducis, with its vetiver plantation and essential-oil distilleries, is a few miles north of Torbeck on the road west of Cayes. It is worth visiting. And so is Boury-sur-Mer, a cocoanut plantation off the Torbeck road that has flat lawns terminating in a fresh-water stream *parallel* to the ocean beach a few yards beyond it. But Camp Perrin, summer resort of the *élite* of Cayes, is the place to visit both for its delightful climate and as the jumping-off-place for a horseback ride to Source Mathurin, Haiti's grandest waterfall. Camp Perrin is no more than an hour's drive on a fairly good dirt road northwest of Cayes. Continue straight through town and you will come to the Ravine-du-Sud Reservoir, with its modern dam and ancient French colonial diversion-canals, which irrigates the Cayes plain as far below as Simon. The water is extraordinarily clear and pure, and provides a stimulating plunge—if you haven't the time for the two-hour horseback trip to the great *chute* whose deep-green catch-basin offers the finest fresh-water swimming in Haiti.

When you are ready to hook up the hill to the right leaving Camp Perrin, you have already covered 15 of the 65 miles to Jérémie, but of the eight hours you should allow as a minimum to cover this most bone-rattling but exalted of Haitian excursions, you have ticked off *only one*. The road, if such it may be called, was built in 1930-1, and being hacked out of solid rock around mountains up to 6000 feet in height, it is a piece of engineering to be marvelled at; but if any upkeep or repairs have been made since, there is no evidence of them. In one place, appropriately named Gouffre Effrayant, the road is exactly a foot wider than the width of a Jeep: above protrudes a jutting cliff, and below yawns a chasm 2000 feet deep. No guard-rail, no retaining wall; and every time there is a heavy rain a little more of that foot af leaway drops soundlessly into the pit beneath. How heavy trucks negotiate this pass is a mystery, but it may be that some don't: nothing that dropped off that precipice would ever be seen again. For at the bottom of the gulf is a mysterious river, the Glace, which ends its icy five-miles of turbulence in a black hole in the cliff just beyond the drop. Where it emerges, if it ever does emerge, no man knows.

One truck in 1950 carried over that road the entire carrousel from the Bicentennial Exposition; it is now set up, and turning, at Dichity, on the divide, the pride of Deputy François Cheron, a man who believes in giving his constituents something different. A little further along is the flourishing coffee-rich-village of Beaumont, a red-mud oasis of peasant industry in that jungle of giant ferns, apricot parasites, airplants and magenta orchids through which you have just mounted. Descending now into the Jérémie plain, prepare for the flooding terrors of the Roseaux, the Voldrogues, the Guinaudée and the Grande Anse! Estimé's folly, a $450,-000 steel suspension bridge, now spans the latter, leaving the three other treacherous rivers to make Jérémie, along with its fearsome approaches by sea and by air, as isolated from the rest of Haiti as it ever was.

> Till finally
> On no fixed date,
> Beyond the promontory
> Where the bay like a great plate
> Empties itself of islands, reefs and boats,
> To meet the barbarous, black-sanded sea,
> We came to Jérémie,
> The "city of poets" . . .

There has to be something a little perverse in one to make one like Jérémie. But those who are smitten will hear no loose talk of the charms of Jacmel or the Cape. Jérémie's streets and houses, they swear, are the strangest; its beach is the best; and its poets are the most Haitian. There is no disputing any of these claims. The question, rather, is, are they worth going to Jérémie for? Visitors isolated here at Haiti's land's-end by the flooding rivers or the crumbling wharf for a matter of days or weeks have been known to go mad. And quite a few of the local citizens *are* mad. These will give you the most fantastic reasons why they *stay* in Jérémie. The average resident, on the other hand, spends most of his time either complaining of his fate, inventing ingenious ways of escaping permanently to the paradise of Port-au-Prince, or asking plaintively whether any of the $26 tax the government places on every bag of his coffee will trickle back before the town completely rots away and its tin-roofed triangular dove-cotes are covered by the abnormally possessive frangipani.

It is a fact that in Jérémie flowers grow even from the cracks in the wall, that people have been known to paint pictures on 48-inch Pathé records, and that the principal café is called the Nirvana. The town is faintly illuminated at night by a venerable private Diesel plant; and there is a movie-house, but when the picture is showing no one else in town is able to read.

The airport, on the rare occasions when Jérémie's unpredictable weather permits flying, is five miles west of the town on an extremely muddy road. 2.7 miles out on the same road (measured from the Garde d'Haiti) is the lovely half-moon beach of Anse d'Azur or Anse à Cochon, depending on your mood. There is no sign pointing to the beach, which lies completely hidden at the foot of a cliff the road traverses; you have to look for it till you find it. And when you do find it you can be sure of one thing: you will be the only person on it.

Other places worth visiting in the Jérémie region are Marché Leon, largest native market in the Grande Anse and scene of a January festival; Anse d'Hainault and Dame-Marie, with white- and black-sand beaches at the end of the Marfranc-Moron road that then cuts back to the rubber plantations at Sources-Chaudes; and the headwaters of the Tiburon River at the Peninsula's tip which I have never visited, but which, Hugh Cave tells me, has rain-forests as dense as any in New Guinea and people 80-90 years old who have never seen a white man.

ST. MARC, GONAÏVES, TORTUGA, AND THE NORTH PENINSULA

Even a Haitian has trouble defining the psychological barrier that separates a man of the "North" from a man of the "South." The differences are subtle. But they are as real, as historical, and no doubt as economic, as the difference between a Welshman and a Scot, or a New England puritan and a Tennessee hillbilly.

The South, a loose geographical expression that includes not only the rugged South Peninsula but also the coastal plains surrounding Léogane and Port-au-Prince, is traditionally "African," self-possessed, easy-going, exuberantly religious, caste-conscious and submissive. Relatively undeveloped by the French, this part of Haiti escaped the libertarian fury of the insurrection, becoming instead a refuge for Mulatto separatism and diversionary English intrigue. To this day it remains unscorched by the winds of politics. It remains also a sanctuary of *vaudou*.

In the same colloquial sense, the North may be said to comprise not only Cap-Haïtien, but also the Artibonite Valley, the barren Môle St. Nicholas peninsula, and the mountainous region that surrounds the central plateau near Hinche, from Christophe's Citadelle overlooking both Cap-Haïtien and the Atlantic to Lascahobas in that eastern enclave of the country once belonging to the King of Spain. The North seems at once more ancient and more contemporary than the South. The crumbling ruins of colonial grandeur are everywhere. The land, for the most part, is poorer than in the South, and where it isn't poor, large-scale cultivation of sisal, sugar and rubber give a visual impression of emptiness, with the result that the sense of swarming activity one so often has in the South is here almost absent. Fort-Liberté, Port-de-Paix and Hinche are almost ghost-towns; and in comparison to Port-au-Prince or Jacmel seem half asleep. Yet this is the part of the country from which all rebellions have sprung, in which all resistance to oppression has smoldered, where even today the eye of the exceptional man looks outward toward the aggressive West rather than inward to the security of ancestral conventions. And the Spaniard, with his fiercely lived beliefs, his political inconstancy and his flair for the theatrical has left a faint but unmistakable imprint on the face of this land.

The paved road from Port-au-Prince to the Cape passes through St. Marc, Gonaïves, Ennery, Plaisance, and Limbé. St. Marc and Gonaïves, flat and architecturally nondescript, are the least attractive of the large towns of Haiti, but St. Marc has a lovely miniature white-sand beach guarded by huge boulders just beyond the banana-loading wharf; it makes an ideal stopping-off place for a picnic lunch. St. Marc was the second city of the French colony and some of the ancient high-sloping roofs with wooden tiles are still standing.

Continuing along the main highway that now runs east along the Artibonite, there is a dirt road to the right that leads to the town of Petite-Rivière-de-l'Artibonite, scene of Dessalines' heroic stand against the French. The walls, the powder magazine and the gun-pits of the fort of Crête-a-Pierrot are still intact on a bluff behind the village, with a commanding view of the fertile river valley, but all but two of the cannon have disappeared. The fort is only ten minutes walk from the village, and on the way to it one passes the Palace of 300 Doors, one of the best preserved of Christophe's provincial headquarters, which now serves as a school. The King's reception chamber has a tablet bearing the date 1816. Roofed over and otherwise restored under Vincent's administration, the palace is constructed of brick in the shape of a stubby cross with exterior galleries on the long arm whose inner walls form an enclosed corridor. By counting the windows as well as the doors, I was able to add up to about 150, but perhaps each should be counted twice for its shutters; anyway there are a lot of doors, and it is fun to count them as I did while a "soccer" game is being played in one of the galleries with a shrivelled orange for a ball. I noticed, while engaged in this higher mathematics, a blackboard on which somebody had written in French "Never put off to tomorrow what you can do today"—a maxim not often honored since Henry commanded these durable wall to rise.

Gonaïves, which lies on the Gulf about fifty miles beyond St. Marc, is in the northernmost corner of the desert, salt flats and marshes which now constitute the Artibonite delta. Irrigation ditches and rice paddies already line the road and when the great dam at Péligre is completed the earth of this whole area will be washed and brought back into cultivation. If you ever have occasion to fly anywhere near this area, ask the pilot to bank over the port of Grande Saline. Here are Haiti's salt "mines" and the chief source of wealth of many a burgher in St. Marc and Gonaïves. From the air this maze of irregularly placed polygonal traps, varying in pastel hues from salmon through mauve and pale green to lemon yellow and sulphuric orange is more beautiful in its sand frame than any non-objective painting.

Just beyond Gonaïves a left fork in the road cuts due north across the thick neck of the North Peninsula to Port-de-Paix. About midway, a brutal road slithers eastward from Gros Morne to Plaisance by way of Pilate, the town the *zombis* are supposed to have built—but this is Hugh Cave's territory and I will not presume to intrude on it. The North Peninsula west of Gros Morne is high, wild, dry, largely roadless and thinly populated. If you wish to visit at its tip the splendid (but unused) harbor of Môle St. Nicholas, guarding the Windward Passage, charter a plane—and even then you will have a good hour's ride over one of the worst roads in Haiti from the desert runway to the isolated fishing port and the ruins of the strategic bunkers General Maitland surrendered to Toussaint in 1797.

Port-de-Paix is best approached by plane in the present condition of the Gros Morne road and the almost non-existent one connecting it with Cap Haïtien. This village is also flanked by the crenalated ruins of colonial forts, but is a substantial port. It is the principal outlet for the coffee and bananas grown on the North Peninsula. The streets are unpaved, but the houses, especially the spidery, weathered pink and blue ones along the waterfront, are a water-colorist's dream. Port-de-Paix is on a good black-sand beach, but because the outhouses on the seawall are built directly over it, the visitor is advised to walk about a kilometre east of the town before bathing. The village's most substantial buildings are the new Garde d'Haiti group built by the Magloire government on a bluff to the west of the wharf.

Directly across from Port-de-Paix, and separated by a 10-mile-wide channel, which is calm in the mornings and wicked at sundown, lies Ile de la Tortue, famous hideout of the buccaneers and richest repository of Arawak relics in the West Indies. Tortuga is rugged and roadless and there are but a few uncapped springs along its 1000-foot-high spine, but it is well-populated except in the wooded western end where wild boar are still to be found. The Atlantic coast of the island is so precipitous that in some places fishermen descend to their ships by rope. There are no good harbors anywhere (one has to be carried ashore pick-a-back as at Ile-à-Vache) but the fishing villages along the channel—Boucan Guepes, La Vallée, Pointe-à-Oiseaux, Cayonne and Basse-Terre, the buccaneers' capital where cannon can still be seen in the shallow water, offer adequate anchorages. The Avant-Poste of the Garde is at Pointe-à-Oiseaux, and from there it is possible to ride (if you are prepared to wait while the entire island is scoured for horses) to Palmiste, the upland capital, past the ruins of the palace where Pauline Buonaparte Leclerc retired with her court in 1802 to escape the ravages of malaria and yellow fever on the main island.

I remember the face of Père Roger Riou, who has been a Catholic missionary in Haiti for 17 years, when he told me about the French archaelogical expedition that had come to Tortuga and stripped Pauline's palace, carrying away with them the statuary and even the stone pillars. I also remember the generosity of this great and good man, who has ministered to all the medical, surgical and dental needs of the people during his seven years at Palmiste, when he offered us his whole collection of the Arawak figurines the natives call *'ti zieux la té* (little eyes of the earth). Could this be the same man, I could not help wondering, who was reputed to have gone so far in stamping out *vaudou* in the region that even the use of drums at dances and *coumbites* was now prohibited?

The character of the Tortugans themselves may be illustrated by two incidents. Coming down the steep mountain trail to Basse-Terre, my horse caught his left hind leg between two roots in such a way that the more I pulled on it the more fastly it became held. Suddenly a peasant, naked except for a loin-cloth, stepped out of the bush and without saying a word began hacking at the roots with his *machete*. The horse stepped free, but when I turned to thank the peasant he was gone.

Justin Sully of Anse Rouge tells the following story, which may be entitled "Gunpowder Lake":

> "Many years ago there were many big birds, half as high as a man, nested on the top of the mountain of La Tortue. They fed on big fish in the channel during the day, each night coming back to the trees in the mountain. One night in 1756 something happened, *je ne sais quoi*, and all the birds died on the mountain. A lake was found where they died. The waters were explosive. A white man discovered the lake many years ago, but he told the secret of its location only to Justin, who, when he needs money badly, will tell it to another person and take him there. Meanwhile—" [the familiar Haitian gesture of washing the hands of the whole business].

CAP HAÏTIEN

If you sail or fly eastward along the north coast of Haiti from Tortuga to Cap Haïtien you will pass a series of rivers that water the fertile valleys around St. Louis du Nord, and then, between Le

Borgne and the rubber plantations of Bayeaux, you will come upon the finest and most extensive white-sand beaches in Haiti. Land has been bought and plans are under way to build an immense luxury hotel behind these gently curving bays, with a natural yacht basin and heavily wooded foothills, but nothing can start without the construction of a road.

While the beaches between the Bay of Acul and Cap Haïtien—La Badie, Cormier and Du Croix—are not king-size, they are splendid too, but only the last is accessible without a 4-wheel-drive Jeep. Now, rounding the Cape itself, you come upon the extensive ruins of another of Pauline Leclerc's pleasure stations, Fort Picolet, said to have been blueprinted by Vauban, Louis XIV's chief of engineers. The harbor of Cap Haïtien lies at your feet.

In the absence of street-maps, or even, as in the case of Jacmel, adequate street-signs, a description of Le Cap's layout must necessarily be vague. Theoretically the avenues parallel the waterfront and are lettered from "A" (the superb esplanade along the seawall built under the administration of President Magloire, himself a Capois) to "Q" which fronts the Champ de Mars and the grounds of the blue Justinian Hospital hung upon the foothills on a straight line running from the new wharf through the metal domes of the Cathedral in the center of town. Le Cap's main street, with the Banque Nationale, Cable Office, Altieri's General Store, the Curaçao Trading Post, the Episcopal Church, etc., is presumably Avenue "D." The Catholic Cathedral, already mentioned, is flanked by Avenues "F" and "H", as is the Place d'Armes in front of it. Driving *west* (back toward Tortuga) Avenue "D" passes between the Casernes of the Garde d'Haiti and the chapel of Notre Dame de Lourdes, high on a hill overlooking the city and surrounded by its convents. Between this hill and the shoreline (Le Carenage) may be found the Hostellerie Roi Christophe and a gay restaurant-bar-dancehall, the Rhumba Club. Turning left, the road ascends abruptly to the Hotel Mont-Joli overlooking everything from the city's red roofs to the Citadelle, thrusting at dawn through Chinese streamer-clouds on its distant peak, and the peak of Dominican Monte Cristi rising from the sea like an island volcano.

The Cap's harbor is well-protected by barrier reefs on which the waves can be seen breaking, giving only two narrow points of entry. In colonial times these passages could be commanded by the guns of Picolet and Petite Anse, hence Cap Français' strategic importance. But in modern times these same reefs have served to insulate Le Cap against both commerce and tourism. Fort Liberté's harbor a few miles up the coast is superior in every way. And Carenage is alive with sharks. Yet the government has been well-advised to spend millions on its 7000-foot waterfront face-lifting. A steel pier for cargo- and cruise-ships drawing up to 26 feet now permits docking right off main street with modern berthing facilities, and this means that tourists have no excuse not to come to Cap Haïtien in droves. The most subtly beautiful city in the West Indies, its streets now completely paved, is there for the taking. The Hotel Mont-Joli, which ranks with the Ibo-Lélé in Port-au-Prince as the finest in Haiti, arranges trips by sea or land to Labadi and its imperial beach at Coco Point; by car and horseback to Sans Souci and the Citadelle.

Of the city of 2000 houses that Christophe set torch to in 1802 only 59 survived. The city he rebuilt was largely shaken down by an earthquake in 1842, and what was left was flattened by a hurricane in 1928. Yet the city of 1954 could not possibly be more mellow, more homogeneous, more seemingly ancient. Indeed part of its charm is in these disasters. Its houses, painted burnt-umber, shell-pink and robbin's-egg-blue in a thousand combinations, are built either out of ruins, on ruins or beside ruins. Past and present meet—with the meeting-place invisible. Hibiscus, orchids and night-blooming cereus guard the fissures. The bricks weather to terra-cotta, matching the semi-circular tiles of the roofs, once happily imported from France as ballast for the empty sugar ships. Christophe's old theatre at Bel-Air, with its polygonal stage and imperial podium is now a Masonic Lodge, its ceiling decorated with clusters of bats; the trees have been chopped down by bureaucratic vandals in the Place d'Armes where Ogé and Chavannes were broken on the wheel in 1791; and the *cacos* of Leconte that Obin painted no longer gallop over President Hyppolite's iron bridge, which needs a new coat of red paint; but the air of Cap Haïtien is still sharp and the spirit of the Capois still as sanguine as the defiant poem on the gravestone of her favorite son:

> Mort à trente-trois ans, trahi comme le Maître,
> Exposé nu sous son drapeau crucifié;
> Comme il avait, un jour, osé nous le promettre,
> Pour le Pays il s'était fait sacrificier
> Face à l'Americain lui seul a crié halte:
> Découvrez-vous devant Charlemagne Péralte!

Two main roads lead out of Cap Haïtien. The road to Limbé and Port-au-Prince crosses the Plaine du Nord in a southwesterly direction. Just beyond the city gates on the right is the battlefield of Vertières where Dessalines defeated the French, making their last stand, and where on January 1, 1954, 150 years later, the battle was stirringly re-enacted by several costumed battalions of the Garde d'Haiti. A little further out, roads to the left lead to Plaine-du-Nord and Acul, villages of the plain, and to the right, in the foothills, is La Voute, only plantation house to survive the insurrection, whose fortress-like walls may antedate the French colony.

The second and more interesting highway follows the coast eastward, passing the airport now being enlarged to permit international airlines to land their biggest ships, to Petite Anse and Limonade. It was in the Limonade Cathedral that Christophe suffered his fatal stroke on August 15, 1820. The road then continues to Fort Liberté, site of the Dauphin sisal plantation, and to Ouanaminthe on the Dominican border. Retracing our steps on this highway past Limonade and just short of a little bridge, a side road to the right leads along a rushing river shaded by giant sabliers to Bord-de-Mer, a fishing village that is not far from the reef on which *Santa Maria* foundered and where the Admiral left the first colony in the New World. The site of the colonists' last stand, perhaps with clues to its fate, remains to be discovered.

The road to Milot branches off the main highway southward, about four miles from the Hyppolite Bridge out of Le Cap. It takes a right turn six miles further. To the right of this part of the road is Bois Caïman, where the *vaudou* ceremony launching the insurrection was held. The Milot road is asphalted right up to Christophe's domed chapel at the base of the ruins of Sans Souci. The dome itself is a restoration, and a good one, of Vincent's regime. But Sans Souci, happily, has not been restored, and those who saw it floodlit the evening of January 1, 1954 with Marian Anderson singing from the grand staircase, while Christophe and his noblemen in full costume paced the battlements above, will pray that this greatest stage-set in the world remains untouched in its crumbling, golden glory.

It is built of brick overlaid with stucco, four stories high, and covers twenty acres of sloping ground from the sentry boxes flanking the regal steps to the royal stables which housed the King's £700 English carriage, and the giant star-apple tree under which Henry dispensed judgments and where now cigarettes, postcards and coffee are dispensed by a little old lady who might well be a descendent of the hard-working but pleasure-loving monarch. Above an arch is a sun in black wood bearing the lordly inscription: "JE VOIS TOUT ET TOUT VOIT PAR MOI DANS L'UNIVERS."

Completed in 1813, Sans Souci in Christophe's time had floors of marble and mosaic, walls of polished mahogany, pictures, tapestries and drapes imported from Europe. Under its floors, conduits carried a cold mountain stream—ancestor of airconditioning—to emerge below as a fountain. Installation of numerous bathrooms was a notable feature for the times.

It has been said that as your horse mounts the steep trail to the Citadelle behind Sans Souci, you can pick a fruit salad as you pass. If your horse is anything like mine, you will be too busy. Oranges, bananas, cashew-nuts, mangoes, grenadine, avocadoes, and cocoa-nuts line the way. Coffee will be found drying in front of the *cailles*, rimmed with bougainvillaea, and mahogany trees provide plenty of shade. When you think you will never arrive—and in the tropical downpours for which the region is famous, it is not unheard of for a traveller to disappear in a murky ravine whose matted floor must contain the bones of many an unfortunate royal hod-carrier—the Citadelle is upon you, its menacing stone prow knifing the rarified 3000-foot air.

They call the red lichen which covers the 140-foot-high walls 'Christophe's Blood.' These walls, 20-30 feet thick, were built to house a garrison of 15,000 men, a modern division. Four gun-corridors, 270 feet long and 30 feet wide, with ports for firing, contain most of the 365 giant cannon that were originally dragged up that trail. English, French and Spanish in origin, some bear such Roman names as Scipio, Romulo and Remo, some the motto of the French Revolution, 'Liberté, Égalité, Fraternité,' and some the 'Honi Soit Qui Mal Y Pense' of the Knights of the Garter. Hundreds of smaller guns and cannon-balls litter the battlements.

A section of 40 rooms was originally set aside for Christophe, his family and his staff. The King's billiard room, with two sentry-boxes at the entrance, was equipped with an open fireplace. Immense storerooms for ammunition, the manufacture of gunpowder, hospitals, dungeons, treasure-chambers, many of them sealed and still unexplored, make up the nether regions. The water problem was solved by building eight huge cisterns, four of them covered for drinking water, in the walls, as well as catch-basins and reservoirs for the storage of rain-water. But although the Citadelle La Ferrière on which tens of thousands toiled for sixteen years, began as a measure of safety, it ended as a monument to vanity as well as pride, encompassing in its ruin the ruin of its builder whose tomb on the ramparts now bears the epitaph:

CI-GIT LE ROI HENRY CHRISTOPHE
NÉ LE 6 OCTOBRE, 1767, MORT LE
20 OCTOBRE, 1820, DONT LA DEVISE
EST: JE RENAIS DE MES CENDRES

DONDON, BASSIN ZIM, PÉLIGRE, VILLE-BONHEUR

Birthplace of Ogé and site of some of the most interesting caves in Haiti, Dondon is 20 miles from Le Cap and an hour's drive. It constitutes the first leg of an alternate route back to Port-au-Prince that is rugged but full of wonders. Dondon is reached by continuing due south and straight ahead along a dirt road two miles short of Milot. The town is not much, but its caves, one directly above the town and another about an hour-and-a-half's ride on horseback up the riverbed to the west of the village, invite exploration. The latter, with many heads in relief, presumably carved by the Indians, on the walls of its first vaulted chamber, is the more interesting.[1]

At San Raphael, about eight miles beyond Dondon, there are more caves, and a branch road to St. Michel de l'Atalaye where Louis Déjoie's most extensive essential oil plantations and distillery are located. Thirty miles more of very bad road southeast lies Hinche, principal town of the Plateau Centrale's cattle-country, and staging-point for a trip to Bassin Zim.

This waterfall, while neither so high as Baril or Saut d'Eau-Ville-Bonheur nor so great in volume as Mathurin, is more beautiful than any in Haiti. It is reached by taking the first right turn af-

[1] Hugh Cave has an informative chapter on the caves of Haiti in his delightful book *Haiti: Highroad to Adventure,* though his description of the "fear" of the natives and the "slipperiness" of the bat guano at Dondon does not jibe with the observations of other travellers. The dreaded Trou Forban near Mont Rouis, which he mentions, has been visited by Henri Borno, a son of the late President Borno, who found nothing in it except two initials and the date 1897. I am indebted to Borno also for a description of Source Balan near Morne Cabrit in the Cul-de-Sac which local *vaudouists* describe as having underground lakes complete with crocodiles and giant birds. Borno attended a ceremony there, following which he was invited to take the plunge. Stepping into a hole of muddy water and ducking under, he was taken by the hand and guided through a lateral hole into a pitch-black cave half-filled with four feet of stinking water—and a dozen panting *serviteurs* as anxious as he was to get out.

ter the bridge on the road east out of Hinche to Thomassique. You turn *left* after the next crossroads, cut across the open fields diagonally and pick up the trail to a gully where there was once a wooden bridge but from which one must now walk for about twenty minutes to reach the falls. The abrupt transition from dusty desert to dripping jungle could not be more spectacular. One is confronted first by the cascade which fans out over a breast-like formation of limestone into a deep milky-blue basin 200 feet wide and 150 feet across, perfect for swimming. There is a trail through the jungle to the right of the falls leading to a cave with a circular opening in the roof of its entrance chamber; deeper recesses can be explored with the aid of a flashlight and a rope ladder. The upper waters of the falls to the left of this cavern enter a tunnel from which they are sucked up into an inaccessible trough before spilling over in their bridal-veil to the main pool below. Care is advised in exploring this area since loose limestone and some very sticky mud in the swamp caused by the cavern-rivulet make the footing treacherous.

Returning to Hinche, the main highway now runs south to Lascahobas where a right fork short of the town leads along a winding road nineteen miles (45 minutes) to Belladère on the Dominican border. When passing the airport just short of the model town, the road divides and an unpromising right fork (which diminshes to the dimensions of a cow-path but is always passable) leads to the little hydroelectric plant at the source of a tributary of the Artibonite which supplies Belladère. Walking along a row of concrete slabs covering the sluiceway, you come to the dammed catchbasin fed by a torrent which pours from a hole in the mountainside. It is a fine place to swim, the water being pure and very cold, but care should be taken not to get caught in the suction where the overflow runs into the sluiceway.

After Lascahobas the main highway continues westward to Mirebalais, but just before entering the latter a branch road several miles long to the right crosses a new suspension bridge over the Artibonite and leads to the Péligre Dam, controlling the headwaters of the big river in a gorge two-hundred feet deep and a quarter of a mile across. When the dam is finished, the big reservoir behind it should provide excellent fishing, swimming and boating.

The first right turn *after* Mirebalais leads to Ville-Bonheur. The side-road, five miles from Mirebalais, is seven miles long; but because it fords two rivers, and in places is nothing but a gully full of rattling boulders, it takes an hour to traverse. Ville-Bonheur is the place where in 1884 a vision of the Virgin Mary appeared to the people in a palm-tree. An incredulous priest, trying to chop the palm down, was cut by his own machete. Miraculous cures followed. And eventually a church was erected on the site, to which, every 15th of July, thousands of pilgrims in hundreds of *camions* journey in the greatest of Haitian festivals. What makes it doubly an attraction, however, is that *vaudou* baptismal rites are held simultaneously under the towering falls of Saut d'Eau two miles away. It is almost an hour's walk across the fertile fields, criss-crossed by canals, and then uphill to the *chute* but the spot is one of the most awe-inspiring in Haiti. The hundred-foot-high cataract, which must be visible from the Dominican border but from nowhere else, descends vertically past grottoes swathed in green algae and *lianes*, into a series of shallow pools separated by pitted limestone tables. The ravine is damp and eerily dark. A single huge silvery tree grows out across the basin. The buttresses of giant *mapous* are decorated with the stumps of thousands of votive candles. If you are lucky you will see a penitent light one. If you are still luckier you will witness the great rites of July 15.

The whole trip from Cap Haïtien to Port-au-Prince by the Hinche road, not allowing for side-trips to any of the waterfalls described, takes eight hours travelling at an average speed of 15 miles per hour. The trip to Bassin Zim and back, from Port-au-Prince, requires a day; to Saut d'Eau and back considerably less.

APPENDIX I

Bibliography

A Selected List of Important Books Dealing with Haiti

ALEXIS, STÉPHAN. *Black Liberator. The Life of Toussaint Louverture.* New York, The Macmillan Co., 1949. English condensation of the Haitian historian's panegyric in French.

ANONYMOUS. *My Odyssey.* Translated and Edited by Althea de Puech Parham. Introduction by Selden Rodman. Louisiana State University Press, 1959. A French Creole's journal. Only eye-witness account of the Revolution of 1791.

BACH, MARCUS. *Strange Altars.* Indianapolis. The Bobbs Merrill Co., 1952. *Vaudou* as seen through the eyes of Doc Stanley Reser. Rapt, somewhat naive, but interesting.

BELLEGARDE, DANTÈS. *Histoire du Peuple Haïtien (1492-1952).* Port-au-Prince, 1953. The best "official" history of Haiti in French by a contemporary Haitian.

CAVE, HUGH B. *Haiti: Highroad to Adventure.* New York, Henry Holt & Co., 1952. The most readable, informative and amusing of recent books on Haiti, with superb photographs by the author.

CAVE, HUGH B. *Black Sun.* New York, Doubleday, 1960. This exciting novel of politics, together with the author's earlier *The Cross on the Drum* and *The Mission,* are the best fiction on contemporary Haiti.

CHRISTOPHE, HENRY AND CLARKSON, THOMAS. *A Correspondence.* Edited by Earl Leslie Griggs and Clifford H. Prator. Berkeley, University of California Press, 1951. Fascinating letters exchanged between the great Haitian and an English Abolitionist.

COURLANDER, HAROLD. *Haiti Singing.* Chapel Hill, 1939. Soon to be brought up to date, this book remains the best in its field. The collection of 185 songs, with melodies of 126 of them, is in itself an outstanding contribution to music. Revised 1960. Out of print.

COURLANDER, HAROLD. *The Drum and the Hoe. Life and Love of the Haitian People.* Berkeley, University of California Press, 1961. A lavish expansion of the above. Songs, dances and other tunes. 90 superb halftone illustrations.

CRAIGE, JOHN H. *Cannibal Cousins.* New York, Minton Balch, 1934. The Marine Occupation as seen through the eyes of a Marine. Hard-boiled but not unsympathetic, and often far more revealing than books by pussy-footing historians. Out of print.

DAVIS, H. P. *Black Democracy; the Story of Haiti.* New York, Dial Press, 1928; revised 1936, 1931. Good account of the early days through the Marine Occupation. Out of print.

DEREN, MAYA. *Divine Horsemen: The Living Gods of Haiti.* New York, Thames & Hudson, 1953. The most detailed and documented account of *vaudou* in English, by an American photographer who became a *serviteur*. Illustrated.

DORSAINVIL, DR. J. C. *Vodou et nèvrose.* Port-au-Prince, 1931. Analysis of the mental phenomena involved in *crises de possessions*.

EDWARDS, BRYAN. *An Historical Survey of the Island of Saint Domingo, etc.* London, 1796. Good eyewitness account of the Insurrection of 1791. Rare.

GOODWIN, JOHN. *The Idols and the Prey.* New York, Harpers Bros., 1953. Satirical novel about Americans in Haiti. Its treatment of Haitians is unsympathetic but sometimes penetrating.

HERSKOVITS, MELVILLE J. *Life in a Haitian Valley.* New York, Knopf, 1937. The ablest account of peasant life, customs and religious beliefs, by an able ethnologist. Out of print.

JAMES, C. L. R. *The Black Jacobins.* New York, Dial Press, no date. Detailed account of the Revolutionary period written from a Marxist-Trotskyist point of view.

JOHNSON, GYNETH. *How the Donkeys Came to Haiti and Other Tales.* New York, Devin-Adair, 1949. Folk tales for children. Illustrated by Angelo di Benedetto.

LEIGH-FERMOR, PATRICK. *The Traveller's Tree.* New York, Harper's Bros., 1952. One of the great travel books, and the best general tour of the West Indies, with a chapter on Haiti.

KORNGOLD, RALPH. *Citizen Toussaint.* Boston, Little, Brown & Co., 1944. A workmanlike biography of the revolutionary leader, though not definitive by any means.

LABAT, LE R. PÈRE. *Nouveau voyage aux îles de l'Amerique.* Paris, 1742. 8 volumes. Penetrating and amusing sidelights on Colonial affairs. Rare.

LACROIX, PAMPHILE DE. *Memoires pour servir à l'histoire de la revolution de Saint-Domingue.* Paris, 1803. 2 volumes. An indispensable source-book on the revolution and Leclerc's invasion, by an eyewitness of the Napoleonic phase. Rare.

LEYBURN, JAMES. *The Haitian People.* Yale University Press, 1941. Though dated in some respects, this remains the best social history of Haiti in English, scholarly, penetrating and sympathetic.

MADIOU, THOMAS. *Histoire d'Haiti.* 4 volumes. Port-au-Prince, 1848, 1904, 1922. The most important historical work by a Haitian scholar, dealing with the early days of independence.

MAXIMILIEN, LOUIS. *Le Vodou Haïtien. Rite Radas-Canzo.* Port-au-Prince, Imprimerie de l'État, 1945. Sympathetic and valuable study by an eminent Haitian.

McCONNELL, H. ORMONDE, AND SWAN, EUGENE JR. *You Can Learn Creole.* Port-au-Prince, Imprimerie de l'État, 1945. An indispensable handbook with a dictionary of basic words and a collection of proverbs (not the saltiest).

METRAUX, ALFRED. Voodoo in Haiti. New York, Oxford, 1959. More objective but less interesting than Maya Deren's account. A well-known French ethnologist's introduction for the layman.

MONTAGUE, LUDWELL LEE. *Haiti and the United States, 1714-1938.* Durham, N. C., University of North Carolina Press, 1940. Source-book of diplomatic relations between the two countries. Definitive, and not unsympathetic to Haiti.

MOREAU DE SAINT-MÉRY, MÉDÉRIC LOUIS ÉLIE. *Description topographique, physique, civile, politique et historique de la partie française de l'île Saint-Domingue.* 2 volumes. Philadelphia, 1797, 1798. The detailed and indispensible source-book on the French colonial period. Rare.

PAN-AMERICAN UNION. *Haiti.* Washington, 1949. Booklet containing comments by Haitians on Haiti's history and culture. Revealing, and not always intentionally.

PRICE-MARS, DR. JEAN. *Ainsi parla l'oncle . . . Essais d'ethnographie.* Port-au-Prince, 1928. Epoch-making study of Haitian folkways by the Republic's leading ethnologist and sociologist. Out of print.

PRICE-MARS, DR. JEAN. *La vocation de l'élite.* Port-au-Prince, 1919. Critique of the *élite* for condemning their African heritage and refusing to participate constructively in Haitian life. Out of print.

RIGAUD, MILO. *Le Voudoo Haïtien et la Tradition Voudoo.* Paris, Editions Niclaus, 1953. Illustrated with fine photographs by Odette Mennesson-Rigaud, the author's wife and herself an authority on the rites, this book is somewhat esoteric but full of fascinating data and theories.

RODMAN, MAIA. *Market Day for 'Ti André.* New York. Viking Press, 1952. Adventures of a Haitian boy from the hills who comes to the big city. For children 5-10. Illustrated with pen drawings by Wilson Bigaud.

HAITI

RODMAN, SELDEN. *Renaissance in Haiti*. New York, Pellegrini & Cudahy, 1948. The early days of the Centre d'Art, with many illustrations in half-tone and color. Out of print.

RODMAN, SELDEN. *The Revolutionists*. New York, Duell, Sloan & Pearce, 1942. Verse play based on the conflict between Toussaint, Christophe and Dessalines. French edition translated by Mme. Camille Lhérisson. Port-au-Prince, Imprimerie de l'État, 1942.

ROUMAIN, JACQUES. *Masters of the Dew*. New York, Reynal & Hitchcock, 1947. Novel concerning a peasant community's search for water, the first of its kind in Haitian literature.

SEABROOK, W. B. *The Magic Island*. New York, Harcourt, Brace & Co., 1929. Cause of resentment and much misunderstanding of *vaudou*, by a brilliant but erratic journalist.

STEEDMAN, MABEL. *Unknown to the World, Haiti*. London, Hurst & Blackett, 1939. Travelogue with some keen observations; *very British*.

STODDARD, T. LOTHROP. *The French Revolution in San Domingo*. New York, Houghton, Mifflin, Co., 1914. A brilliant account of the Revolution marred only by a racist antipathy to the Negro.

SYLVAIN, GEORGES. *Cric? Crac!* Paris, 1901. Port-au-Prince, 1929. Collection of the fables of 'Ti Malice and Bouqui, in Creole.

THÉARD, GASTON. *Le Jacot de Madame Ciceron*. Port-au-Prince, Henri Deschamps, 1944. Charming folk-tales told with humor and feeling.

THOBY-MARCELIN, PHILIPPE AND MARCELIN, PIERRE. *Canapé-Vert*. New York, Farrar & Rinehart, 1944. First and best of the brothers' satirical novels of Haitian peasant life.

THOBY-MARCELIN, PHILIPPE AND MARCELIN, PIERRE. *The Beast of the Haitian Hills*. New York, Rhinehart & Co., 1946. Novel purporting to expose the superstitions of *vaudou*.

UNITED NATIONS MISSION OF TECHNICAL ASSISTANCE TO HAITI. *Mission to Haiti*. Lake Success, New York, 1949. Statistics available nowhere else, and advice.

VANDERCOOK, JOHN W. *Black Majesty*. New York, Literary Guild, 1928. Fictionalized but for the most part documented and accurate story of Christophe's life. Good reading.

WIMPFFEN, FELIX BARON DE. *A Voyage to Santo Domingo in the Years 1788, 1789, and 1790*. London, 1797. Fascinating revelation of Haiti just before the Revolution. Rare.

WIRKUS, FAUSTIN AND DUDLEY, TANEY. *The White King of La Gonave*. Garden City, New York, Doubleday, Doran & Co., 1931. Account of the Marine Sergeant's "reign" written in a surprisingly unsensational vein. Out of print.

Bibliography

Additional Titles: 1955–1973

COLE, HUBERT. *Christophe King of Haiti*. New York, Viking Press, 1967. First full-dress treatment of the great Haitian builder. Objective and exhaustively researched.

COURLANDER, HAROLD. *The Drum and the Hoe: Life and Lore of the Haitian People*. Berkeley, University of California Press, 1960. Greatly expanded version of the author's *Haiti Singing*.

DIEDERICH, BERNARD & BURT, AL. *Papa Doc. The Truth About Haiti Today*. New York, McGraw-Hill, 1969. Polemical and superficial account of the controversial period by two journalists.

DUNHAM, KATHERINE. *Island Possessed*. New York, Doubleday, 1969. Memoir of the dancer's Haitian years, with insights into Dumarsais Estimé and his personality.

GREENE, GRAHAM. *The Comedians*. New York, Viking Press, 1966. Haiti in the Duvalier years as filtered through the neuroses of the well-known English novelist.

GRIGGS, E. L. & PRATOR, C. H. *Henry Christophe & Thomas Clarkson, A Correspondence*. Berkeley, University of California Press, 1952. Fascinating correspondence between the British Abolitionist and his royal friend.

HUXLEY, FRANCIS. *The Invisibles*. New York, McGraw-Hill, 1966. Personal and not altogether sympathetic probe of *vaudou* and black magic by a clever young anthropologist.

METRAUX, ALFRED. *Voodoo in Haiti*. New York, Oxford, 1959. One of the important books on the subject by the French ethnologist. Sympathetic and learned.

RIGAUD, MILO. *Secrets of Voodoo*. New York, Arco, 1969. Interesting sidelights on the cult, with photographs by the author's wife, Odette Mennesson-Rigaud, herself a Mambo.

RODMAN, SELDEN. *The Miracle of Haitian Art*. New York, Doubleday, 1974. *Renaissance in Haiti* brought up to date. Ten colorplates and twenty-one black-and-white illustrations.

ROTBERG, ROBERT L. *Haiti: The Politics of Squalor*. New York, Houghton Mifflin, 1971. Badly written, exhaustive account of Haitian problems by a heartless statistician.

SCHMIDT, HANS. *The United States Occupation of Haiti, 1915–1934*. New Brunswick, N.J., 1971. Basic research revealing the good intentions and unhappy consequences of the intervention.

WILLIAMS, SHELDON. *Voodoo and the Art of Haiti*. Nottingham, England: Morland Lee Ltd., 1971. Historically shaky but aesthetically perceptive. Twelve colorplates, twenty-five black-and-white illustrations.

APPENDIX II

150 Common Creole-French Words

(Not including *vaudou* terms, etc. already translated in the text)

ampil   very, a lot, plenty

assisté   attend

ba   give, provide; down, low; stocking; bar

bagaille   thing, gadget, article, object

b'am nouvelle   What's new? (greeting)

bamboche   party

besoin   need; want (noun & verb)

bo   kiss

bordreau   bill

bouchon radiaté   radiator cap

bouké   bushed, tired

bourik   donkey

boutik   shop

caché   hide; to search for

capab   can, able, might (*Li pas capab*, he can't)

chadek   shaddock, grapefruit

chargé   loaded

chaudié   pot

carrefour   crossroads

camion   bus, truck

caotchou   tire, rubber

citron   lime; lemon

clé anglaise   monkey wrench

commandé   order

coument   how

condui   lead, guide

coné   know (as in *M'pas coné*, I don't know)

connaissance   skill, knowledge

controlé   check up on

coulé   run; leak, pour

coulevre   snake

couté   cost; listen

coté   where (as in *Coté ou yé?* where are you?)

crazé   crush

cui   cook, bake

dégoutant   disgusting

dépensé   spend

déposé   lay, put down

dérangé   disturb, annoy, interrupt

derrière   behind

di ri   rice

dirigé   direct

douche   shower-bath

doucement   gently, slowly

droite   right (*tout droite*, straight ahead)

en avant   forward, ahead

en pann   out of order (generally of a car, or tire)

en principe   theoretically (term of evasion)

en retard   late

144

épi and

étang lake

fé mal harm, hurt, ache

fé réclam advertise

fé vit hurry

fig banana

fillé (fillet) steak

fixé fix

frain brake

frigidaire icebox

gadé look at; keep; store

gain get, have, win (as in *Yo gain argent*, they have money)

garage garage

gaspilé waste

gaté spoil, wreck

gauche left

gazon lawn

glace ice; mirror; ice-cream

grand-gou hunger

guide (pronounce "geed") guide

icit here

jodia today

kob penny

la lign taxi

la police police

la pli rain

la rad laundry; harbor

lèd ugly

let milk; letter

leti lettuce

loin distant, away

Madame Sara crow, woman peddler in markets

makak monkey

mal elevé rude

m'ap vini I am coming

Marie-Claire pink-blossoming vine

maré bind, strap; tide

misèr poverty

moun people, person, one

mouyé wet

morne mountain

moin I

net thorough, absolutely

ou you (singular); or; August

paré ready, prepare

piès coin; room, hall

pistache peanut

piti mi millet

pou ki moun whose

pouki why

poussière dust

préjijé prejudice

pressé hurry (verb); rushed

qualité quality, class, sort

qui coté where

quitté leave (verb); allow; depart

quimbé li tie it

rapadou brown sugar

reglé arrange, settle, fix

rélé shout, call

remerciement thanks

reté stop

savane desolée desert

semblé seem; like, similar

serré press, squeeze; tight

sik (sucre) sugar

tap-tap station-wagon to Carrefour

tambour drum

ti bèt insect

ti moun child

ti boss superintendent (patronizing but friendly)

ti back reverse-gear (*fé ti back*, back up!)

tiré shoot

tonton uncle (term of endearment for any old man)

traca trouble, nuisance

travaille work, industry

rroquette roll of cloth to support head-burden
tué kill
usine factory
veritable breadfruit
vidé empty; pour; spill
vini come; become
vlé wish
volan steering-wheel
voyagé travel
yo they
you a, an
you seul one only, single

youn one
zaffaire business
zeb grass
zé egg
zégui needle
zépingles pins
zéprongs spurs
zin or *zim* iron pot
zoranges oranges
zouti tools
zonyons onions
zuit oysters
zwazos birds

APPENDIX III

Balance Sheet:

How to get there; Where to stay; What to see and buy—

TOURIST AGENCIES AND SOURCES OF INFORMATION

New York: The Haiti Government Tourist Bureau, 30 Rockefeller Plaza

Washington, D.C.: The Haitian Embassy, 4842 16th Street, N.W.

Miami: Newman, Shulte and Reese Public Relations

Port-au-Prince: National Tourist Office, Ave. Marie-Jeanne. ABC Tours, Agence Citadelle, Southerland, others.

Cap Haïtien: Cap Haïtien Travel Service, Rue A-23. Léopold Sanchez, Director.

REQUIRED DOCUMENTS AND CUSTOMS REGULATIONS

Citizens of the United States and Canada are not required to show passports or vaccination certificates, but should have some proof of citizenship, a birth certificate or its equivalent, and a round trip ticket or a ticket for transportation beyond Haiti. All visitors will be issued a tourist card (cost $2) on arrival which is valid for 30 days and may be renewed for longer periods.

There are no restrictions upon the amount of money or personal effects to be brought in, but firearms and ammunition may not be imported without prior written authorization from the Haitian Army Chief of Staff. Each visitor may import 1 quart of liquor and 200 cigarettes or 50 cigars. Dogs and cats must be properly vaccinated and accompanied by certificates of good health.

It is not advisable to have packages sent to you in Haiti if it can possibly be avoided. All letters should be sent Air Mail.

Haitian authorities place no limit on exports, but Americans may bring home only 1 quart of liquor and $100.00 worth of goods without paying duty. Works of art are exempt.

WHAT TO TAKE ALONG—CLIMATE, HEALTH, SOCIAL CUSTOMS

Clothing: The Haitian climate is uniformly warm (70 degree average in winter, 85 in summer) so that lightweight, loose clothing will prove most comfortable. Sweaters will be needed only for mountain trips, an exceptionally cool evening, or excessive air conditioning.

The rainy season in Port-au-Prince and the South comes in spring and fall (April–May, September–October) and is usually in the form of showers rather than all day downpours. Rainfall in the North, near Cap Haïtien, is heaviest January through March, when raincoats are recommended.

Haitians tend to be casual in their dress, yet conservative. Women have only recently been able to wear slacks in town without occasioning stares, and may not yet wear shorts. Stockings and girdles are, on the other hand, never worn, as the climate is more conducive to bare legs and sandals. Most hotel dining rooms and night clubs request that gentlemen wear jackets and ties, although the injunction is not always enforced, and women wear long skirts and cocktail dresses in the evening. Long hair and beards have not yet spread to Haiti and hippie types are regarded with suspicion.

Medical: Those required to take prescription drugs are advised to bring an adequate supply as Haitian drugstores often stock European brands, and the precise compound may not be recognizable. (Drugstores, however, are able to dispense what they have without a physician's prescription.)

An extra pair of glasses is good security against breakage. Sunglasses, suntan lotion, and bug repellant will be useful and while available locally, finding them may be time consuming. (The best source of bug repellant, for example, is the supermarket; suntan lotion, a drugstore; and sunglasses, the Iron Market.)

Everybody visiting the tropics gets dysentery sooner or later— even if the water is boiled and the green vegetables washed in potassium permanganate. Take along (or buy in Haiti) paregoric or lomotil, kaomycin for extreme cases.

Malaria, once virtually stamped out in Haiti, is reappearing. Although Port-au-Prince is still considered safe, those venturing into the country would be wise to take twice weekly doses of a quinine blend (helioquin and paleoquin are popular) as a preventive. Most doctors recommend that the drug be taken several weeks before contagion is likely and several weeks afterward.

Cash: American money, up to and including the $20 bill, is accepted throughout Haiti. The Haitian unit, the *gourde,* is pegged to the dollar, one dollar being worth five *gourdes.* The one-gourde note is small, brown, and tired from great use. Two *gourdes,* small and blue, are worth 40¢, and five *gourdes,* large and orange, $1. Fifty centimes (10¢) is a coin the size of a half-dollar, and so on down to 5 centimes (*cinq kob*) the equivalent of our penny. American Express Traveler's checks are, of course, accepted by all stores and hotels, and the American Express and Master Charge credit cards can be used in many places.

Misc.: A French phrasebook may be of some help as French is the official language and is used by the *élite* and the government. The Haitian peasant, however, speaks Creole, a French-African patois, and may, or may not, understand tourist French. A list of Creole phrases is included elsewhere in this book.

Film of every variety is available in Haiti, but it is expensive and developing is both costly and slow. Imported cigarettes, cigars, liquor and canned goods are also expensive.

Sports lovers should remember to bring their tennis racquets, fishing rods, golf clubs, and snorkeling gear. Hunters will discover that guns are prohibited.

AIR LINES SERVING PORT-AU-PRINCE

American Airlines flies direct from New York every day but Wednesday, leaving at 10:30 A.M. and arriving at 2:04, with the return flight in the late afternoon. Pan Am and Air France stop over in Miami. Pan Am's daily flight leaves Miami at 3:30 P.M. and arrives at 4:15 P.M.; Air France at 2:45 P.M., arriving at 4:35 P.M. The round trip NYC-PaP 21-day excursion rate in winter is $266 on weekdays and $309 weekends. In summer it is $248 weekdays and $291 weekends.

INTERNAL AIRLINES

Jet prop daily service, except Sunday, to Cap-Haïtien, Jérémie, Les Cayes, by Haiti Air-Inter. Round trip rates are $34 Cap-Haïtien; $40 Jérémie; $42 Les Cayes.

CRUISE LINES

Many cruise ships stop in Port-au-Prince and two in Cap Haïtien, giving tourists a day's time for sightseeing. However, ships are reluctant to book passage only to Haiti, as long as there's a chance of selling space for an entire cruise. Among the steamship lines running cruises through Port-au-Prince are Flagship Lines, Norwegian Caribbean Lines, Lykes Line, Eastern Steamship Lines, Atlantic Cruise Line, and Royal Netherlands Lines. Norwegian Lines and La Bohème, which leave from Miami, dock in Cap Haïtien.

HOTELS

There is a hotel in Haiti for every taste. The *Ibo Lélé*, in the mountains above Pétion-Ville, is the highest and coolest and offers the best view. Its adjunct resort, *Ibo Beach*, allows visitors to split their time between the mountains and the sea. The cuisine at the hotel is French, but the charm and decor pure Haitian. *Villa Créole*, also in Pétion-Ville, allows the traveler to escape from the city's heat and bustle, and provides superlative food in especially attractive surroundings. *El Rancho*, the most Americanized of the hotels, provides tourists with the kind of decor and service they'd expect in Miami or Las Vegas. Formerly the most expensive, it is now being challenged by the *Habitation Le Clerc*, a group of villas with private swimming pools, conceived for the jet set by Olivier Coquelin, owner of New York's famed Hippopotamus night club.

The *Hotel Oloffson*, most famous of Haiti's hotels, is the darling of intellectuals for its casual chic and Haitian "gingerbread" atmosphere. The *Sans Souci*, *Splendid* and *Plaza*, provide proximity to the city, the respite of their pools, and their own individual charms. An especially good smaller hotel is *Villa Quisqueya* in Pétion-Ville, whose courtyard is shaded by a giant mango, and whose food is memorable.

Cap Haïtien has three fine hotels. *The Mont Joli*, the newest and most modern establishment, has an attractive setting and view, good food, a nice pool, and exclusive access to the finest beaches on the north coast of Haiti: Cormier, Coco Point, Labadi. The

Beck's mountain terraces and spacious pool are bathed in cool breezes. Occupying a former governor's palace, the *Roi Christophe* has old world charm and proximity to downtown shopping. *Brise de Mer*, on Carenage Beach, is a fine pension with family cuisine and hospitality.

The guest houses at *Cormier Plage*, an appendage of the Mont-Joli on the road to Labadi, offer Cap Haïtien's only tennis court and a magnificent sea-food cuisine.

Jacmel, in addition to the Pensions *Manoire Alexandre* and *Craft*, late in 1978 opened its first big hotel, the *Jacmellienne*, on the hill town's black sand beach. Situated in a coconut grove, it has both a swimming pool and tennis courts. For students and other travelers of modest means, Jacmel offers at least three guest houses that serve good food, all in the $4–12 range: Serge Lemaistre's *L'Amitié* on the Cathedral Square, *Guy's Guest House* and *Choubeloute* both on the way into town.

Michel Monnin's beachside cabanas at Port Salut near Les Cayes, to which guests are flown from Port-au-Prince via Haiti Air-Inter, offers the most in far-away comfort and privacy. More accessible is Carmelle Oland's *Taïno Beach Hotel*, an exquisitely crafted resort near Grand Goâve.

Turning north from the capital along the new superhighway to Cap Haïtien, many such luxurious resorts are to be found, of which *Ibo Beach* and *Kyona* offer the best facilities in Haiti for skin-diving and water-skiing. *Ibo* offers additionally three tennis courts, two salt-water pools, miniature golf, and Haiti's first marina for incoming yachts with every imaginable facility for docking, fresh drinking water, restaurants and telephones.

Further along the Cap highway, Mont-Ruis is shaping up as a bayside luxury resort of the future, with one Hilton-size hotel already nearing completion, and smaller ones nearby along the white sand beach. But this area may be surpassed in chic by Labadi on the Atlantic where a 400-room hotel is projected for Coco Point within sight of Tortuga Island.

Hotel	Address	No. Rooms	Winter Rates MAP Double	Remarks
Port-au-Prince				
Beau Rivage	Blvd. Harry Truman	40	*$33	pool, restaurant, club, tennis
Castel Haiti	Ave. St. Gérard	100	$42–55	pool, restaurant, club
Oloffson	Ave. Christophe	26	$48–75	pool, restaurant, club
Park	Champ de Mars	38	$26–30	pool, restaurant
Plaza	Champ de Mars	62	$33–39	pool, restaurant
Sans Souci	Ave. C. Summer	18	$32–42	pool, restaurant, club
Santos Guest House	Pacot Rue 4	20	$16–20	pool, restaurant
Splendid	Ave. "N"	40	$25–31	pool, restaurant
Habitation Le Clerc	Martisse	44	$72.50–80	private pools and maids, restaurant
International	Laboule	58	$50–52	pool, restaurant, bar
Coconut Villa	V. Lamothe	31	$30	pool, restaurant, bar
Pétion-Ville				
Dambala	Rue Montagne	75	$30	pool, restaurant, club
Green Garden	Lamarre 73	15	$26	pool
Choucoune	Lamarre	42	$45–50	pool, restaurant, club
Marabout	Rue Gregoire	17	*$20–26	
Ibo Lélé	Box 1237	70	$55–75	pool, restaurant, club
Villa Créole	Ave. Pan American	80	$60–70	pool, restaurant
El Rancho	Ave. Pan American	105	$50–95	pool, restaurant, club
Hispaniola	Tête de l'eau	30	$35–40	pool, restaurant
Montana	Box 523	48	$42–48	pool, restaurant, club

* Breakfast only

Hotel	Address	No. Rooms	Winter Rates MAP Double	Remarks
Cap Haïtien				
Beck	Bel Air	12	$40–45	pool, restaurant
Brise de Mer	Carenage	10	$25	restaurant, small beach
Mont-Joli	P.O. Box 12	35	$34–45	pool, restaurant, villas
Roi Christophe	Rue 24-B	19	$35–48	pool, restaurant
Imperial	P.O. Box 31	18	$28–36	pool, restaurant, club
Beach Hotels				
Ibo Beach	Box 1237 (20 min. from Port-au-Prince)	100	$55–65	3 salt pools, restaurant, tennis, mini golf, marina
Kyona Beach	Box W-47 (30 min. from Port-au-Prince)	16	$48	calm sea waters, restaurant, boats, horses for hire
Ouanga Bay	Box W5	50	$32–50	lunch included, boats
Taino Beach	Grande Goâve	15	$70–90	restaurant
Cormier	(see page 151)			
Jacmel	(see page 151)			

RESTAURANTS AND FOOD

Most Haitian hotels are operated on the Modified American Plan, e.g. with breakfast and dinner included, leaving the tourist free to experiment at lunch. While hotels and top restaurants are careful about using bottled drinking water and about washing their salad ingredients in chlorine water, street vendors and corner soda fountains are not likely to do so. Some caution is desirable.

Good places to lunch downtown are *LeRond Point* or *The Casino* in the Exposition grounds, Blvd. Harry Truman, or at the Hotel Oloffson, a 15-minute walk from the Champ de Mars, where a full course lunch costs $2.

Pétion-Ville boasts two gourmet restaurants in garden settings. *Chez Gerard* is one block off the square at 52 Rue Pinchinat and *La Lanterne* is just beyond the Hotel Hispaniola at 14 Rue Borno. A la carte entries start at $3.50 and an average full course meal comes to about $9. Try La Lanterne's cream of shrimp soup, red snapper à la lanterne and saboyon au porto. *Le Picardie*, a few blocks below the Pétion-Ville square, specializes in Haitian food. Almost all hotels operate restaurants and are open for lunch.

Economy-minded tourists may prefer to put their own picnics together from the supermarket. George *Cole* operates a chain of these modern establishments, the most obvious on Lalue, the main road between Port-au-Prince and Pétion-Ville. Prices are a little higher than smaller local groceries, but quality is assured.

Haitian specialty dishes include *Lambi* (conch stew); *Riz djon-djon* (rice with black mushrooms); *Salade chou-palmiste* (heart of palm salad); *Griot* (fried pork); *Pain patate* (sweet potato pudding); *Tassot de d'inde* (dried turkey); *Croquettes veritables* (bread-fruit cakes); *Riz et pois* (rice and kidney-beans); *Bananes frit à la Haïtienne* (plantains sliced and fried in coconut oil); *Zoeuf-au-lait* (burnt caramel custard); *Casave royale* (dried manioc pancakes dipped in salt water and rolled up with peanuts and watercress); *Langouste flambee* (flaming lobster); *Salaise, sauce 'Ti Malice* (dried beef with avocadoes and plantains, the sauce being sour-orange and lime juice, with shallots, hot peppers, and salt); *Poule creole* (chicken flavored with lime-juice and served with plantains and bread fruit.

INTERNAL TRANSPORTATION

Taxis, with English-speaking guides have "L" on their license plates and were authorized in 1973 to charge the following rates:

Airport to Port-au-Prince hotel, $3.50 per car
Airport to Pétion-Ville hotel, $5 per car
Within Port-au-Prince, 50¢ per person
Within Pétion-Ville, 75¢ per person
Between Port-au-Prince and Pétion-Ville, 75¢ per person
Between Port-au-Prince and Pétion-Ville (1–2 persons), $2 per car; (3 to 5 persons), $4 per car.
Tour of Port-au-Prince, $9 or $3 per hour
Boutilliers and Kenscoff, $16
Théâtre de Verdure, round trip, $6
Voodoo Dance near Port-au-Prince, $8 round trip
Night Club, round trip, $15
Ibo Beach, round trip with 3 hour waiting time, $12
Kyona Beach, round trip with 3 hour waiting time, $16
Cap Haïtien, round trip with one night stopover, $100
Cap Haïtien, round trip with two night stopover, $150
All day sightseeing (approximately 8 hours) $20
All day and all evening sightseeing, $30

Publiques are older taxicabs with a "P" on their license plates. They will pick up several fares at a time and may give you a "tour" en route to your destination. They can be had for as low as 14¢ but bargaining is in order. Be sure to agree on the price to be paid before you get in.

Camionettes are the Peugeot stationwagons which operate on a bus-like schedule between Pétion-Ville and Port-au-Prince. Fares are similar to "publiques" and very reasonable.

Camions are truck-like affairs with open seats, usually gaily painted. They all converge upon the Grand Rue, and are the cheapest possible way to go on an excursion out of the city. Seats must often be shared, however, with live pigs, active chickens and even pieces of furniture. Small camions will take you to Carrefour for 6¢, larger ones to Jacmel (a five hour trip) for $1 or even to Cap Haïtien (10 hours) for $3.

PRIVATE CARS

Cars may be rented by showing one's home driver's license and generally leaving a $50 deposit. Gasoline, not included, runs between 70 and 80 cents a gallon. *Avis*, the largest rent-a-car agency, has a desk at the airport and an office at Rue Pan Americaine on Lalue, Pétion-Ville. Volkswagens rent for $9 a day or $45 a week plus 10¢ a mile. Plymouths and Datsuns are slightly higher. Required insurance costs an additional $1.50 per day or $7.50 a week. Smaller rental agencies include Haiti Car Rental, Bourdon, Lalue; Perry's Car Rental, 123 Rue du Centre, Port-au-Prince; National Car Rentals, 130 Rue Dantes Destouches, Port-au-Prince. ABC Tours provides Land-Rovers with chauffeurs for long trips.

You can bring your own car to Haiti without paying any import duty, provided you remove it in 90 days. Antillean Line, 3050 N.W. North River Drive, Miami, will ship a car for $280 one way, and other freight for 75¢ a cubic foot. The voyage takes six days and leaves twice a week.

BEACHES AND WATER SPORTS

Most of Haiti's best beaches are still inaccessible or at any rate accessible only to the adventurous who'll venture forth by jeep. However, development programs now in progress may soon open up Carrefour Raymond and Petit Mouage, which lie near Jacmel, and Labadie and Chou Chou Bay in the North. The three beaches currently available are, in order of their proximity:

Ibo Beach: Developed by Robert Baussan, owner of the Ibo Lélé, the beach lies on Cacique Island, a half hour's drive plus 5 minute boatride from Port-au-Prince. In addition to ocean bathing there are three salt water swimming pools, a tennis court, shuffleboard, ping pong, water skiing and snorkeling. Thatched roof "cailles" rent on the MAP, but those who come for the day pay only $1.50 for adults and 50¢ for children. There is a well-stocked bar, native music, and ample Haitian food with lunches beginning at $2.50.

Kyona Beach: Fifteen minutes beyond Ibo, Kyona is a pretty, palm-lined oasis, with calm seas and good food. In addition to its hotel guests, picnickers are admitted for $2 daily; others for $1 plus the luncheon tab. Horseback riding and boating are available.

Ouanga Bay: About an hour's drive from Port-au-Prince, Ouanga is most easily reached via its daily package tour for Scuba Divers. Guests meet at 8:45 at Le Rond Point Restaurant for a complimentary breakfast, drive to Ouanga, where they may swim and have a cool drink before proceeding by boat to the diving area. There, between "Les Arcadins" islands the visibility is 80 to 100 feet. A full course tropical lunch is served before the return trip to Port-au-Prince. The day costs $20 per person and all snorkeling and scuba equipment is available for rental.

Sand Cay: A short distance out in Port-au-Prince's harbor lies Sand Cay, a reef notable for its tropical fish and vegetation. Glass-bottomed boats leave the pier behind the Casino at 10 A.M., returning at 1. Those who wish to don face masks to snorkel the reef may do so. Non-swimmers are provided with floating equipment. The trip costs $7 per person.

SAILING

The Lady Lise, leaves at 10 A.M. and returns at 2 P.M. daily with a stop at "The Grand Banc" for swimming in a 4 to 20 foot deep sea. Make reservations at the Park Hotel, 25 Champ de Mars, where free transportation is available to the pier at 9:15 A.M. $5 per person.

Iwalani, 41-foot catamaran, sails Monday through Friday, 9 A.M. to 5 P.M. with a stop for swimming at Ibo Beach. $20 per person, lunch included. Boat leaves from the dock across the street from Hotel Beau Rivage, about ¼ mile south of the Casino. Week-end trips can be arranged to Kyona Beach and Ouanga Bay.

Dog Star, 62-foot schooner, and *Maria Luisa,* 50 foot yawl, operated by the Greater Antilles Charter Association, out of Columbus Gate, Port-au-Prince harbor. Daily 9 to 5 sails to Ibo Beach with food and drink included, $25 for adults, $15 for children. Three day weekend sails to Kyona at $100 per person. Daily 9 to 2 sails to Pelican Reef for snorkeling. $15 for adults, $10 for children with sandwich lunch and rum punch included. Individual charters can be arranged.

LAND SPORTS

Tennis: Ibo Beach and the Hotel Beau Rivage have their own courts. Private clubs include Turgeau, the Cercle Bellevue, the Port-au-Prince Tennis Club and the American Club.

Golf: Although Ouanga Bay and Kaloa Beach both plan to construct golf courses, the only one currently in existence is the nine-hole course which belongs to the American Club. One must be invited by a member in order to play.

Horseback Riding: Haiti is a great place for riding as many of its roads are more conducive to horses than automobiles. Kyona Beach advertises riding and horses can be had in Cap Haïtien for the journey to the Citadelle and in Jacmel for the picturesque trip to Bassin Bleu.

SIGHTSEEING

Most sightseeing in Port-au-Prince is done by private taxi with English-speaking guide. These guides are inclined to waste one's time at (commissioning) gift shops and art galleries unless the tourist demands to be taken to see the following major sights:

Cathedral St. Trinité, Rue Pavé, where the Haitian art movement came to its flowering. Brilliantly painted murals in tempera by famous primitive artists decorate the apse and transepts of this Episcopal Church and a series of cut-out ceramic sculptures form the choir screen.

Musée de l'Art Haïtien, a new modern structure on the Champ de Mars, built to house a permanent collection of Haitian masterpieces. Traveling shows are also on view.

Le Centre d'Art. While the Centre is also a commercial gallery, it is of special interest because it is the place where the Haitian art movement began. Preliminary murals, a "testing" for the murals in the cathedral, can be seen and special exhibits are displayed on the ground floor.

The Presidential Palace, a grand white mansion on the Champ de Mars, where the president lives and history is enacted. Also on the Champ de Mars is the parade viewing stand, statues of Haitian heroes, and a memorial to the Revolution.

Pacot, an expensive residential area. Haitian "gingerbread" architecture as dramatized in the Hotel Oloffson and Le Manoir on Lalue, can be seen in all its variations by a drive through this section above the Champ de Mars.

The Exposition. Modern buildings beside the harbor, built in 1953–4 to celebrate the 150th anniversary of Haitian independence, now house shops and government buildings, as well as the American Embassy, the Post Office, and the National Tourist Office.

Kenscoff and Boutilliers. This mountain area above Pétion-Ville offers panoramic views of the Cul-de-Sac and Port-au-Prince (especially from the restaurant, Le Perchoir). Country boys sell bouquets of mountain flowers which grow on every side. Stops can be made at several art galleries and at the Jane Barbancourt Rum Factory, where you can sample 17 varieties of rum liquors, buy what you like at $2 a fifth. The tasting rooms are housed in an attractive reconstructed castle, and equipment used a century ago in the distillation of rum is on display.

CAP HAÏTIEN AND THE CITADELLE

Citadelle Tour: A visit to the Citadelle is a good six hour expedition from Cap Haïtien by taxi and horseback. It is wise to leave at 7:30 in the morning to ensure good visibility, to wear slacks and hiking shoes, and to carry a camera, plenty of film, and a sweater. The cost of the trip can vary from $20 for one person to $47 for five, broken down as follows (for one person): taxi to Milot, $12; entrance fee, $1; horse, $3; carry boy, $1; guide, $3.

Sightseeing Tour of Cap Haïtien: Two hours with a chauffeur-guide, visiting the ruins of Pauline Bonaparte's Palace, Fort Magny, Saint Joseph, Picolet Point, the 17th Century Cathedral, the old plantation homes, $6 for one person, $4 each for two, $3 each for three.

Coffee Plantation Tour: A five hour trip into the country including exploration of a coffee estate by foot or horseback and a free bag of coffee beans, $8 per person.

NIGHT LIFE

Le Péristyle de Mariani, half an hour's drive beyond Port-au-Prince on the main paved highway to Jacmel and the South, offers the most exciting (and educational) evening's entertainment available in Haiti. After a lucid introduction delivered in English, French and Spanish by the *houngan*-proprietor, Max Beauvoir, there follows a genuine (but compressed and therefore highly dramatic) *vaudou* ceremony, complete with invocation, *vevers*, dancing, drumming, and possessions. To achieve the last nightly, *hounsis* are selected from those most susceptible to trance. So electrifying is the ceremony that guests have been known to go into a trance inadvertently. On certain nights the rite is held across the road in a jungle setting around which a Greek-style amphitheatre has been built. 9:30 nightly except Sundays. $5 per person, drinks additional.

Folkloric night club shows are presented on Monday night at the *Hotel Oloffson* (with choreography by Lavinia Williams, founder of the Haitian School of ballet and modern dance), on Tuesday at the *Sans Souci,* Thursday at *El Rancho,* and Saturday at *Cabanne Choucoune.* The average cover charge is $2–$3 per person and shows begin at 11 P.M. The *Théâtre de Verdure* (non-nightclub) presents a program of Haitian songs and dances Thursdays at 8:30 P.M. in the Exposition Grounds at $1 per person.

There are dance bands Wednesdays at *Castel Haiti* and the *Bacalou Night Club,* Thursday at *Villa Créole,* and Friday at *Ibo Lélé;* dancing nightly at *El Rancho,* at the Oloffson, 6:30 to 9 P.M. and on Saturdays at *"Le Cave,"* a Discothèque.

The *Casino International* is open all night every night for gambling.

SHOPPING

Haitian handicrafts:

Carlos, around the corner from the Post Office in the Exposition Grounds, has a wide variety of embroidered dresses, blouses, and shirts for men, women, and children; coffee bean sandals, belts and necklaces; mahogany salad bowls, plates, candlesticks; straw handbags, placemats and coasters. Also imported perfumes, scarfs, jewelry, Haitian rum, paintings.

Le Manoir, Lalue, has a courtyard full of craft shops, where tourists can watch artisans at work, then make their purchases in the main house.

Cathedral Ste. Trinité Gift Shop, best in downtown area, features books, handicrafts, embroidery.

Baptist Mission Gift Shop, at Fermat on road to Kenscoff, has all of the above, plus an excellent restaurant and small museum.

Joe Etienne, 1377 Carlstroem St., off Lalue, specializes in sporting goods, and is the best place to find the tennis racquet or diving mask you left at home. Gifts for men, women, and children.

The Iron Market, Grand Rue, is a bargainer's dream. Every imaginable tourist item, article of clothing, and bit of food, is displayed by hawkers who speak an amazing amount of English. A good rule is to offer at the start about ⅓ of what you actually expect to pay. Persistence will be rewarded if you don't mind the smells, the heat, or the crowded conditions.

Art Works:

Le Centre d'Art, Rue de la Revolution. Oldest and best known abroad. Handles Liautaud, Antonio Joseph and Benoit exclusively; Damien Paul, Philippe-Auguste, Brierre, Antoine Obin, Isméus.

Galerie Issa, Avenue Chile, near the Oloffson. Largest selection and supplier of European museums and collectors. Handles Janvier Louisjuste exclusively; best of André Pierre, Gerard Valcin, J. B. Chéry, Casimir, Normil, Bottex brothers.

Georges Nader's, Rue Bonne Foi, near the Iron Market. Very large selection with gallery connections in Puerto Rico, and the Dominican Republic. Best of Ducasse, Raymond, Cédor, H. J. Laurent.

Rainbow Gallery, off road to Pétion-Ville (Lalue) handles many of the best primitive and nonprimitive Haitian painters.

The Red Carpet with galleries on Lalue, Pétion-Ville, and Rue Bonne Fois, downtown. Handles metal sculptures by Seresier Louisjuste exclusively, and works by most of the other well-known artists along with a wide variety of clothes, Haitian handicrafts and jewelry.

Galerie Monnin on the Grand Rue, with a branch called "Thomasaint" off the Kenscoff Road at Boutillier, handles Roland Blain and Gerard Paul exclusively; best of recent Wilson Bigauds.

Claire's Gallery in Pacot, up the hill from the Sacré-Coeur Church. Specializes in primitive expressionists like Robert St. Brice and St. Pierre of Kenscoff.

National Gallery of Art on Lalue near Pétion-Ville, specializes in pictures by Wilmino Domond and the Vital brothers of Jacmel.

Museum Gift Shop, in the rear of the Musée de l'Art Haïtien on the Champ de Mars, sells superb *papier-maché* sculptures and a wide variety of art objects.

CAP HAÏTIEN. Works of Philomé, Senêque and Antoine Obin and their talented progeny are best found in the studios of these artists. Philomé paints only on commission.

Cookoo's Nest, on main shopping street, has developed and sells a wide variety of ceramic planters, sisal macramé, plates, and *objets d'art.*

JACMEL. Selden Rodman's gallery, Renaissance II, on the Rue de Commerce carries the best of the painters and sculptors from every part of Haiti, and such local talents as Wilmino Domond.

Imports

La Belle Créole, Rue Bonne Fois, specializes in Swiss watches, French perfumes, cameras, china, gold jewelry.

Little Europe, Rue du Quai, offers Movado watches, Lalique crystal, French perfumes, Japanese cameras.

Film and camera equipment: Photo Kahn, Rue Bonne Fois, is recommended for its complete stock, its comparative speed, and its proximity (between La Belle Créole and Little Europe, near the Iron Market).

Music: Paul Anson's, Rue Pavée, recordings of Haitian folk music, meringues, and drumming.

Souvenir d'Haïti

Méringue Populaire

Paroles et Musique
du Dr Othello Bayard

Allegretto ♩ : 86

Ha.ï.ti ché rie...... pi bon pa.ys pas.sé ou lan point Foc moin té quit_

_té ou pou moin té cap com.pren'n va.leur'ou Foc moin té man qué ou pou'm'

té cap ap_pré_cié' ou Pou'm sen_ti vrai_ment tout ça ou té yé pou moin Gangn

bon so_leil bon ri_viè et bon breu_va_ge En bas pié ois

ou tou_jou join'n bon l'om_bra_ge Gangn bon ti vent qui ban nou bon

li frai_chè.... Ha_ï_ti Tho_mas cè gnou pa_ys qui m'est chè.........

D.C.

D.C.

INDEX

These entries include all Haitian names and most other names mentioned in the text; together with major references to principal towns and islands; aspects of "Haiti"; "peasants," "élite," "Catholicism," "vaudou," "Creole," "Citadelle," "Mardi Gras," "Ra-Ra," "coumbite," etc.

Index

Index